820.935 D257f   FV
DAVIES
THE FEMININE RECLAIMED : THE
IDEA OF WOMAN IN SPENSER,
SHAKESPEARE, ...   25.00

The Feminine Reclaimed

The Feminine Reclaimed

THE IDEA OF WOMAN IN SPENSER, SHAKESPEARE AND MILTON

Stevie Davies

THE UNIVERSITY PRESS OF KENTUCKY

Published by the University Press of Kentucky
Scholarly publisher for the Commonwealth,
serving Bellarmine College, Berea College, Centre
College of Kentucky, Eastern Kentucky University,
The Filson Club, Georgetown College, Kentucky
Historical Society, Kentucky State University,
Morehead State University, Murray State University,
Northern Kentucky University, Transylvania University,
University of Kentucky, University of Louisville,
and Western Kentucky University.
Printed in Great Britain by Anchor Brendon Ltd, Tiptree, Essex

Editorial and Sales Offices: Lexington, Kentucky 40506-0024

Library of Congress Cataloging-in-Publication Data

Davies, Stevie.
    The feminine reclaimed.

    Previously published as: The idea of woman in
Renaissance literature. 1986.
Bibliography: p.
    Includes index.
    1. English literature—Early modern, 1500–1700—
History and criticism.   2. Women in literature.
3. Spenser, Edmund, 1552?–1599—Characters—Women.
4. Shakespeare, William, 1564–1616—Characters—Women.
5. Milton, John, 1608–1674—Characters—Women.
I. Title.
PR429.W64D38   1986   820'.9'352042   85–22482
ISBN 0–8131–1589–2

For Harry and Monica Davies

So seemd those two, as growne together quite

Contents

Preface   ix
Note on Texts and Abbreviations   xii

1. Introduction   1

2. Spenser   37
        The Four Graces   37
        Britomart to Florimell   55
        Diana and Venus   77
        Art and Amoret   93

3. Shakespeare   105
        Hamnet and Judith   105
        Isis and Ceres   120
        Marina and Eleusis   129
        The Temple of Demeter Hermion   152
        Woman as Magus   165

4. Milton   175
        Deborah   175
        The Muse and the Maenads   186
        Mother Earth   221
        Ceres and Proserpina   231

Notes   248
Select Bibliography   262
Index   266

Preface

The considerable scope of a work such as this required a principle of selection in order to avoid the twin dangers of being overwhelmed by seas of generalisation on the one hand or mountains of detail on the other. I have therefore limited my study to consideration of three Renaissance English poets—Spenser, Shakespeare and Milton—choosing within their works areas which seemed to me comparable both in the material out of which they are shaped and in the manner of treatment. My book concentrates on Book III of Spenser's *Faerie Queene*, Shakespeare's tragi-comedies, especially *Pericles* and *The Winter's Tale*, and certain areas of Milton's *Paradise Lost*, though I have naturally referred to other parts of the authors' works, other poets, and multitudinous background works to elucidate the traditions in which I felt that 'the feminine' (defined in a specialised way for the purposes of this book) was 'reclaimed' for Renaissance literature. The title of my book was intended to disclose a Platonist nuance. This is the Idea, not just the idea, of woman, a person made of air or thought, real on paper and in the mind's eye rather than representative of everyday experience in an imagined Golden Age.

I am aware that in undertaking to write on such a topic as this, I am entering into a most controversial contemporary debate, that being played out between discrepant feminist readings of history and literature. I therefore thought it right to provide a substantial introduction to define the position from which this book proceeds, as well as to give account of some of the abstruser, odder forms of Platonising and Hermeticist thought which caught the Renaissance imagination enough to contribute to the conjuring of the impossible into being by some artists, both on the page and in the theatre. The perspective from which I began to contemplate these ideas was broadly Jungian, and this may still be perceptible in the final work; the manner is personal, showing a lack of deconstructive zeal for which I cannot apologise. Generic problems are naturally raised when survey is made of a poetic dramatist alongside two epic poets, and here perhaps some apology is due. I have tended to treat Shakespeare's drama with emphasis on the poetry because of the company in which I read him for the purposes of this book. Whilst I believe this inclination to be apt for the symbolic and mythic mode in which his Last Plays are agreed to be written, I have tried not to ignore the dramatic dimension without which interpretation is seriously incomplete.

Finally, I have accused Shakespeare of possessing more learning than is commonly thought quite compatible with the joy of drama and the slanders of history ('small Latin and less Greek'). It seems to me extraordinary that the present generation still likes to view Shakespeare as so inadequately endowed with information which was common knowledge and vitally interesting to the enquiring minds of his generation. The Hermetic and Platonistic secrets were the gossip of the intelligentsia of his day: you did not have to live with your head in an antique book to know what was in the air.

I should like to take this opportunity of thanking my friend Douglas Brooks-Davies of the University of Manchester for many wonderful conversations about Renaissance mythography and iconography, which enlarged my understanding and suggested clues and possibilities; perhaps all the more precious was his undertaking the drudgery of hunting elusive references and inaccessible books on my behalf on many occasions.

I must thank several generations of students of Renaissance English literature at the University of Manchester for sharing with me their responses and insights. Here I might especially mention Grace Timmins, Katherine Spearman, Mark Fairey, Caroline Redmond, Marilyn Tolhurst and Teresa Flower. I am grateful to my friend Andrew Howdle for sharing with me his scholarly love of Renaissance literature in many illuminating conversations.

I owe a great debt to the generous interest taken in my work by Professor William B. Hunter Jr. of the University of Houston, though of course I attribute to that eminent and learned man none of the positions adopted in this book, which I hope he will look upon with his customary charity.

Lastly, I should like to thank my friend Rosalie Wilkins for her loving support during the writing of the book; and I need to thank my friend Joy Watkin of the University of Manchester for her treasured friendship and encouragement.

Manchester, September 1984

Note on Texts and Abbreviations

I have used A.C. Hamilton's edition of Spenser's *The Faerie Queene* (London and New York, 1977), and in citing references to Spenser's other works I have used E. de Selincourt's edition of *The Poetic Works of Edmund Spenser*. References to plays by Shakespeare are to the Arden editions of individual plays. I have referred to John Carey and Alastair Fowler's edition of *The Poems of John Milton* (Oxford, 1968). References to Milton's prose works are to the Yale edition of *Complete Prose Works of John Milton*, general editor A.S.P. Woodhouse, 8 volumes (New Haven, 1953–83), abbreviated to *CPW*. The Bible alluded to is the King James version, unless otherwise specified.

1

Introduction

Had ye them seene, ye would have surely thought,
That they had beene that faire *Hermaphrodite*...
So seemd those two, as growne together quite...

(Spenser)

  Hang there like fruit, my soul,
Till the tree die.

(Shakespeare)

Part of my soul I seek thee, and thee claim
My other half...

(Milton)[1]

Woman in life and woman in art are not the same person. The
ancient androgynous dream of two becoming one, gender
dissolving into gender, has been fulfilled neither in Renaissance
England nor in any other state of culture. All this book will
claim is that in Renaissance poetry such dreams are familiar and
powerful: man's affinity with woman, along with a high
valuation of the feminine and a wish to incorporate and emulate
it, appears to be an obsession of the period. I shall call Spenser,
Shakespeare and Milton's art 'feminist' in this sense, though
with very different individual emphases. I shall link it to the
humanist and Platonist revival, which yielded ideas, impulses
and images to this radical view, but not in the belief that women
were actually and literally emancipated by humanism, except in
an important minority of cases.[2] It is said by modern writers on
the sociology of the period and its literary manifestations that the
Reformation forced woman's status down to that of passive
handmaiden, with the duty of silence, removing the iconography
of the female from religion in the persons of Virgin and saints;[3]
that property rights reflected man's primary interest in her; that
the stage presented her eloquence and pretensions as those of
rebellious 'scolds' who had to be punished and muted. But even

1

if there were not a free, or slightly free, woman in England in 1590, we would not be at liberty to claim that its literature of eloquent, right-thinking, strong-willed womanhood could not be an authentic dream. Shakespeare's Posthumus in *Cymbeline* sees Imogen as 'my soul'; Milton's Adam before his fall into rancour and misogyny knows Eve as 'part of my soul'; for Spenser, the two-in-one vision of human nature's opposites growing together into one nature is a 'faire Hermaphrodite'. These longings and symbolisms exist on the page we inherit, if not in the homes that have been long emptied. Platonism, humanism, alchemy, cabbala, Orphism and Hermeticism passed on to the insatiably enquiring mind of the Renaissance bodies of literature which claimed an unexpectedly divine nature for woman, and asserted the elusive existence of 'woman' within the male nature in a way which it was in his interests to seek. It may be that the same poet who wrote of man and woman 'growne together quite' took advantage of his leisure hours to kick his wife, incarcerate his daughter or impregnate mistresses. We know little about that. The present book is concerned with the words on the page, and I assume that they relate to some psychic reality, however oblique, within the poet's mind. The unpleasant behaviour of history towards womankind on a day-to-day basis I take as read; but I am also convinced that the discourtesies of the male, his codified abuse of woman in buying, selling and owning her, sniggering at her 'faults' and caricaturing her sexuality, is not all there is to say about male traditions. In art we may be free to express our dearest prejudices; we are also free to do justice and to desecrate socially sanctified lies. Therefore the book is entitled the '*Idea*' of woman. It makes no claim to exhume the reality, who has been 350 years in her grave.

There are other, more peculiar but equally obligatory perspectives to be sought in Renaissance belief than that of sociological enquiry. With the humanist discovery of lost, misdated bodies of literature, new relations and affinities were postulated between sets of values which under old Aristotelian systems had been kept neatly and comfortably separate. The *Hermetica*, misdated by scholars so as to suggest that they were either concurrent with or pre-dated Moses (and the older the better, the more 'original' as far as the Renaissance was concerned),[4] and the *Orphic Hymns*, actually second- or third-century incantations to the sun, as well as the whole body of Plato's works and that of Neoplatonists, undid the cosmos. They did it back up again in new fluid forms which fundamentally rearranged each constituent part of the universe, including that 'fair defect', woman. The universe was reformed magically, according to the philosophical researches of the fifteenth-century Florentine Platonists Marsilio Ficino and G. Pico della Mirandola, and according to the sixteenth-century Paolini and Bruno. It does not signify that 'Hermes Trismegistus' was not an Egyptian from thousands of years before but a collection of first-to-third-century gnostic Greek revivalists, nor that Orpheus may never have existed. The Renaissance thought it had inherited a philosophical and theological revelation. That is what counts. The philosopher became a magician, using Hermetic and Orphic magic to conjure the many into the One, to marry the earth to the heavens. When we learn that one of the foremost philosophers of his age, Marsilio Ficino, translator of Plato and Hermes, commentator and academist, spent a considerable proportion of his philosophising life accompanying himself singing the Orphic hymns on a *lira de braccio*, and whilst he warbled burning frankincense, sipping at an astrologically appropriate wine, contemplating a talisman,[5] we are bound to revise the assumptions with which we approach Renaissance images of anything, let alone woman. For Ficino was not a solitary crank, conjuring in safe isolation, but a mighty representative of, and influence on, the 'Greek' heritage of Renaissance humanism. (The Latin part, being on the whole more sensible and concerned with accurate datings of accurate texts, is also less flamboyantly radical and peculiar.) Ficino's waylaying of astral influences and his directing them through secret knowledge of sympathetic magic into the desired channels represented an age's commitment to imaginative and philosophical spell-casting. Spenser, Shakespeare and Milton were all profoundly influenced by the influx of new imagery which came like light from stange planets to illumine new ways of seeing. The paths these generations chose were not those of common sense: their map is of a world in which philosophy is close to magic, magic to poetry, poetry to love, love to philosophy. A magic circle surrounds the élite of humanistic artists, who were all conjuring for the same ends: to set forth an enigmatic, extraordinary, occultly secret wisdom, which can be done through any of these sister arts. When we open the door on the sage philosopher, he will tell us that through singing Orphic hymns he is seriously attempting to tune in to the music of the spheres. When we consult the great astronomer, Kepler, we find that stumbling upon the laws of motion came as a bitter personal disappointment, for he was eagerly seeking to prove the existence of the music of the spheres.[6] Thus it will not come as a shock to find Shakespeare representing on the London stage an aged gentleman whose claim to hear that music is the climax of the play: 'The music of the spheres! List, my Marina.' (V.i. 228). That Pericles should hear this music through loving a woman is true both to the spirit and the letter of the Orphic, Hermetic, Platonist philosophies through which Pythagoras' good idea that the universe was measured in the ratio of notes and octave was mediated. For at the centre of these systems is not Aristotle's abstract supreme Intellect, whose 'thinking is a thinking of thinking',[7] but something essentially more human, simple and mysteriously personal. It is Love. If we are considering Renaissance Platonism, we find that it is through Love (by Ficino out of the *Phaedrus* and the *Symposium*) that we ascend to the divine One. If we think of the cabbala, the *mors osculi* (kiss of death) draws us out of the body to enraptured vision; if we consider Hermeticism, we learn from the *Pimander* that the Divine, in erotic embrace with Nature, created the world; if we enquire into Ophism, we find the centrality of Venus (Amor, Eros) to the world.[8] Old stereotypes pass; new dreams succeed. For since in the Renaissance period, Love was at the centre, and since the days of idealistic pederasty had gone with the Greeks, so it followed that the female principle was at the centre, invested with a new sanctity which came not so much from the Cult of the Blessed Virgin as from the mystery religions of the ancient world, supposed to have been founded by Orpheus. The new philosophy, with its doctrines of emanation, the coincidence of opposites and the existence of the whole in the part and the part in the whole, naturally overflowed into art. The poet is Orphic in an obvious way. He sings creation. In singing it, he fulfills a sacred role of priest, and a magus role as creator. Spenser and Milton play this Orphic role explicitly; Shakespeare's magus figures, surrounded with powerful lyricism, culminating in Prospero in *The Tempest*, show his awareness of that role for the dramatic poet.

In the new mystical philosophies, the cardinal precept is that All is One. The Orphic theogony quaintly but picturesquely represents this by showing Zeus swallowing the first-born god, Phanes, and thus ingesting the whole multiplicity of the universe into himself.[9] In the *Orphic Hymns* Protogonos (Phanes) is 'born of the egg, delighting in his golden wings' (6: 2). Out of the Orphic egg the bisexual first-born comes, bringing light into the dark;[10] Creation is then reabsorbed, outside becoming inside. The system is one of dynamic process rather than static machine. The flow of forms in Renaissance visual and literary art reflects their organic view of the cosmos. Like Spenser's Garden of Adonis in Book III of the *Faerie Queene*, the Orphic universe is in constant process of recycling, going out, coming back. *Pammateira* ('the mother of everything') and *Spermeia* ('he who rules over the seeds of life') communicate not just as opposed pairings but as aspects of one another. The image of the hermaphrodite (particularly within the feminine nature) prevails, for the Orphic aim is vision of wholeness. Thus Mother Nature, in *To Physis*, is addressed:

> Father and mother of all, nurturer and nurse,
> you bring swift birth, o blessed one, and a wealth
> of seeds... *(The Orphic Hymns)*[11]

Queen Mise, likewise, is composed of a 'twofold nature... male and female' (42: 3–4), evidencing this urge towards a *coincidentia oppositorum* expressed in the sexually complete nature of a female-and-male origin. In all the mystical philosophies which dominated the period, we find this image of androgyny not just as a minor by-product but as a major preoccupation. So, for instance, the Hermetic *Pimander* yields a Creation myth, with a bisexual Father, bisexual Man (in the father's image) and bisexual Nature, whose relevance I shall show to Milton's androgynous Creation in *Paradise Lost* (see pp. 198ff below). On the coarser and more practical level, the alchemist was engaged in exploiting this science of the chemical union of genders, heating 'hermaphroditic' compounds in his crucible; compounds which had their own human variants in Donne's 'Loves Alchymie', or his 'new Alchimie' completed in the *Nocturnall upon S. Lucies Day*. In Christian cabbalistic traditions of angelology drawn on by Milton, angels could be both sexes or either, as a condition, and surely a rather convincing proof, of their bliss. With mystical philosophy moving towards this reincorporation of the feminine in the divine, and the hermaphroditic as divine, it is natural that these motifs should shed their influence on the poetry of Spenser, Shakespeare and Milton. The world of *The Faerie Queene* is transformed by the poet's miraculous reintegration of gender, and its possibilities. Britomart, the warrior-maiden of Book III, is an inclusive image of perfection, touching all the female, and all the male characters in the book in her mirroring of nature. Her hair burns long and golden and her skin is soft as a child's beneath the hard surface of the armour in which she pursues her ends. She is the coincidence of opposites in person, Venus and Diana, war and love, male and female: numinous, mysterious, carrying unaccountable energy, all power and all gentleness. Androgynous, often double-named transvestite personalities recur throughout Shakespeare's plays: Rosalind/Ganymede, Viola/Cesario, Portia/Jessica, Imogen/Fidelio. Though it is interesting to speculate on whether through these figures dramatists 'reinforced the feminism of the masculine woman' in the contemporary debate about woman's nature and place, or that conversely they reinforced prevailing patriarchal attitudes to women threatening to get out of hand (Jardine),[12] the argument may well be inconclusive, for want of women and playwrights to interrogate. What is undeniable is that the image of the bisexual heroine coincided with that of the bisexual cosmos of the mystical philosophies. The Idea of woman was being revalued upwards in a range of disciplines, as an essential constituent part of the God-reflecting universe. The boundaries of the female nature were being opened and redefined in terms of greater inclusiveness and fluidity. This did not happen as a result of 'feminism'. Most women still endured short, painful, hard-working and undignified lives, dying in childbirth or of untreatable disease. They had no vote, few rights, little choice and minimal education, and mostly died without knowing that divine hermaphroditism was available to be believed in, or that the female mystery religions of the Ancient World and the Greek Pantheon of powerful female goddesses had been disinterred from time and Platonistically reinvented for the edification of the modern world. But to say that women did not know about the Idea of woman adds little to the universal assumption we have to make in studying ideas in a period of low literacy. Spenser's soaring Platonisms were aimed at a 'noble' clan of men, and one or two women, as the *Letter to Raleigh* explains; Shakespeare's plays catered to the particular audience; Milton's readership must inevitably, and proudly, be 'fit... though few' (*Paradise Lost*, VII. 31).

Such caustic ironies of history do not seem especially peculiar when they are read in terms of the other outrageous oddities of our period, such as the foundation of the massive schools of Ficino and Bruno upon a credulous mistake in dating texts, to the tune of 4,000 years. Upon this basis the heliocentric theory of the universe ('science' and thus 'true') was first predicated. I shall assume that we can bear to read the new ideas about women ('egalitarian' and thus 'true') upon such gratuitous foundations. Thus Renaissance Egyptologists, falsely interpreting the hieroglyphs on the ancient tombs as enshrining a secret pictorial language containing delicious secret wisdom, went running after all things Egyptian and brought back with them the goddess Isis, a central manifestation of the reclaimed image of the feminine as the inclusive and powerful white goddess. The syncretistic tendency of the Renaissance scholar was not to substitute one image or idea for items in the existing collection and declare it 'true', but to accumulate as many as possible. The business of the Church Fathers and the medieval church had been scrupulously to pick out and discard or sterilise accretions from the old female lunar religions, on the grounds of danger of contamination. St. Paul had raised a despotic voice against the ancient cult of the many-breasted Diana at Ephesus: 'Wives, submit yourselves unto your own husbands, as unto the Lord'. (Ephesians 5:22). Four centuries later, Augustine remembered with nausea in *De Civitate Dei* the obscenity of the 'sacrilegious sacrifices' to the Great Mother Deity,'the shameless games in honour of... the Virgo Caelestis and Berecynthia, mother of all'.[13] But a thousand years after Augustine there was no need to be quite as irascible. Though

Protestants and Catholics alike still worried about the potential clash between Christian orthodoxy and the pagan past, the fascinating gods and goddesses no longer threatened an actual come-back. They could be allegorised into the modern world, coaxed in as images, hints, clues to truth. Wisdom lies strewn across our planet in bright fragments of multiplicity, Pico argued, so our job must be to resemble Isis searching out the scattered remains of her god-brother, to recollect and unify it. Naturally, the 'feminine' would come along with the 'masculine' aspects of truth, since we want it all. Within the humanist's great magpie-hoard lie heaped the excavated fragments of the mother-religions, man's most venerable traditions. More completely than the humanists knew, they were putting the Renaissance in touch with its most original roots. From Pico's extravagant fits of elation at man's godlike capacity to recapture and comprehend the whole body of lost learning, the *Oration: On the Dignity of Man* (1486), to Milton's call for freedom to press forward with this search in *Areopagitica* (1644), is a span of two centuries of the same quest. Each envisages humanity as a searcher, or re-searcher, participating in a huge joint enterprise to lift and assimilate the whole past into the present. The process is a dynamic movement between opposites:

> Sometimes we shall descend, and, as in the myth of Osiris, unity will be scattered into multiplicity with titanic strength, and sometimes we shall ascend, with the force of Phoebus, turning multiplicity into unity as when the limbs of Osiris were collected together
>
> (*Oration: On the Dignity of Man*)[14]

> Truth indeed came once into the world with her Divine Master...but...how they dealt with the good *Osiris*, took the virgin Truth, hewd her lovely form into a thousand peeces, and scatter'd them to the four winds. From that time ever since, the sad friends of Truth, such as durst appear, imitating the carefull search that *Isis* made for the mangl'd body of *Osiris,* went up and down gathering up limb by limb still as they could find them. We have not yet found them all, Lords and Commons[15]
>
> (*Areopagitica*)[15]

It is not only in the definition of man's quest, the hopeful attitude, the wish to synthesise and universalise, that Pico and Milton are comparable. Most significantly, their metaphors speak the same language, in this case Egyptian and feminine. Milton is unexpectedly more sedate than Pico, crashing up and down the ladder of being at top mental speed between the One and the many. But for an image of quest as redemption of lost unity (in Milton's case, more elegiac) each instinctively chooses the story of Isis and Osiris, the double god of the Egyptian mystery religion. Isis is associated with loss succeeded by healing, restoration and unification. She represents the power of the feminine principle (accessible in minds of either gender) to compose reality against the destructive forces that confuse and darken. The evolutionary nature of truth is figured in Milton's adaptation of her patient, painstaking search. We note with a slight shock that he has altered the balance of the whole story by choosing, instead of the male Osiris, a Spenserian feminine personification for the body of restored Truth: 'the virgin Truth' scattered upon the the winds. Both the searcher and the sought are feminine. Thus the great misogynist of Renaissance England confirms a double loyalty to what Ficino used to call 'the sacred mysteries of Minerva',[16] an idea of truth reformulated according to feminine images and structures made newly available from the Old World.

It has become fashionable to deny that humanism was as explosively radical as used to be assumed. Continuity with the medieval period is stressed, and the Christian commitment of the humanists. Yet even such continuity helps us to understand where the pagan religious iconography, which is such a feature of the 'feminine' revival, comes from: it was never actually lost at all, but survived within the Middle Ages as an allegorised hybrid with Christianity, though without the aesthetic beauty of the authentic Hellenic tradition.[17] The reclamation of the feminine in the Renaissance is in good part a redemption of the magnificent classic form for the female deities, and then a re-imagining of these original possibilities in new variations and compounds. While it is important to recognise this continuity, it may be overemphasised. The schools of humanism which concern this study eagerly researched the secrets of the Ancient World so as often to prize them heretically alongside or on the wrong side of the Christian belief. The findings of alchemists stood in contradiction to the clear message of the Bible, for instance, on Eve's guilt and woman's inferiority. Paracelsus, dealing as his art must with an androgynous universe, and highly valuing its fertility, does not so much contradict as elude Genesis. Woman is 'man's world, from which he is born...How can one be an enemy of woman—whatever she may be?...woman is also superior to man. Man is to her what the pear is to the tree. The pear falls, but the tree remains standing.'[18] If we read this against the surviving Aristotelian and scholastic traditions which put in doubt not just her equality but also her humanity and her creation in the image of God, we are aware of how vast a leap Paracelsus and the Platonists are making. Valens Acidalius' pamphlet of 1595 entitled 'A new disputation against women, in which it is proved that they are not human beings' represents a good old-fashioned view, which, however, while many might secretly consult as a cherished prejudice, few Renaissance thinkers felt to be an elegant theory which it did one credit to argue.[19] But the medievalism, which stubbornly prevailed, even amongst Puritans whose political radicalism one might imagine threatening to the sexual status quo,[20] was contradicted in theories of Creation based on androgyny, and (Platonist) theories of the universe based on Love.[21] In combination with political events in Europe which concentrated power in the hands of individual women of great mental scope (Elizabeth I, Catherine de Medici), I think these factors magnified the image of women in art and literature to sometimes heretical or blasphemous proportions. The pagan goddesses of Greece, Rome and Egypt were revived in their authentic majesty to focus this reconceived image. The extent of the potential heresy is suggested in this apparently casual remark in a letter from the humanist Mutianus Rufus to a friend:

Est unus deus et una dea. Sed sunt multa uti numina ita et nomina: Jupiter, Sol, Apollo, Moses, Christus, Luna, Ceres, Proserpina, Tellus, Maria. Sed haec cave enuntes. Sunt enim occulta silentio tamquam Eleusinarum dearum mysteria.[22]

Giordano Bruno was burned on the Inquisition's bonfire for less than this. 'There is one god *and one goddess*': Mutianus seems to think this rather a tame article of faith. He is more interested in the 'many divinities' and 'many names', which he goes on to

enumerate with Christ impertinently listed between Moses and
the Moon, and Mary the mother of God dragging along in the
rear after the discreditable earth-goddess Tellus. This casual
semblance of polytheism is only equalled by the parity implied
between male and female divinities. Both the Christian and
classical gods are interpreted as being equally as credible and
philosophically relevant as the sum of the stories they can tell
us about reality. Renaissance syncretism perhaps reaches its
most extreme expression here. Within the female half of his
Pantheon, Rufus names Ceres and Proserpina, a duality he then
picks up in his warning that it is as well to keep this knowledge
of the fascinating multiplicity of gods to oneself, 'as the initiates
kept secret the Eleusinian mysteries'. It was at Eleusis, the
sacred temple of Ceres/Demeter that the Renaissance authors I
study in this book found a spiritual home where human life
could be freshly interpreted, through the mother-daughter
relationship, as a pattern of growth and civilisation.

But it is essential to remember that the goddess is always
one of many; that is, '*Est...una dea*', but equally, '*sunt
multa...nomina*'. In Renaissance mythography all the goddesses
of the classical Pantheon stand linked, their faces and gestures
echoing, opposing, circling back to one another, like Botticelli's
Graces in the *Primavera* (1476–81). The goddesses resemble the
whole spectrum of expressions available to a single face; they
cross the entire range of experience and emotion possible to
human nature. Thus Venus and Diana—Love and Chastity,
reconciler and warrior—are natural opposites. But each goddess
has many aspects, as stars have conjunctions, as types of people
have ranges of moods. The mythographers—Giraldi in *De deis
gentium varia* (1548), Natale Conti in *Mythologiae* (1551),
Cartari in *Le imagini* (1571)—were encyclopedic to a fault: they
did not like to leave things out. The Romans had left their gods
in a very confused condition. There were dozens of kinds of
each major deity, according to attributes, place of origin or
combination with Oriental or Egyptian analogies. Renaissance
mythographers welcomed this incomprehensible muddle with
childlike joy and reproduced it in its fullest complication. To
synthesise in the interests of the One was not to reduce to a
simple unity; it was rather to aggregate the largest imaginable
whole. Thus Pico hungrily prepared no fewer than 900

propositions, to be discussed at Rome, and Cartari assembled the list of Apollos and Dianas with special reference to the 'Triforme, Trigemina, e Trivia' Diana, or the Egyptian Diana with three animal heads.[23] The goddesses combine and interlace in bewilderingly miscellaneous forms. There is, for instance, a variant of Venus who is very like her own opposite, Diana, as *Venus virgo* or as the *Venus armata*, displaying a pugnacious and unreassuring aspect of Love. Venus with Diana's bow, helmet and quiver exemplifies the *coincidentia oppositorum*,[24] as does the threefold nature of the lunar deity, Proserpina—Ceres—Hecate, in which we can read the sequence which rounds both human life and the seasonal cycle: maiden—mother—old woman. The Renaissance taste for large structures as elaborate permutations of single units may be seen both in the hieroglyphic art of the emblem books and that of the epic poetry from Tasso and Ariosto to Spenser. To disentangle the multiple meanings of the composite goddesses alluded in *The Faerie Queene,* the modern reader may sometimes feel the need of the patience of a saint. The structure is a tissue of thread-fine distinctions based on a desire to figure the *una dea* according to her million reflections within the visible world. A glance through the popular emblem books reveals that, statistically, feminine images of the vices and virtues outnumber their masculine counterparts. The influential Cesare Ripa in his *Iconologia* (1593) shows a greater taste for reading the world through a feminine hieroglyphic glass than through male images. A bizarre female squirting milk from both breasts whilst holding armfuls of corn and grapes enacts the virtue of *Sostanza* (Abundance), while a surprising individual wearing an elephant's head, holding a scorpion in one hand and a cornucopia in the other, impersonates the moral and material nature of the continent of Africa.[25] The male personifications are both more rare and less enterprising. Nothing more graphically illustrates the bias of the age towards the female than the priority she enjoys in both mythographies and emblem books, which were such a basic influence on Spenserian and post-Spenserian art in England.

Est una dea. The Platonising art of Florence shows her face through infinite refractions of her image, as Venus, Diana, Juno, Minerva, Ceres, and clusters such as Graces and Muses, who mediate between the world of the goddess and the world of men,

as well the 'raped maidens' like Flora and Proserpina who perform
a three-fold mediation, linking upper, middle and lower worlds.
Botticelli's *Primavera* powerfully conveys this sense of infinitely
mirroring forms and faces which informs humanistic Italian visual
art (which has to be 'read' as if it were literature) and English
poetry (which asks to be viewed as a kind of written picture).[26]
The lyricism, care for detail and otherworldly Platonising of
Botticelli's learned dream-picture is very close to Spenser's art
in the 'Aprill' eclogue of *The Shepheardes Calender* (IV) and *The
Faerie Queene*. Equally, it is close to the flower world of the
pastoral Act of Shakespeare's *Winter's Tale*, Act IV, and to
Milton's Eden in *Paradise Lost*, where Pan and the Graces play
and dance, again Book IV. The Renaissance feminine is
profoundly rooted in the pastoral, and its traditions, conceived
not as an escapist fantasy world where an idle poet may happily
squander time but as the embodiment of the growing-principle
itself, the mystery of childbirth and the annual recurrence of the
colour of green. Botticelli's *Primavera*, which seems so
otherworldly, records a total of forty species of herbs, flowers and
plants, exactly recorded from nature, with fidelity not only to
emblematic meaning of each in relation to Venus and the events
which encircle her but also to their appearance in the natural
world. M.L. D'Ancona's recent beautiful monograph *Botticelli's
'Primavera'* identifies the simple plants of spring, from cress to
colt's foot and starwort, which pattern the ground in a living
tapestry.[27] Each bears a distinct meaning, or group of meanings,
associated with the Garden of Venus. To read these meanings is
to be initiated into the deepest allusions the picture makes to a
world which is both beyond the world, and also speaking through
it: a world dominated by Ficino's *Venus Urania*, Love the
reconciler, and the feminine composition of her reign, with six
female figures (Venus, the Graces, Chloris-and-Flora) standing to
three male (Mercury, Cupid, Zephyrus).

But equally, given the microscopic accuracy with which
Botticelli renders the galaxies of flowers in his picture's world, we
are reading the Book of Nature itself. The feminine pastoral
celebrates Mother Earth, and humanity as her child; it also
initiates the contemplating observer into the harmonious
patterning which is the Idea upon which appearances so
beautifully vary. The faces of the female figures in the *Primavera*

are all variations on one model; the bodies rhythmically echo one body. The events enact cataclysmic change at a moment when eternity enters time so that time stills (poised upon the central stillness of Venus) into an eternal insight. Venus' reconciliation of time and eternity, her revelation of their mutual compatibility, is a twofold epiphany, expressed in the structure of the whole work. Two groups of three figures balance nearly symmetrically: on her left, the dance of the Graces in a circle mimes the planetary dance, as art mimes the Ideal World. Venus seems to become almost a fourth Grace in her stance echoing their rhythm. On her right, the entrance of eternity into time is expressed as Zephyrus' (the spring god's) rape of Chloris, who looks back at the fat-faced and swarthy rapist with an expression that has not had time to turn into horror; out at her mouth springs a surprising cascade of flowers where words should have come, and her form spills down upon the tranquil figure of her future metamorphosis, Flora. Flora is the plentitude of nature, her gown elaborately woven with spring flowers, swollen gracefully with pregnancy. She steps free of her own identity, as in Ovid's account of the fertility myth in the *Fasti*: '*Chloris eram quae Flora vocor*'—'I who was Chloris am now named Flora.'[28] The elegy for the dead self is also the birth-song celebrating the new. The Mercury figure on the extreme left, reaching back up to heaven with his caduceus, reinforces the link between the world of nature and the world beyond. And because he is a god so often imaged as bisexual, or able to combine with other gods, as in Herm-Athene, or Herm-Aphrodite, he speaks of the secret alchemical transformation in the crucible of gender. As Zephyrus combines with Chloris, and Amor with Castitas (there is an obese, malign Cupid aiming at the central Grace), so Mercury combines with Venus (Herm-Aphrodite) in Hermetic, Platonic and alchemical marriage into the One.[29] Botticelli paints the *coincidentia oppositorum* as a union of extreme sensuality with spiritual *ekstasis;* male with female; violent action with perfect stasis. The rhythm of his picture is a rhythm of female bodies and echoing female faces; if we think of his other pictures from this classicist period, the *Mars and Venus,* the *Birth of Venus,* the pictures are seen to echo the same faces wearing a similarly abstracted, wistful expression. A secret is being partly shown, partly veiled; an erudite dream, based on the *una dea,* who can only be known through her many different names, translations and manifestations.

Most deeply, this dream is of a new kind of power, standing in opposition to the old warrior culture. In *Mars and Venus* the goddess watches with sarcastic composure while Mars, quelled into the sleep of postcoital torpor, violates his own stormy nature, despite the bellowing efforts to arouse him made by the boy-satyr blowing into his ear through a shell. This motif, of the triumph of the subtle and cosmic power of Love over the martial and aggressive power of the heroic tradition of arms, is a favourite one in the period. In Spenser's *Faerie Queene* and Milton's *Paradise Lost* the erotic radically qualifies the heroic as the subject of epic. The berserk male world of the battlefield gives way to the feminised epic of Spenser, in which Gloriana is more important than Arthur, and Florimell in her constantly vanishing evanescence a more forceful image of divine glory than pious knights like Red Crosse and Guyon eternally hacking at the bones of their enemies, as if God had designed the world to be nothing but a battlefield. Milton's Eve is a development of the Homeric figure of the 'beloved companion', in whom epic heroism is redefined in female terms.[30] Milton, 'Not sedulous by nature to indite/Wars' (IX. 27–8), presents his readers with an Eden where Eros 'Reigns...and revels' (IV. 765). The Fall in *Paradise Lost* involves the forfeiture of some such Garden of Venus as Botticelli paints: the telling of the loss is inspired by a Muse who is named as Urania (VII. 1) and recognisable as in part inspired by Ficino's Venus Urania. In Shakespeare's histories, given the fratricidal character of the English past, Mars naturally predominates over Venus, and 'feathered Mercury' is employed not uniting with Venus but vaulting onto a war-horse, in the person of Prince Henry (*Henry IV*, Pt 1, IV. i. 106). In *Henry V*, the Chorus requires 'a Muse of fire' in order to represent 'war-like Harry, like himself', as Mars (1–5), a Martial posture which seems to have it explicitly in mind to make war on women and children:

> The gates of mercy shall be all shut up,
> And the flesh'd soldier, rough and hard of heart,
> In liberty of bloody hand shall range
> With conscience wide as hell, mowing like grass
> Your fresh-fair virgins and your flowering infants.
> (*Henry V*, III. iii. 10-14).

The martial King Henry knows far too intimately the hateful rhetoric of war, outdoing Tamburlaine in vaunts and threats. Here Death the Reaper seems to raise his sickle to make a pointless harvest of the Botticellian floral dream. Black-armoured, faceless soldiers are invoked to de-flower women and children. But where in the histories genre dictates the victory of Mars and the suppression of the 'woman in man' (*Henry V*, IV. v. 28–33), in comedy Mars is seen as little better than an idiot and a thug, Armado's 'armipotent Mars, of lances the almighty' who cannot speak a grammatical sentence (*Love's Labour's Lost*, V. ii. 642). This is true to the original Greek spirit: in the élite of the Greek Pantheon, Ares/Mars was looked down on by his fellow gods as a brainless degenerate.[31] Venus, whose 'true Promethean fire' Platonically illumines the universe not from books but from women's eyes (IV. iii. 301),[32] conquers the comedies in ring-dances, festive songs or marriage festivities, overwhelming Mars. This motif is developed through *Lear* and into the tragi-comedies less in terms of the Venus-motif than through the Ceres/Proserpina myth. As Vulcan to the urbane laughter of his fellow gods netted Mars and Venus in *flagrante delicto*, where the 'man-murderer' struggled impotently in nude embarrassment, so the Renaissance artist casts the subtle net of his harmonious craft over the truculent warrior-god. In the chapter on Shakespeare I shall claim that this represents a return to the original authentic Greek spirit, not the Roman, for the Romans were rather fond of Mars and valued his violent character rather as an asset to the state than an intimation of spiritual failure.

The feminine principle as the Renaissance recognises it often stands in fierce (even, paradoxically, embattled) opposition to the ethos of war. As Queen Elizabeth I calculated her policies so as to avoid warfare as an expense a state should do without wherever possible, so even Spenser's Britomart, the warrior-woman, is a hermaphrodite within the female not the male nature and culture, and seeks across the world of the poem for a loved-one (Arthegall) rather than spoiling for a fight. The desirable end for both male and female protagonists is not to kill enemies but to make peace in the soul (the poem being a *psychomachia*, an internal moral battle);[33] peace in the body, preferably in the union of marriage; peace in Church and state (the Red Crosse Knight married to

Una, the One herself). I do not here dismiss cavalierly the militant nature of the whole period in Europe, its Protestant and nationalistic militancy, nor facts such as that the protector of Michelangelo was the 'warrior-pope', Julius II; nor should one regard this background of perpetual hostilities as inconvenient to the case which is to be made for Venus against Mars, Ceres against Jupiter. For in an age of violent oppositions and vociferous debates, the 'feminine' and pacifist ideal originates as a direct result of a dialectical turn of mind. We have to read the myths of feminised power against the realities of power exerted (even by female monarchs) as it has always been exerted, against fellow human beings, conceived as 'food for powder'. The Elizabethan peace bred the monster Tamburlaine; the poet of Eden would be a regicide whose pen endorsed the shedding of royal blood.

But the secrets which had been unearthed from the Ancient World, whose products could be grafted on to modern life, were myths of female creativity, care and reconciliation, appropriate to the Christian ideal of Charity and the idea of Grace (both by tradition iconographically represented as female, and both at least partially Hellenic in origin). Synthesis between the story of Christ's loss and man's redemption, and the Eleusinian story of Ceres' loss of Proserpina, her grief and reclamation, was easy and natural. The stories did not have to be coerced or mutilated to yield analogous emotions and meanings. An age gifted at forging arguments to prove that classical black was really (allegorically speaking) Christian white (say, that Odysseus' titillating episode with Circe was really an example of Christian wisdom), would have to afford very little ingenuity to the equation of Christ's love of man's soul with Orpheus' for Eurydice, or with Ceres' for her daughter. Both visit the grave, out of pure love; both retrieve the beloved one from the grasp of the underworld; both achieve a (however temporary) rebirth of the soul. And both promise the believer mysterious consolation, life after death, the ritual illumination of the present moment in vision and sacrament. Besides, the initiation rites at Eleusis were a secret, perhaps the best-kept secret of the Ancient World; and the Renaissance humanist could not resist the temptation to pry into secrets, to become a member of the élite of all time who were 'in the know'. The ancient sources of information about the Eleusinian Mysteries were very numerous indeed, but they were also uniquely cryptic. For minds used to exercising themselves upon the Egyptian hieroglyphs (with the added difficulty caused by their use of a wholly erroneous principle of approach which assumed the hieroglyphs to be a system of ideograms), the secret of what happened at the Eleusinian Mysteries, and what it meant, would not seem an insuperable challenge, rather a stimulus to invention. Additionally, the authorities were, according to a humanist perspective, so impeccable. One level of curiosity is aroused when Pausanias in his *Description of Greece* tells the reader that a dream has forbidden him to describe 'the things within the wall of the sanctuary' of Eleusis, 'and the uninitiated are of course not permitted to learn that which they are prevented from seeing'.[34] But quite another is excited when the venerated Roman Cicero, whom the humanist Petrarch had wished to count as a Catholic,[35] gives vent in *On the Laws,* to the assertion, 'We have been given a reason not only to live in joy but also to die with better hope'.[36] The rational, just and pious Cicero could not be imagined as being taken in by a vulgar fraud. This testimony by one of the greatest of the Romans was corroborated by that of the greatest Greeks. Sophocles testifies 'Thrice blessed are those among men who, after beholding these rites, go down to Hades. Only for them is there life',[37] and his Oedipus concludes his life in *Oedipus at Colonus* (Sophocles' final and most personal play, set in the author's birthplace and written in extreme old age) with a vision of Persephone (1551). Other authorities were Herodotus, Pindar, Isocrates, Krinagoras, Euripides and Aristophanes—in fact, all the authorities one would be most disposed to credit in the Greek and Roman world, the virtuous pagans upon whose solid foundations the Renaissance was built. Their testimony was further endorsed by the preservation of various poems on the theme including the ancient *Homeric Hymn to Demeter* (in which the basic ritual is coded as the story of the two goddesses), the beautiful Orphic *Hymn to Persephone* and *Hymn to Eleusinian Demeter,* the unfinished *De Raptu Proserpinae* of Claudian, and, of course, Ovid's account in the *Metamorphoses.* The incantation of names in the *Orphic Hymns* shows how important the manifold nature of the *una dea* was felt to be, both in classical and Renaissance periods. Persephone is the queen of death, who in miraculous paradox gives birth, 'maiden rich in fruits'.[38] She is both the fullness of the old year, in 'fruits', and the childhood of the new spring, whose ' holy figure' is shown in the year's first green shoots (13). She is the young girl across the river of old age, the seed within the burial chamber. Mysteriously, she is one with her mother, the friend of humanity, as *To Eleusinian Demeter* reminds us:

> Deo, divine mother of all, goddess of many names,
> august Demeter, nurturer of youths and giver of prosperity
> and wealth. You nourish the ears of corn...
>
> From beneath the earth you appear and to all you are gentle[39]

The fascination of the Eleusinian faith for the Renaissance lay partly in the secrecy of its cult (obtained by oaths made at initiation, and sanctioned by the penalty of loss of that eternal hope and bliss which Cicero and Sophocles recorded. The beauty of the vision which all the pilgrims experienced at Eleusis—the 'light at Eleusis' during the nocturnal vigil—presses out against the barrier of their shared silence. You have a feeling of the participants' longing to speak: their restraint evidencing the strength of their motivation. Eleusis for Christians also has the glow of forbidden fruit: the early Church fought for centuries to stamp its mystery out, as a very aggravating rival. Partly the fascination lay in Renaissance awareness that Eleusis *was* in a very deep way Greece. Its faith had bound man, gods and underworld in mutual balance; the epiphany obtained there by men and women, bond and free, included insight into the harmonious law binding all existence, without which civilised life was not thinkable. The Christian emperor who sought to suppress the Mysteries was told that without them life would be to the Greeks 'unlivable', *abios.*[40] Renaissance recognition of the place of natural and divine law in the Demeter/Persephone cult is evidenced in Shakespeare's adaptation of the myth in *The Winter's Tale* to the mother-and-daughter relationship of Hermione and Perdita and the idea of the restoration of justice in the state. Personal emotion of an overwhelming kind is one with public and cosmic awareness. And, partly, the appeal of the mother-daughter cult lies simply in its uniqueness as being a religious story about a mother and daughter.[41] There are plenty of father-and-son and mother-and-son, and some father-and-daughter cults in Western religions. Christianity has its divine patriarchy, God the Father and God the Son, and its Holy Family of Madonna and boy-child. Egypt has its sister-and-brother variant in the Isis and Osiris myth. The Renaissance was happy to conflate all these. But Eleusis is unique in lacking a central male component. It uniquely offers to religion a structure yielding insights based on the continuum of female experience, the affinity between mother and daughter providing a new metaphor for experience of the holy. It is a myth which incorporates the universal experience of suffering as an essential part of the divine: the goddess in her bereavement suffers basic human loss, is one with man in being subject to painful, inexplicable procedures dictated by higher and lower powers (Jupiter and Pluto, respectively). Proserpina is one with humanity in being subject to violent death in her prime. But the two goddesses set man an example of hope by their power to round out their catastrophe to a tragi-comic conclusion, and by the significance and productiveness of their mutual suffering. In Claudian's *De Raptu Proserpinae* the air is thick with feminine questionings of the divine plan. Pallas Athene's *'quid viva sepultis/admisces?'* (why mix the quick with the dead?)[42] as Pluto tears the young girl out of the garden gives way to Ceres' storming questioning of the divine order (III. 407-18). But from this agony proceeds purgation in recognition and acceptance (the tragic *anagnorisis*); understanding is gained as well as the gift to the natural order of the new season's vegetation and corn harvest. The Renaissance mythographers understood the vegetation symbolism of the story very well. Rationalising the myth, Abraham Fraunce in *The Third Part of the Countesse of Pembrokes Yvychurch* (1592) explains:

> Pluto then, you see, the third brother, ravished *Proserpina*: the naturall efficacie and vertue of the earth...drawing unto it the rootes of corne, growing and increasing in the bowels of the earth. *Ceres* her mother seeketh *Proserpina*, and mourneth for her absence: the corne pursueth and foloweth the reede...*Proserpina* was ravished in *Cicil*, the dearest soyle to *Ceres:* that was a most fruitful

and fertile Island. *Arethusa* (signifying the natural power and virtue of the seede and roote) is the first that tolde Ceres tidings of *Proserpina*[43]

Inheriting the rationalising and allegorising approach initiated by Cicero in *De Natura Deorum,* Fraunce sets out the structure of the Ceres story as a fertility myth and documents the stages of the feminine pastoral. Arethusa, the growing spirit of the corn, appears as a healing agent in Milton's *Lycidas*, in company with multitudes of benign female spirits of nature, from Orpheus' mother, the Muse Calliope, to the flower catalogue, which includes Proserpina's flower, the daffodil (150)—Cymoent's flower in Spenser's *Faerie Queene,* Perdita's in the pastoral Act of *The Winter's Tale.* The connection between Ceres and the other fertility goddesses, Pales, Pomona and Flora, is also methodically noted by Fraunce.[44] Pastoral elegy, associated with the Sicilian Theocritus, is—because of this deep association of woman with flowers, fruits, grain yield—a genre in which the feminine plays a focal part. At the root of structures within *The Faerie Queene,* Shakespeare's Last Plays, Milton's *Paradise Lost,* we shall find the transforming presence of Eleusis, asserting the principle of the feminine as the vitality of our mother-planet—the most tangible hope to which human nature can reach.

Beyond the home-planet, the feminine principle was located in the moon. All the goddesses are connected in being lunar rather than solar. Richard Linche's translation of Cartari, *The Fountaine of Ancient Fiction* (1599) explains in simple form the threefold nature of the goddess in terms of her heavenly name Luna, her earthly name Diana and her extension 'down even to the bowels of Erebus, where shee is called Hecate and Proserpina',[45] the latter because when the moon is fully waned she is considered to be under the earth's surface, in the realm of Hecate, the grave. This detail is a perfect example of the mythographers' intricate network of divinities, which they work on like a crafty but laborious piece of knitting with a view to showing that every deity is a manifestation of every other deity. Thus the myths of Diana meet and interweave with the myths of Ceres/Proserpina in the lunar symbol; also, the Hecate and Proserpina figures (crone/virgin maiden) are expressed as

attributes of one another. The generalisation may be made that
in the mythographers' view everything is finally everything else.
It is to this identification of All and One that their vastly
detailed accumulations of elaborate variants are heaped. And for
this reason there is a preference for the large inclusive
manifestations of the *una dea*, such as the Egyptian Isis, within
the literature of the period. The most crucial texts for study of
the Renaissance revival of the Isis cult are Plutarch's *De Iside et
Osiride* and Apuleius' *The Golden Asse*, translated into English
by William Adlington in 1566, the version which was known to
Lyly, Spenser and Shakespeare, casting white light over the
world of *A Midsummer Night's Dream*. Isis is associated with
revelation, insight, a new method of being human. (These
experiences are also expressed in the interpolated tale of 'Cupid
and Psyche', which figures human nature in the feminine person
of Psyche—Greek for both 'soul' and 'butterfly'—unfolding
through the stress of many metamorphoses towards, in final
form, unification with its 'other self', Eros. Psyche is the *anima*
searching out wholeness through union with the twin *animus*.)
Apuleius' Lucius has his own rather pressing reasons for seeking
metamorphosis, since he has been humiliatingly transformed
into an ass. In the famous eleventh book, Lucius experiences a
vision and a soul-change.

> When midnight came, that I had slept my first sleepe, I awaked with
> suddein feare, and sawe the Moone shininge bright, as when she is at
> the full, and seeming as though she leaped out of the Sea.
> (*The Golden Asse*, p.257)[46]

Here the visionary element so crucial in the retrieved mystery
cults is powerfully interpreted into English in the sudden 'leap'
from the sea of the moon's radiance. Though Lucius claims to
be awake, the experience has the hallucinatory strangeness of a
dream, with the telescoping of time as the feminine rushes out
of the matrix of the sea. It is midnight, the time of transition,
and the deep hour of the night at which time itself, and causal
relation, seem abolished. Lucius' perception is fraught with fear,
for he knows that this visionary planet has to do not only with
birth but with death and the underworld; yet equally he
apprehends that she comes as friend and reconciler, who 'doest

luminate al the borders of the yearth by thy feminine shape' (258). In the vision, Isis responds to Lucius' querying of her name or names by taking on a more fully distinct form as a goddess; 'planet' metamorphoses in the dream-medium to 'woman' (a process of metamorphosis which is recurrently associated with the feminine in Renaissance literature) and defines herself to him in a classic statement of the inclusiveness of the Isis-image. Her huge sentence is worth quoting in full because it conveys the importance of the multitudinous *nomina* and *numina* of the *una dea* whilst collecting all those fragmentary units of deity into one single whole. Of all the female deities, Isis is seen as the most inclusive. That, after all, is her story and function. She collects together the dismembered fragments of her brother-god, Osiris, makes them potent and impregnates herself with the recreated phallus. Like Proserpina, who bears the divine child to the god of the underworld, Isis through her united fidelity and art gives birth to the new god. Thus the significance of the goddess Isis is not just that she reclaims what has been lost (so does Ceres) but that she physically puts it back together again. This synthesis of disparate elements, and the fact that she is also the daughter of Thoth (Hermes Trismegistus, hence the association with Asclepius, healing, and Egyptian occultism) makes Isis central as a magically healing, cleansing, reconciling figure. As she tells Apuleius:

I am she that is the natural mother of all thinges, mistris and governesse of all the Elementes, the initiall progeny of worldes, chiefe of powers divine, Queene of heaven, the principall of the Goddes celestiall, the light of the Goddesses: at my wil the Planettes of the ayre, the holsome windes of the Seas, and the silences of Hell be disposed, my name, my divinitie is adored thoughout all the worlde in divers manners, in variable customes and in many names, for the Phrigiens call me the mother of the Goddes: the Atheniens, Minerve: the Cypriens, Venus: the Candians Diana: the Sicilians, Proserpina: the Eleusians, Ceres: some Juno, other Bellona, other Hecate: and principally the Ethiopians whiche dwell in the Orient, the Egyptians whiche are excellent in all kinde of auncient doctrine, and by their propre ceremonies accustome to worshippe me, doo call me Queen Isis. Behold I am come to take pitie

(*The Golden Asse*, p. 260)

Plutarch also refers to Isis as 'myriad-named' (53. 372E), and he
stresses the attribute Apuleius implies in the name 'Minerva', for
his Isis is 'exceptionally wise and devoted to wisdom' (2. 351E).[47]
She is a goddess of wisdom, whose mysteries lead Platonistically
to *gnosis* of the highest being, the otherwise unapprehensible
Osiris.[48] From Apuleius' more personal account, however, it is
clear that Isis represents a specific kind of wisdom, a turn of
mind radically different from that of the rational, daylight
world: an inner seeing, from which perception of time being
cancelled, a fundamentally altered kind of power 'comes to take
pitty' rather than to bully. The power exerted by Isis is a
matriarchal power, for she declares herself 'the natural mother of
all thinges'. It incorporates change and diversity, mediatorial
between life and death, inner and outer ('the Planettes of the
ayre...the silences of Hell'). It both terrifies and simultaneously
reassures the dreamer. After his vision at the festival of Isis, 'my
deforme and Assy face abated' (265): Bottom is translated, so to
speak, by moonlight.

Apuleius' symbols of moon and sea are central focuses of the
feminine in the literature of the English Renaissance. In the
Elizabethan period they partly cover for us, in the cult of the
Virgin Queen as Cynthia, Phoebe, Belphoebe, Diana, Astraea,
that difficult area which lies like an abyss between the world of
art and the world of life. The mythographers themselves
covered some of this gap by their rationalising insistence that
the myths they describe relate to 'real life' as allegory and
proverb. Thus Linche's *Fountain of Ancient Fiction* deals with
Aristotle's belittling interpretation of Minerva as indicating the
witless and inconstant mind of woman, by justifying 'that
praise-worthie sexe':

> there are in the world women of as great spirit, wit, capacitie, and
> setled resolutions as most men are, and are as eloquent in delivery of
> their thoughts, and as scholler-like in chusing fit and significant
> words, in composing and annexing their pithie, sententious, and
> well-placed phrases, as most men are whatsoever (exempting some
> professed Doctors, and daily Students.)
>
> (*Fountaine of Ancient Fiction*, 5. iv.)

In 1599 this is not particularly revolutionary. Throughout the sixteenth century a small number of learned patrician women had been educated as humanists, from the daughters of Sir Thomas More, for whom he set up a school run on the best humanist educational principles of linguistic and textual as well as scientific studies, to Queen Elizabeth herself, educated in the humanities by Roger Ascham so as to be a practising poet, an argumentative philosopher and an eloquent and self-congratulating classical linguist.[49] It has been objected that this élite of female Minervas was not only small but patronised both in the curriculum and in the motivation for its education; which was to reconstruct the feeble intellect natural to woman so as to present the humanist male with a worthy helpmeet.[50] While it is the case that Sir Thomas More quipped about woman's brain as liable to bear 'bracken' rather than 'corn'[51] (a nice irony when the age's preoccupation with corn-goddesses is considered), his image suggests, and he insists, that the fern-yielding wasteland is essentially cultivable. And even if he and his friend Erasmus (whose *A devout treatise upon the Pater Noster* his daughter Margaret translated and published) had insisted that woman's brain was the size of a pea and should only be educated as a kind of learned freak, this would not have altered the fact that in the sixteenth-century England women learned, they wrote and they governed. Certain attitudes towards the minority of women scholars changed. The tragic loss of nearly all Margaret Roper's humanistic works, the fact that Queen Elizabeth's poems are somewhat minor in quality and her colloquial Latin not quite as prodigious as she thought it, do not alter this simple fact of the attainment of learning and power by some women.[52] The questioning occurred of attitudes and theories of woman's nature and place held to be self-evident over hundreds or thousands of years. The discrepancy between what some women actually achieved and what the Church, the law and public opinion said was permissible and possible is a gap which must be acknowledged by all writers on this subject.[53] But what the status quo denied was, we have to remember, contradicted first by practice, second by extraordinary libertarian male thinkers and thirdly by the mythographers and the myth-making imaginativeness of politics, art and literature. Cornelius Agrippa argued in *De nobilitate et præcellentia foeminei sexus* (1529) that woman was outrageously discriminated against in law; that Eve,

so loaded with her scapegoat burden, was actually superior to
Adam. Her Hebrew name meant 'life' itself, Adam's just 'red
earth'; as last-created, fabricated from flesh not dust, in Paradise,
and able to bear God, which Adam's sons are not biologically
fitted to do, she was man's superior.[54] Comparable heresies
entered literature in the form of the imaginative exuberance, say,
of Beatrice, in *Much Ado About Nothing:*

> *Leonato.* Well, niece, I hope to see you one day fitted with a
> husband.
> *Beatrice.* Not till God make men of some other metal than earth.
> Would it not grieve a woman to be over-mastered with a piece of
> valiant dust? to make an account of her life to a clod of wayward
> marl? No, uncle, I'll none: Adam's sons are my brethren; and,
> truly, I hold it a sin to match in my kindred.
>
> (II. i. 53-60)

The kind of thing that Cornelius Agrippa could argue in the
Latin of juristic and theological discourse, Beatrice argues in the
English of a play, and Spenser's Una demonstrates in Book I of
The Faerie Queene in an 'angels face' which 'made a sunshine in the
shadie place' (I. iii. 4) and seems immune to the recurrent
pattern of stumblings and fallings of her male counterpart.
Woman comes free of the clay and dust out of which man is
formed in *The Faerie Queene,* as though one Eve had been exiled
but another remained at home within the original garden.
Belphoebe is born free of original sin (III. vi. 3). Even in Milton's
Paradise Lost this Agrippan awareness of woman as life itself, as
last, dearest and most redemptive of God's creations, is allowed
to escape the author's own sourest curse upon her. Where
Adam cannot give birth, Eve and the poet can: 'By me the
promised seed shall all restore' (XIII. 623).

A familiar expression on the Renaissance face is one of
duplicity. Its Janus temperament sees with dual vision and
maintains a vehemently self-contradictory set of opinions. Eve
the first criminal whose daughters we may still punish with
impunity is accompanied by Eve whose body is not made of
earth and whose birth-canal is the channel of redemption. The
pagan goddesses are all lies and humbug; on the contrary, they
allegorise deep truths. Woman is a bane and a fool, and a scold:
she is the highest being we can know or imagine. She is the

alienated other; she is, like Psyche, our truest self. Once this duplicity is grasped, our optic nerves may be trained to see two of everything. We can perceive, for instance, the two Venuses of Ficino: Venus Urania, heavenly and spiritual; Venus Pandemos, of the earth and less trustworthy. There are two Floras: the Botticellian and Ovidian flower-spirit of the new year; the Roman prostitute whom it is not nice to mention in good company. There are even two Pandoras: the first a regrettable mistake on the part of her creator, Prometheus, whose inquisitive opening of the box of all gifts lost the race all good things save Hope; the scond 'the all-gifted' or 'the gift of all' who is in herself a cornucopia bestowed upon a lucky species.[55] In literature this dual vision relates to the theme of doubling, twinning and mirror-reflection. In Spenser's *The Faerie Queene* Una's false double, Duessa, reflects the problem all encounter in life of distinguishing reality from fiction; the two Floras are suggested in Book III by the witch's manufacture of a false Florimell out of an amazing factory of materials in the way of golden wire for hair and burning lamps in silver sockets for eyes (III. viii. 7), animating this stuffed doll with such art 'That who so then her saw, would surely say,/It was her selfe' (9). Spenser exposes a shadow-world of false copies which plays upon the moral eyesight of his characters like the flame-cast shadows upon the wall of Plato's cave of the senses in the *Republic*.

Double vision, as I shall show, became not only a possible way of measuring the gap between art or philosophy and reality but practically inescapable when the young Tudor princess Elizabeth ascended the throne in 1557 and seemed against all the odds likely to survive in this volatile position, not to wish to share her seat with a Spanish or a French husband, able to keep the peace, make money and remain Protestant. This fact of a forty-six year reign by a woman, mythologised in her own time, informed the Idea of woman not only in Spenser and Shakespeare, who, writing in her reign would be supposed to have a vested interest in supporting the floral 'Aprill' of her rule and in worshipping whatever moon-goddesses were considered politically desirable, but also artists practising years after the lonely and autocratic monarch's death in 1603. 'Spenserians' continued to write poetry and drama under Stuarts and Protectorate, including Milton. Nearly fifty years of myth-making do not terminate with the life of that merely human being who is their pretext. Art does not absolutely mistake its dreams for life. 'There is one goddess', as Martianus Rufus wrote, despite the fact that one conspicuous example goes into the dark. Thus, though in James I and VI's reign the white Isis-magic of the inviolable queen's reign was reinterpreted by that woman-hating, hag-ridden Scot as black and demonic,[56] and under his influence witch-hunting flared, the feminine power was still in the air. The *una dea*, feared as Hecate, was still remembered even in the baleful, curdled atmosphere of Jacobean revenge drama, as having once enjoyed existence as Gloriana. Thus Tourneur in *The Revengers Tragedy* (1607) gives us a heroine who features on stage as an exhumed skull. This lady, whose name is Gloriana, has been mouldering for a total of nine years. She was deflowered before her death. The nine-year period between the conception and birth of Vindice's revenge for her rape and death evokes the nine months of pregnancy; but the process is reversed. Woman is a 'thing',[57] which returns the man who kisses her poisoned mouth to the condition of a 'thing'. To name this unpleasing lady 'Gloriana' is to lament the death of the glorious Eliza, Spenser's sacred lady: it is to deplore the corruption of the Jacobean court. But, more deeply, it is to remember her and wish her back. Jacobean cynicism may be viewed as another manifestation of the Tudor Idea of woman; Webster's *White Devil* personifies a bad dream of female demonism, which the tragedy purges, but it remembers a diamond-whiteness in the image. An Arthurian Elizabethan revival centred around the persons of James I's children, Prince Henry and Princess Elizabeth, a Protestant and humanist chivalry that came to grief with the death of the nineteen-year-old prince in 1612.[58]

Elizabeth's motto had been *semper eadem*. As her childbearing years ran out, and the sterile throne became a self-referring monument to a unique longevity of personal power, the myths of Elizabeth elaborated themselves as Protestant versions of the cult of the Virgin Mary,[59] female versions of the new Arthur, Christian versions of the pagan deities, especially Astræa and Diana, modern versions of the viragos of the Old Testament, Judith and Deborah.[60] Lyly, Peele, Dekker, Greene, Raleigh, Spenser, Nashe, Sabie, Davies and Shakespeare all

colluded in the weaving of this huge mutual tapestry of art and
myth. Of all the testimonials to the beauty of the idea of the
miraculous lady, none is more movingly eloquent than this
snatch of prose from Dekker's *The Wonderfull Yeare* (1603),
Gloriana's epitaph:

> Shee came in with the falle of the leafe, and went away in the Spring:
> her life (which was dedicated to Virginitie,) both beginning &
> closing vp a miraculous Mayden circle: for she was borne vpon a
> Lady Eve, and died vpon a Lady Eve.[61]

The graceful, courteous sentence closes round its paradox with
the sense of a completed, ultimate statement. It conveys the
satisfaction of a life well measured, reposing upon the perfection
of its own grammar. It is a pastoral life, which has to do with
seasonal circularity. Its statement dictates against the closing of
the calendar upon human aspirations—the cold waning of the
year in the December eclogue of Spenser's *Shepheardes Calender:*
'Winter is come, that blowes the balefull breath,/And after
Winter commeth timely death' (XII. 149-50). Elizabeth
challenges the natural close of the pastoral year in Dekker's
celebration both by entering as a visitor to mortality rather than
as inmate and by challenging the calendar and therefore the
genre of our lives. At her birth the year was dying; at her death,
the year was being born. The pattern is recreative, the structure
of her life tragi-comic. Lady Eve, the Virgin Mary's sacred time,
reinforces this miraculous association with virgin
motherhood—a life mysteriously linked to the harvest and the
floralia of the Age of Peace. Shakespeare's tragi-comedies,
beginning in winter and turning towards spring, come like a late
tribute to the departed image of the virgin-mother. The 'Mayden
circle' of Elizabeth's reign is encompassed in John Lyly's
Endimion. The Man in the Moone (1591), where Elizabeth as
moon-and-sea goddess is '*Cynthia* of all cyrcles the most
absolute';[62] in Raleigh's lyric 'Praised be Dianas faire and
harmles light' as 'Eternitie in her oft chaunge she beares'.[63] The
aged, querulous and cadaverous queen of the 1590's renews
herself in eternal recurrence to youth, waxing and waning
rhythmically between fullness, crescent and the *dea abscondita*
transiently set under the earth or in the sea. When the time

came for Elizabeth I to die, she could still be apprehended in this role of *dea abscondita*, real though imperceptible. The connection lingered as long as humanism in England—or a shade longer.[64]

Personified in Elizabeth, or in Catherine de Medici, the feminine is an image of glorified power. In a period which was frequently given to picturing the gory extremes of human behaviour, images such as that of the bliblical figure of God's chosen avenger, Judith, severing His enemy Holofernes' head, or holding it aloft, were much favoured. A savage *Judith and Holofernes* (1614-20) by the female artist Artemisia Gentileschi hangs in the Uffizi: Judith carves at the neck with her right hand; her left fist clutching the still-living victim's hair; his blood squirts in thin fountains. Judith concentrates hard, her face and busy arms irradiated.[65] In England, Michael Drayton celebrated Judith's holy butchering in 'The Song of Judith' with the incomparable bathos of 'Her beautie hath bewitcht his mind, her sword cut off his head'.[66] Power politics and the art of slaughter are no nicer when women rather than men exercise them. Elizabeth was the English and Protestant Judith, to whose Holofernes—whether in the person of Pope, Spaniard or Catholic Stuart cousin—pity was not considered due. She was a warrior-queen, furtive sponsor of pirates[67] and leader of her army. Riding into Tilbury before the Armada in 1588, her speech capitalised on the apparent contradiction between her woman's physique and the martial spirit of her role and bearing as the defender of her nation:

> being resolved in the midst of the heat of the battle to live or die amongst you all; to lay down for my God and for my Kingdom and for my people my honour and my blood even in the dust.[68]

If a male monarch addressed the same words to his troops prior to a great battle, they would surely seem completely unremarkable. Something might be thought lacking in the way of the Agincourt rhetoric. But the words are transformed by the fact of being spoken by a woman—consciously so. Elizabeth flaunts and exploits her gender throughout her long life of public oratory. In a speech of 1566 she alludes disarmingly to her 'petticoat' condition: she has the body of 'a weak and feeble woman', but as a 'prince of England' she claims an epic nature. Elizabeth claims not an unnatural but a supernatural status as a warrior-queen. She embodies the realm as does the king in her 'body politic', but since her mortal 'body natural' is female, she incarnates England in a specifically female incorporation.[69] A queen who can be believed when she asserts her willingness to 'lay down...my blood even in the dust' is exploiting sexual stereotypes so as to claim, like Jeanne d'Arc, a talismanic power and virtue. Yet it is important to note that Elizabeth does not offer directly to hack off the enemy's head like a Judith. She does not envisage herself as taking an aggressive but rather a defensive role. The paid (or, as it turned out, unpaid) soldiers are hired to do the killing; the epic role of the warrior-maiden if to *be* there 'to live or die...to lay down'.

Thus the terminology of power, and the whole meaning of power in the state, is translated by the gender of the ruler. Feminine traditions assimilated to the world of power politics radically alter the agreed perception of that world. Power becomes easier to idealise. The filth of bloodshed (given Elizabeth's restraint in the exercise of that art) is distanced. Personal values are brought into the public world. An example may clarify this. In English law the sovereign is conventionally *pater patriae*, father of his country. This is said at his coronation and used in legal definitions of his relationship to his people. As their 'author' he must cherish, govern and be responsible for them. To kill him is parricide; to obey him a matter not just of civil law but of 'natural law'.[70] But, as her coronation oath and the Bible gave her the obligation of doing, Elizabeth becomes not just the *sponsus regni* whose ceremonial ring signifies her marriage to the realm, but also *mater patriae* (mother of her nation). The sacramental relationship between monarch and realm is redefined according to the peculiar traditions, taboos and mystiques attaching to the mother-bond. The Book of Isaiah told her that 'kynges shalbe thy nursyng fathers, and queenes shalbe thy nursyng mothers' (49:23). This meant that she fed the nation with the political equivalent of her own breast-milk, a feat which with the best will in the world it is easier to imagine a woman undertaking than a man. The queen gives birth to, nurtures, fosters and 'loves' her nation (as Elizabeth's speeches claim) with a deeply personal love, as of mother to her children. As virgin mother, being of an allegorical turn of mind as regards both clothes and poems, she often dressed in white; as nursing mother, she enacted the role of pelican, the bird which feeds its young upon its own blood, the emblem of the atoning Christ. Thus, though England was never, and would never have dreamed of being, a matri-linear state, for a brief and idealised period of its history it perceived itself as being a matriarchy.

It is a strange consideration that this individual, Elizabeth Tudor, is the one indisputable link between living 'feminism' and the 'feminism' of the art-world. The hair-fine endurance of one person's life, mythologised, was enough to stretch across that gulf to reflect its own dominant image into the world of poetry. Humanists knew that if we were all cast into alternative forms (like Ulysses' men, say, transformed by Circe into different animal species) and given free choice, it is highly unlikely that we should actively choose to come back into human form as a woman. In his brilliant dialogue, *Circe* (1549), Giovanni Battista Gelli adapted the familiar Renaissance habit of exploring through impersonation other modes of being, to the question of what it feels like to be a woman. Disguise, as in Spenser and Shakespeare, makes free and reveals. Ulysses interviews the talking animals on Circe's island, inviting them back to the mainland of their original human being. No one will come. The oyster would rather stay safe and comatose in his shell than encounter the risks run by the sensitive skin of humanity. The afflictions of class and gender in society are active deterrents to the return of all but Gelli's philosophically inclined elephant. From behind the security of her disguise as a deer, a woman speaks out:

Hind. . . .ask us, or ask experience, and you will find us as fit to govern, nay, preside, in affairs of the highest importance. Consider the kingdom of the *Amazons*, how long was that preserved without their being indebted to any of you, either in Politicks or in War? To relate how the bounds of the *Babylonish* empire was extended by *Semiramis,* or the *Scythian* by *Tomyris,* were to transcribe your histories, which abound with their exploits.
Ul. And how many more such can you name? I fancy you may count them all upon the fingers of one hand.

Hind. For which we may thank you; who never give us an opportunity of exercising these faculties, but keep us immured within your own houses, employed in all the low offices that the care of a family brings with it; for which our sole reward is, to hear you say magisterially, that a Woman's fame and her employment should begin and end within the compass of her *own walls.*

(Circe, p.110)[71]

Tantalising vistas of epic fields for female endeavour are glimpsed by the ex-woman far in the past. Nowadays woman is tamed and quartered in her own personal prison-house. Better, she feels, to live as a deer grazing the fields of the outdoor world than risk not only confinement but also the perplexing public insistence that inequality and constriction are natural and pleasant to you, and the cancellation of your traditions and history by the male pen. For the deer, history is 'your histories', but even there she can resentfully point out the examples of autonomous women: Amazons, Semiramis, Tomyris. Female voices in Renaissance drama by men are constantly raised to echo the deer's point of view. 'The best condition is but bad enough' is their theme, like Middleton's Isabella in *Women Beware Women* (c. 1620), pitted against the economic basis of the marital bond, in which 'when women have their choices, commonly/They do but buy their thraldoms'.[72] The plays do not necessarily endorse such views, neither do they deny them. Like Gelli, they vividly imagine and impersonate them. Gelli's ex-woman recollects two insults to her nature with a peculiar force: her suffocation in the indoor world; the scandalous degrading of her nature through the miswriting of her history. She has been written off, or written out.

Nearly forty years later, Spenser tried to write womankind back into the epic, outdoor world. The incentive to do so included, naturally enough, self-interest: the wish to ingratiate himself with the female 'prince' of her nation. Perhaps *The Faerie Queene* is the longest unfinished compliment to autocracy in any language. But surely, also, Spenser shows a deep temperamental affinity with the feminine, likely to have stemmed from more than ambitious motives; a desire to do justice to the Idea of woman. In Book III, Spenser portrays Elizabeth as Britomart, a warrior-maiden whose military exploits, judgment and courage are more than equal to the skills of the male Arthurian knights furiously questing, jousting, riddling and quarrelling around her. The androgynous Britomart is not a *lusus naturae* but the representative of an original free and heroic womanhood entitled to rule and adjusted to forceful action. As Britomart she is 'British Mars', summing up in a paradoxically lyrical and sensitive nature the talent for organised ferocity which the British have shown throughout history. As a variant of 'Britomartis', she is based on a Cretan manifestation of the goddess Diana, and thence of Elizabeth the warrior-virgin. Gelli's Ulysses had argued that the number of able women in history could be counted on the fingers of one hand. Spenser, the epic poet both of Protestant and matriarchal Britain explains why. History itself is a male fabrication. History is written by men, and it has been in their interest either to minimise or score out the contributions of woman. He links this with woman's confinement to the indoor world, from which, however, they are already showing such disconcerting signs of intellectual and political precocity that their captors are having to think up more drastic means of subjecting them:

> Here have I cause, in men just blame to find,
> > That in their proper prayse too partiall bee,
> > And not indifferent to woman kind,
> > To whom no share in armes and chevalrie
> > They do impart, ne maken memorie
> > Of their brave gestes and prowesse martiall;
> > Scarse do they spare to one or two or three,
> > Rowme in their writs; yet the same writing small
> Does all their deeds deface, and dims their glories all.

> But by record of antique times I find,
> > That women wont in warres to beare most sway,
> > And to all great exploits them selves inclind:
> > Of which they still the girlond bore away,
> > Till envious Men fearing their rules decay,
> > Gan coyne streight lawes to curb their liberty;
> > Yet sith they warlike armes have layd away,
> > They have exceld in artes and pollicy,
> That now we foolish men that prayse gin eke t'envy.
> > > > > > (*The Faerie Queene*, III. ii. 1-2)

It is a myth, of course; but then, we are concerned with myths. The probability that there has never been a Golden Age of Womankind, noble and free, and the probable accuracy of misogynistic historians whom we with Spenser despise, does not detract from the value of the idea itself. If such women had existed, we know that historians would have unaccountably found their paper and ink running out, so as to necessitate cramped 'writing small', in Spenser's brilliant phrase. There is a special irony in the verb 'deface' when applied to the heroic deeds of women. They are conventionally valued for their faces, but not very highly; their names and deeds are willingly written out of the book of life, their features and characters rubbed out. In 'defacing' woman, the human race in the person of its spokesman over time, the historian, has desecrated something of rare value. With its 'streit lawes' it has bound her. Spenser's poem lifts these laws, to let its female heroes onto the battlefield and the pilgrim's way in pursuit of wisdom and experience. He lifts the constraints placed on their lives in the real world by 'envious Men', as Shakespeare will do in defining the cardinal sin of the masculine mind as forms of jealousy; Lear's irate self-love in disowning Cordelia; Othello's, and Leontes', and Posthumus' murderous jealousy. The crime against women is also seen as an offence against the mother-tongue. Each author seeks to cure 'diseased opinion' (*The Winters' Tale*, I. ii. 297) and reform a corrupted language. The language of poetry is this redeemed mother-tongue. The Muse has to be recognised as feminine. When Milton wrote *Paradise Lost*, the Spenserian influence, or a buried temperamental affinity, was still so strong in him that at the same time as, in the fortifying company of Jehovah and Adam, he condemns Eve as 'Defaced, deflowered, and now to death devote' (IX. 901), his poetry redeems her image from the spite of the false etymologies he liked to share with his age. 'O woe to man, that woman thus can move!' cried out Sir William Alexander not very originally in 'The first Houre' of his *Doomes-Day* (1637).[73] Milton's habitual spelling of woman, which seems to have given him repeated pleasure was 'Woeman' woe to man (see pp. 180–1 below). 'Eve' was a feasible root of 'evil'. But in the great game between the self that loves and the self that hates, Milton may be said to have preferred 'Queen Truth'[74] and her language to the vituperative rant of the tyrannies against whom his writings fought. *Paradise Lost* spells a return to the Platonistic dream of the original androgyne:

> Part of my soul I seek thee, and thee claim
> My other half.

2

Spenser

THE FOUR GRACES

The poet who was to celebrate the virgin queen of England as the Gloriana of his unfinished epic, *The Faerie Queene,* was by a graceful coincidence framed during his life by a group of four Elizabeths. The first is his mother, Elizabeth Spenser, with whom in the beautiful *Prothalamion* he perhaps indentifies London as his 'Lifes first native sourse' (129), associating the place of his origin with the person who originated him. A sister was also named Elizabeth. The third Elizabeth, whose power dominates his public and poetic life, is Queen Elizabeth I, to whom he dedicates the art of his 'life-resembling pencill' (*Faerie Queene,* III. Proem, 2) in the darkening hope of public recognition. The fourth and final Elizabeth, who completes the nominal symmetry of Spenser's personal life—a symmetry which, as a lover of numerological patternings he would surely have enjoyed—is Elizabeth Boyle, with whom he fell in love comparatively late in life, married in 1594 (he being about forty, she in her early twenties), and celebrated both in his sonnet-sequence, the *Amoretti,* and his *Epithalamion.* This last Elizabeth is figured by him as a home-coming, in whom the poet of wanderings achieves 'the joyous safety of so sweet a rest' (*Amoretti,* LXIII). During the restless passages between the court of Queen Elizabeth and virtual public exile in Ireland, and during the writing of the literally endless odysseys of the many heroes of *The Faerie Queene,* a poem without an end, Elizabeth Boyle is felt as the Ithaca to his Odysseus, the mainland of home after 'long stormes and tempests'.

Spenser's son by Elizabeth Boyle was aptly name Peregrine, 'the wanderer', an eloquent living testimony to the poet's obsession with existence as a journey across one's lifetime in

search of some imperfectly imagined ideal, or ideal self. The
globe spreads out in all directions in *The Faerie Queene*, to be
encountered without reliable map or compass, like the landscape
of a dream,[1] shifting in and out of focus, with a dream's intricate
but elusive precisions of name and structure, but with dilations
of space and time, immeasurably unfolding before Spenser's
pilgrims and travellers. All is unstable and deceptive. The past
curls up behind them as they walk; persons they meet are
suddenly and inexplicably lost to them; they gallop in and out of
forests, visit mesmerising houses, fight gory battles with
unknown knights they do not have particular reason to hate.
The whole unfinished journey ends in 'Mutabilitie', and 'The
VIII. Canto, unperfite' concludes in a prayer, the monumental
line 'O that great Sabboth God, graunt me that Sabaoths
sight.' The poem ends in change and pleads for rest. Ten years
after Spenser's death, Ben Jonson told Drummond of
Hawthornden that when the Irish rebels burnt him out of his
Irish home in 1598, 'a little child new born' was also burnt in the
holocaust.[2] Spenser and Elizabeth escaped to Cork, and fled
from there to court in London; but he died 'for lake of bread' in
King Street, in bitterness and destitution, and exile in 'mery
London, my most kyndly Nurse' (*Prothalamion*, 128). Camden
said that the poets threw their pens and verses into his grave in
Westminster Abbey. These are such haunting and unsettling
images of the conclusion of Spenser's quest that the poet might
almost have dreamed them up himself in sardonic self-
allegorisation: a new-born baby burning; Gloriana's unthanked
poet starving; the graceful but vapid tribute of the pen-throwing
poets gathered at the burial ceremony.

But throughout Spenser's writings, against the volatile
surfaces of reality stands a composing principle of impartial
stabilisation: metaphorically, the four Elizabeths, both in art
and in life. The mercurial and ambitious nature which naturally
gravitated to its like in his aggressive friend, Raleigh, sought its
opposite as a way of alleviating a raw sense of the landslide
quality latent in things. The recurrent symbol of the
hermaphrodite centralises the emotional meanings of *The Faerie
Queene:* it mysteriously fuses the contradictions of the poem,
whose polarities pour through the hermaphroditic Venus of
Book IV and the hermaphroditic goddess Nature of

'Mutabilitie'. This happens too with individual persons, the androgynous Britomart in Books III and IV, and with couples, Venus and Adonis, Scudamore and Amoret, Psyche and Cupid. The poem's opposites always flow towards and occasionally enter deeply into one another, like strong currents meeting. In the 1590 ending of Book III, Scudamore and Amoret are compared with a 'faire Hermaphrodite' (xii. 46a). This is the mysteriously perfect way to be. There are secret and occult meetings to this symbolism, which will be glanced at later, but the most important message is simple and personal. Any child could read it: under all the fuss, theology and hard words, there is only love to make us one.

The present section is entitled 'The Four Graces', which must be seen as very peculiar arithmetic by any standards, since everyone has always known that only three Graces are available and necessary. Spenser's arithmetic is very strange, not only in the abstruse numerological preoccupations which excited him and amaze us as modern readers. He was fascinated by the odd numbers of human experience, its apparent randomness and the imbalances of the multitudinous cosmos. Like all Platonists, he was forever trying to make these numbers add up to One, in the end. But his liking for 'odd' numbers is opposed by a perhaps even stronger wish for 'evenness' of number. Odd numbers are male by tradition and generally thought to be better than the suspect female 'even' numbers. When Eve was created from Adam's side, that made two—a bad thing. But Spenser, in this as in so many ways, both reverences the tradition and quietly reverses the system of values attaching to it. Triads are certainly functional in his poem, though very dreary (the Sansloy and Triamond brothers, Medina and her sisters);[3] Christianity, after all, has a Trinity of male gods, and triads were very popular with Aristotle, so threesomes would be obligatory. But rather than accept the three Graces intact, Spenser both at the beginning and the end of his poetic career suggested that it would be more satisfactory to add a fourth, in the person of an Elizabeth. In the fourth eclogue of his *Shepheardes Calender* (1579) 'Elisa' features as a pastoral image of 'Her Grace' the queen, whom he thinks to add to the three Graces whose eternal dance brings the celestial music within the compass of the sublunary world:

Wants not a fourth grace, to make the daunce even?
Let that rowme to my Lady be yeven:
    She shalbe a grace,
    To fyll the fourth place,
And reigne with the rest in heaven.
              (*The Shepheardes Calender*, IV. 113-17)

Nearly twenty years later Spenser allowed the uninitiated eye of
Sir Calidore, and that of the reader, to penetrate the secret
vision of the poet upon Mount Acidale. Within the dancing ring
of the hundred naked maidens (*The Faerie Queene*, VI. x. 11),
there dances concentrically an inner ring of the Three Graces
like the Crown of Ariadne in the firmament. Enclosed within the
circle-within-a-circle is an initially unnamed fourth. (12–15)
The vision perishes as soon as Calidore stumbles out of hiding
and shows himself, the gauche voyeur of the wheeling cosmos
itself. Colin, the pastoral poet and Spenser's mask for himself,
breaks his pipe in a fury (18). But who was the woman he saw in
the middle, Calidore pesters him? Colin replies that this is
'another Grace' (26–7), Gloriana herself, Elizabeth. The
longing is being expressed for a life that is 'even' rather than
'odd', based on Spenser's sense of a want or vacancy in the
pattern of reality, an asymmetry requiring a new mathematics
of amendment. Such a gap or unevenness in the plenitude of
creation, as it is experienced day by day, Spenser seeks to amend
through the even feminine principle. As in the emblem books,
so in *The Faerie Queene*, female personages outweigh male in
emotional stress of meaning. As C.S. Lewis saw, Spenser
reverses mythological norms in making the mother principle
dominate the father principle in *The Faerie Queene*, a
hair-raising proposition for many patriarchs of criticism who,
however, like Fowler, found that 'it is possible to escape the
many difficulties this theory gives rise to'.[4]

    There is no real need to run for the escape route. As Beatrice
was to Dante, so 'Elizabeth', fourfold or singular, is to Spenser.
The 'four Graces' of *The Shepheardes Calender* and of *The Faerie
Queene* represent the *quaternio*, called by the Pythagoreans 'the
perpetual fountain of nature',[5] figuring amity and the idea of the
cosmos itself. The feminine in Colin's vision, circle within circle,
centring inwards to the most sacred Lady of all, figures the

mystery of the All.

At the same time, the dancing ring of spheres of the cosmos, the Botticellian circling maidens on Mount Acidale like moving garlands of flowers, represent the world within—the mind, in its integrity and wholeness. Calidore pushes forwards, excitedly gesticulating. The vision perishes. The dreamer crossly awakens to break his pipe. But Spenser's implication is that the vision of Venus the reconciler at the centre of the world is always a possibility; we may sleep and dream again, live to sing again. Spenser internalises the feminine principle. He seems to locate and see, not an image of the 'other'—foreign, alien, antithetical—but fugitive reflections of the psyche itself. The search for identification of man with woman (Spenser with Elizabeth in the *Amoretti* and *Epithalamion;* epic heroes with epic heroines in *The Faerie Queene*) is also a journey inwards, to educate and elucidate the most richly yielding sources of creativity. The beloved woman is repeatedly understood as an image of that which is most precious and restorative within the self. As Apuleius' Psyche seeks herself in Cupid in *The Golden Asse,* as the souls in Ficino's Plato seek their other halves and as the cosmos in the *Hermetica* androgynously embraces itself (see pp. 2–6 above), so Spenser seeks himself in the Elizabeths.

This is clear in the *Amoretti,* whose story is Spenser's long courtship of Elizabeth Boyle, bearing fruit in the mighty central sonnets in which the lover, upon renouncing claim to possession, paradoxically achieves union. The good, austere grammar of the sonnets characterises the departure Spenser has made from the Petrarchan profanities satirised by Milton as:

> serenade, which the starved lover sings
> To his proud fair, best quitted with disdain.
> (*Paradise Lost,* IV, 769–70)

The affinity in which the lovers meet is 'simple truth and mutuall good will' (*Amoretti,* LXV). In the great Easter sonnet beginning 'Most glorious Lord of lyfe' (LXVIII), the poet dedicates their equal, atoned and adjusted lives to a sacred kinship in Christ's love. The fourth Elizabeth is understood both as a sacred sanctuary and as a guiding, structuring principle of education—a mind within his mind:

You frame my thoughts and fashion me within,
you stop my toung, and teach my heart to speake,
you calm the storme that passion did begin
                                        (*Amoretti*, VIII)

To 'frame' and 'fashion' is to recreate the inmost nature of the
poet: to his intemperately verbose character she is the agent of
quietening; to his passive and undirected nature she is active and
constructive. The fourth Elizabeth becomes the architect of the
private soul, like Temperance itself (or actually herself,
Temperantia) in *The Faerie Queene*: 'this goodly frame...
grounded...fast setteled' (II.xii.1). This 'framing' of the
soul signifies the provision of a home. Both the questing hero,
Sir Guyon, and the poem on the page are 'this goodly frame of
Temperance', being built on firm foundations. The significance
of this identification of the feminine with the power to 'frame'
and 'fashion' will not be clear unless we realise the extent of the
poet's sense of protean homelessness. Like his friend Sir Philip
Sidney's poet in *An Apology for Poetry*, Spenser 'lifted up with
the vigour of his own invention, doth grow in effect into
another nature' (but he does not know what that nature is); like
Sidney's poet, Spenser's imagination is not constrained by the
limitations of the natural world but flies 'freely ranging only
within the zodiac of his own wit'[6] (but is deeply confused as to
where he is going). The humanist dream, bequeathed by Pico
(see pp. 8–9 above) of man's boundless capacity to take any shape
at any time has the potentiality to turn to agitated nightmare.
To be boundless is to be without boundaries, eternally out-of-
doors.

Spenser writes exceptionally well of Proteus (e.g. *Faerie
Queene*, III.viii). He writes so magnificently about shape-
changing that he bears the label the English Ovid.[7] He is a poet
of abundant, promiscuous talent; the sheer length of *The Faerie
Queene* and its infinity of stories testify to this. His Odyssean
curiosity was endless; his reading omnivorous; his imagination
and insights fertile and teeming. It is as if this very abundance
engendered feelings of fatal insecurity. The wanderers in *The
Faerie Queene* recurrently enter houses which are never homes
but intricate systems of rooms which might not be there again if
you turn round. They are carefully described, and then left

behind: the House of Pride (intimately known and authoritatively described by the poet) with its bad foundations; the House of Holiness, all solidity and improving conversation; Alma's Castle besieged by restless enemies; the House of Busyrane with its salacious tapestries and its enchanted room where a man is writing using a girl's blood for ink. More than the journey itself, the houses testify to an insecurity which is not only a metaphor for general human loneliness or the wanderings of the poetic imagination, but the thrusting male ego's bafflement as it seeks targets and spoils and then is surprised not to find a resting-place. *The Faerie Queene* speaks against the ethos of love-conquest in which woman is taken as a possession. It should not be attempted and it cannot be done. In Book V, at Isis Church, Britomart's dream in which she stands on the symbol of Osirian patriarchal law (the crocodile) signifies the transcendence of male by female law (vii. 3–24). The Book of Justice thus teaches the same message as the *Amoretti*: 'you frame...teach...calm' (surprisingly, perhaps, for love sonnets might be supposed to tell of experience that arouses, deranges, overwhelms). Spenser figures the work of poetic composition as the reflex of a hard-won inner composure, born of conjunction of male and female. The feminine is both the poet's inspiration, the Platonic *ekstasis* which in the *Fowre Hymnes* initiates in the 'ravisht soule' the power to see through 'bright radiant eyes' (*Heavenly Love*, 281, 283), but she is also the *techne*, the framing craft through whose skill the poet shapes his material. The skill is Orphic, the measured power to sing the dead alive, reversing Euridice's double death.

In the beautiful *Epithalamion*, which Spenser wrote for his own marriage to Elizabeth Boyle, the Orphic poet associates himself unmistakably with an élite in possession of ancient secret knowledge, spelt out in the hieroglyphs of Orpheus's story. It is an esoteric and also a private poem:

> So Orpheus did for his owne bride,
> So I unto my selfe alone will sing,
> The woods shall to me answer and my Eccho ring.
> (*Epithalamion*, 16–18)

The occultly private truth he sings is the bride. It may also be understood as the Euridice-in-himself, who must be retrieved from the mind's underworld (as Orpheus did for his own bride). The refrain alludes to the gist of Orpheus' coming tragedy, for 'my Eccho ring' associates the poet with the myth of Narcissus whose sterile self-admiration for 'my selfe alone' was fatal for the nymph, Echo. Disembodied Euridice fleeing back into the grave is like disembodied Echo, dwindled to a voice in a cave.[8] As the marriage poem unfolds from the wedding rituals to nightfall, the poet learns the art of cancelling the self-proclaiming echo, as he imagines the fertile love-making which is followed by shared sleep in the 'one flesh' of the marriage-bed: 'Ne let the woods us answere, nor our Eccho ring' (389). This shared sleep, like that enjoyed by the lovers in Milton's Eden,[9] is *gnosis*, the mysterious knowledge Ficino conjured for and which Botticelli's paint sought to recreate on canvas. It is a knowledge of eternity in the moment:

> Be unto her a goodly ornament,
> And for short time an endlesse moniment.
> (*Epithalamion*, 432-3)

With its 24 stanzas and 365 long lines not counted for many centuries, until a modern scholar told them over,[10] the *Epithalamion* was a secret and silent monument to the mortal brevity of those few timeless and sacred hours. It celebrated with consciously secretive Orphism a fertile, generative love which for Spenser was always intrinsic to the Idea of woman as the source of creativity. The nameless, newly born baby which was generated by that union is said to have been burnt to ash in its crib; the 'endless moniment' was left to the young widow of a destitute poet whose grave was the receptacle of other poets' pens. Spenser in this less enviable sense, of abundant losses, was authentically Orphic.

The image of wholeness remains when all its constituent realities have gone their separate ways in the process of decomposition. The great symbol of the hermaphrodite dominates *The Faerie Queene*. The figure is not that of the male hermaphrodite, the gelded effeminate of old and often lewd imagining, which made Ovid's Hermaphroditus both a teasing riddle and a joke for the Renaissance.[11] Spenser's hermaphrodites are predicated on the 'Aphrodite' constituent, taking her as the inclusive and major figure. The male is taken into the Venerean female, as he is before birth, as he returns in the act of love and (since 'Mother Nature' is archetypally implied) as he expects to re-enter her after death.[12] By her very nature Spenser's hermaphroditic divinity relates to literally everyone and everything else in the poem. The androgynous individuals like Britomart, and androgynous couples like Amoret and Scudamore, correspond most closely, like mirror-reflections from a central, living source. The two major hermaphroditic deities are the bisexual goddess at the Temple of Venus in Book IV and the goddess Nature in the 'Mutabilitie' cantos. Both are intensely secret. Their faces are veiled, and Spenser does not gesture towards lifting the veil so that his readers can pry. One implication is that he cannot lift the veil. Perhaps, too, there is the feeling that he does not wish to. This central mystery of his poem's world contains elements that to mortal eyesight are not only bizarre or freakish (like the bearded Venus whose learned Latin title, *Venus barbata*, cannot rescue her from association with the circus-ring) but also terrifying. She evokes that quality in the gods which the Greeks caught in epithets like *Pallas Athene Parthenos Gorgo* (Pallas Athene Maiden Terrible), and which they feared in the ruthless moods of the earth-mother, Cybele. In 'Mutabilitie' the air is electric not only with a sense of the numinous radiating from Nature but also with primitive horror and the will to avoid seeing the expression on her face:

> Then forth issewed (great goddesse) great dame *Nature*,
>> With goodly port and gracious Majesty;
>> Being far greater and more tall of stature
>> Then any of the gods or Powers on hie:
>> Yet certes by her face and physnomy
>> Whether she man or woman inly were,
>> That could not any creature well descry:
>> For, with a veile that wimpled every where,
> Her head and face was hid, that mote to none appeare.
>
> That some doe say was so by skill devized,
>> To hide the terror of her uncouth hew,
>> From mortal eyes
>>> (*The Faerie Queene*, Mutabilitie, vii. 5–6)

This figure evokes the terrible energies of the bisexual mother-goddesses of the *Orphic Hymns* (see p. 5 above), fond of 'drums and cymbals' like the 'frenzy-loving' Rhea with her chthonic power ('To Rhea', 3), or simultaneously vicious and gentle like the maiden-mother Persephone, or Athena whom the Orphic poet somewhat oddly praises as 'maiden vigorous and horrid-tempered' and goes on to congratulate on being 'Male and female, begetter of war, counselor,/she-dragon of many shapes' ('To Athena', 7, 10–11). Equally, Spenser's 'great dame Nature' corresponds to the archetype of the 'great mother Venus' of Book III, 'reaping' Adonis in the Garden through a sexual possession which makes him, and us, 'eterne in mutabilitie' (III. vi. 40, 47) but which does not deny the terrible aspects of our dedication to time—the hyacinthine and narcissistic aspects of existence which bleeds human nature like the red flowers of those names seasonally back into the originating soil (45). *Venus genetrix* 'reaps' man both in the erotic passion that pours him out seminally into herself and in the draining of his 'purple gore' in death. More closely still, the Nature of 'Mutabilitie' resembles the hermaphroditic Venus of Book IV, in the Temple of Venus, who causes the 'daedale earth' (IV. x. 45) to flower. Here Daedalus, the greatest human artist of antiquity, has changed his gender: through 'mother wit' (x. 21) the earth herself is the supreme artist, mothering the 'abundant flowres' into being. The natural world in each of these numinous areas of the poem is all power and energy. Never have flowers seemed less pretty and lyrical than these which 'voluntary grew/Out of the ground' (Mutabilitie, vii. 10) under the goddess's feet. A field of flowers becomes a force-field. Venus in Book IV is called 'Mother of laughter' (47), but mother also of the savage need to procreate that impels all animals, humanity included, to mate in the breeding season like 'raging Bulls' that 'rebellow through the wood'.

The veil which conceals the goddess Nature's face is comforting to the poet's assumptions, for it enables him to abstain from telling 'Whether she man or woman inly were', or both, or neither, questions which border on our sense of the perverted. The oxymoron 'she man' is already threatening. Through this *coincidentia oppositorum*, all civilised categories, and the accepted structures of meaning within the language itself, are potentially upset. In stanza 6, Spenser hazards two explanations of why Nature wears a veil. 'Some doe say' it is to conceal the leonine horror of her face; but 'others tell' that the veil is worn because the naked beauty of that face having a thousand times the radiation of the sun could not be seen by the human eye. When horror and beauty, birth and destruction, male and female, vision and the invisible are indeterminate, words fail—and are allowed to fail in the 'transfiguration' (7) of her presence. Failure of words may reveal the divine: God is by definition unutterable and inconceivable, veiled from common sight and sense. Through radical, even absurd, play with our notions of a world structured on certain given norms of gender, Spenser leads the imagination round Christian dogma to an extraordinary image of the One.[13] The *una dea* for whom there are so many names figures God Himself but cannot be reduced back to 'Him'. 'He' and 'Him' become, in the light of Spenser's imagery, inadequate terms in which to personify God. It is not that he blasphemously denies the doctrine of the male Creator; he makes no doctrinal statement at all. Rather, the bisexual imagery recreates our sense of the divine, generating awareness of the extraordinary basis of life itself, the miraculous creative power of the mother-planet on which we play such a limited part. The religious challenge of the image resembles that made on the Renaissance by the 'Nature' of Hermes Trismegistus' *Pimander*, who, falling in love with man's divine image, 'wrapped him in her clasp, and they were mingled in one...And that is why man...is bisexual, as his Father is bisexual' (*Pimander*, 14–15 in *Hermetica*, pp. 121–3). Spenser goes one step further in spicing theology with erotic glamour by making our source seem to be a bisexual Mother as a change from the familiar Father.

In Book IV, the image is more lyrical. Scudamore tells his own story of the fulfilment of his quest for Amoret at the Temple of Venus. We enter with him into the beauty of a remembered landscape, the sensuous green abundance of whose vegetation carries with it a sense that this is a place in which meaning collects, as in dream. It is typical of Spenser's descriptions of the 'greenewood' world (IV. x. 22) of juniper and cedar that they convey not merely the surface beauty of a natural scene but that the poetry breathes out a kind of resinous and aromatic scent of

meaning, and especially of numinous meaning, intrinsic in the
planet we inhabit and available through the senses. Infinite
varieties of flowers 'throw' their scents out into the garden-
world (22); 'fresh shadowes, fit to shroud from sunny ray' are
areas of retreat from the lawns in full sunlight; there are 'soft
rombling brooks' and labyrinths of high-hedged mazes (24). The
unpuritanical love of nature Spenser shows here prefigures
Milton's celebration of the same principle of 'enormous bliss' in
the Eden of *Paradise Lost*, which constantly echoes Spenser's
'second paradise' (23); the Platonism that can admire 'fresh
shadowes', whose dark unreality automatically impels a more
conventional Platonist to disapproval, is unique to Spenser and
inimitable. As Scudamore enters the Temple itself, the sense of
the divine intensifies further, but does so sensually, in the
frankincense that floats on the air, the carpet of flowers of May
(37) and the girl-priests 'in soft linnen dight' (38). Both the
Garden's vegetation and the circularity of the Temple itself are
images of the creative feminine principle. Typically, we move
'Into the inmost' (37), 'Right in the midst' (39), towards the
luminous, glass-like statue of the hermaphroditic Venus glowing
through the thin tissue of its encompassing veil:

> The cause why she was covered with a vele,
>   Was hard to know, for that her Priests the same
>   From people's knowledge labour'd to concele.
>   But sooth it was not sure for womanish shame,
>   Nor for any blemish, which the worke mote blame;
>   But for, they say, she hath both kinds in one,
>   Both male and female, both under one name:
>   She syre and mother is her selfe alone,
> Begets and eke conceives, ne needeth other none.
>   (*The Faerie Queene*, IV. x. 41)

The labyrinth has led to an image of God. The shadows on the
grass have been emblems of God, like Cusa's cloud of
unknowing.[14] The pairs of lovers roaming in the Garden, man
and woman, or homosexual, know God. Now, at the centre, the
work of art (veiled as an allegorical poem is veiled) signifies God.
But if we hope at this central moment for revelation, we are
disappointed. Translucent as glass, the statue's form and light

are veiled away, and the reader is only passed the conjecture that 'she syre and mother is her selfe alone'. Spenser cannot or will not reveal the image of the divine in herself; he both shows and withholds her, leading us to a central truth that cannot be told.

In Shakespeare's *The Winter's Tale* the veil can be lifted from the 'statue' of Hermione because she is human, not a goddess, not an art-work. In a comparable way, Spenser can make the revelation of Venus through unveiling his female (and particularly his androgynously female) human characters. The epic tradition already incorporated a figure of the androgynously arms-bearing maiden, from Virgil's Camilla to Tasso's Clorinda. Into an epic world these figures bring a lyricism, accompanied by a pastoral and elegiac language which speaks of a timeless, transforming world beyond the limits of the battling tribes fighting it out on the plains of Troy. Yet they are warriors and take part in the bloodshed. Before their unhelmeting, they are generally taken to be male. When they are unhelmeted (often when mortally wounded) there is an increased sense of the numinous in the poetry, and an epiphany within the poem for the beholders who perceive the beauty of the girl-self within the pugilistic male exterior.[15] Heaven for a split second is glimpsed in the world of matter; eternity in time; the 'feminine' soul comes clean of the 'masculine' body. Such figures are carefully distinguished from the Amazons and their wild bellicosity, *ululante tumultu/feminea* (*Aeneid*, XI. 647–63). Virgil's Camilla is a slight, fluid, tempered girl-hero, linking in herself the opposites of gentleness and warrior-power. She is all speed and light: she might, Virgil comments, have skimmed the tops of unmown cornfields without bursting a single ear of corn; like Mercury, perhaps, she might have sped across the sea's surface without touching the waves at any point (VII. 808–11). This imagery powerfully illustrates the curious aura of harmlessness that characterises the figure, a vulnerable insubstantiality, and an association with nurture (the cornfields are of course the world of Ceres). In Virgil the predominantly male ethos of the poetry dooms her to violent death in battle. The miracle dies. The epic voice drowns out the pastoral in the drumbeat of Roman militarism. In the later Italian romance-epics of Boiardo, Ariosto and Tasso, so important to Spenser's concept of epic, this feminine androgynous figure is more fully centralised, particularly in the moment of unhelmeting. Ruggiero in Boiardo's *Orlando Innamorato* recognises in Bradamante's revealed face and hair an '*angelico aspetto*' (III. 5. 41–2), but sees her at the same time as deeply unknown. Gender, name, relationship, identity itself are put in doubt. When in Tasso's *Gerusalemme Liberata* Tancredi kills Clorinda, words fail before her revealed beauty. Stasis interrupts the hectic action of the epic world; visionary light is let in; opposites are reconciled and a dream of perfection fractionally glimpsed in the midst of the laboured mathematics of epic activity.

It is by adapting this epic archtype that Spenser is able to allow us to see what is ideally perfect in Venus and therefore invisible. Britomart's emotional, excited, sometimes touchingly childlike and at others nobly certain personality humanises her virtue so that it can reflect images of perfection intelligible to the merely human eye. There are four major instances of such unveiling in the poem (III. i. 42–3, ix. 20; IV. i. 13–15, vi. 19f.)

> With that her glistring helmet she unlaced;
> > Which doft, her golden lockes, that were up bound
> > Still in a knot, unto her heeles downe traced,
> > And like a silken veile in compasse round
> > About her backe and all her bodie wound:
> > Like as the shining skie in summers night,
> > What time the dayes with scorching heat abound,
> > Is creasted all with lines of firie light,
> > That it prodigious seems in common peoples sight.
>
> *(The Faerie Queene, IV. i. 13)*

The devastating gold of Britomart's hair falls to cover her from head to foot. She has just been fighting, and has won, a fairly routine battle, and the watchers have naturally assumed that she was a perfectly normal male knight. But the unhelmeting is more than a revelation of gender, though that is central to its meaning. We say of hair that it catches the light: the hair of Britomart somehow is the sun itself, sun burns and shines in it. Thus too Florimell's hair, though she is in one sense Britomart's opposite, glimpsed in flight, rays out behind her 'as a blazing starre' (III. i. 16; see pp. 70–2 below). Opposites within the feminine principle (the extreme of activity, the extreme of passivity) reveal one divine power. Both have the power to terrify, like demonic portents in the sky which no one understands. Britomart's hair appears like the night sky 'creasted all with lines of firie light', and 'common people' see this as a prodigy, perhaps as an omen. We too are 'common people' in Spenser's usage, for as common readers we do not understand the status and meaning of what we are seeing. The moment of illumination shocks and threatens, for how can a woman's hair be seen like this? What is presented as a simile has the force and directness of metaphor or literal description at such moments of passionate narration. Spenser seems to contract his perception of the whole cosmos into the shaking out of a woman's hair. The molten force of Helios declares against the powers of night in golden fire, as the beauty of Britomart's girlhood declares against the saturnine armour of the male.

The Platonist Ficino had set traps for the divine in the hope of conjuring the sun's rays (Sol, Jupiter and Venus all together, preferably, or 'The Three Graces' as he liked to call them)[16] to mitigate the lugubrious atmosphere of the scholar's study. A gold bowl, a yellow crocus, a solar song and a sun-figuring talisman might encourage the influx of the sun to pour its healing in through the window of human experience. His generation expended some energy in trying to make statues speak with similar art, such as Hermes recommends in the *Asclepius* (III. 37 in *Hermetica*, pp. 121–3). Spenser's art does not make the statue of Venus speak; tacitly, she draws the light into her lucent nature from the cosmos and veils it in. It is through the talismanic human heroine that Spenser enables eternity to speak into time. The watchers who see her hair cascading from its shroud become *illuminati*, filled with a truth which, however, they cannot translate into common usage. Britomart is the means through which *spiritus* travels into *materia:* the flood of cosmic love pours into her, and for a moment she *is* this love, terrible and inhuman as well as beautiful and soft. We could say that here Britomart is Venus, for us more fully so than the immobile statue in the Temple. Beauty for Spenser is not static but flowing, active and living within time; the fact that Britomart in personifying it is mutable and able to die only increases our sense of its preciousness. Unlike Virgil and Tasso, Spenser does not kill the androgynous heroine of his poem. In its passionate Platonism, his poem sustains the images of Britomart and her sister-selves, Florimell, Belphoebe and Amoret, alive within a conception that is more fully tragi-comic than any previous epic with regard to the androgynous motif. Giordano Bruno in *Lo Spaccio* (1584) had seen 'the sun in the Crocus, in the narcissus, in the heliotrope, in the rooster, in the lion':[17] a universe woven through all species with the royal gold of the Creator. Spenser catches the sun in the hair of Britomart in such a way that she links the lower world's golden flora, simple and small, with the highest burning helium of the sun. The hidden oneness of the cosmos is demonstrated through her, and we are momentarily released from the cave of the senses so that, with Plato's cave-dweller we 'stand up suddenly, turn the head, walk and look up towards the sunlight' with seared eyesight for 'doing all that would give [us] pain, the flash of the fire would make it impossible to see the objects of which [we] had earlier seen the shadows' (*Republic*, 515c-d). Spenser reproduces the pain and fearfulness involved in the experience of total revelation.

At the same time he intensifies the sense of mystery. Something is left unsaid, and unsayable. When Britomart removes her helmet, the imagery is associated with life as a knot, or binding, of experience which cannot normally be undone and seen for what it is. At rare moments of epiphany the hair beneath the helmet comes 'unlaced'; the 'bound...knot' is untied, and an inner reality released. But at the moment of exposure the inner reality is converted into an outer reality; hence in turn it encloses something newly hidden. Britomart's hair is let loose in order to become 'a silken veil in compasse round'. The alchemical gold pours from the crucible. A girl's hair and the night sky are lit through by identical energy. The human battle stops at this revelation of the divine. But what is seen is always only an image, a 'veil'; beyond this layer of reality, it is felt, lies yet another which human nature continues to need to perceive. Spenser thus reties the knot of narrative, and the remembered miracle, seen within time, is at once distanced in the search for fuller vision. Britomart's armour as male warrior is again adopted.

As equestrian warrior at Tilbury in 1588, Queen Elizabeth I's heroic posture had asserted an epic destiny for the island of

England against the Spanish and Catholic aggressor. The figure of Britomart leads us naturally to this image of Elizabeth the sacred warior making history happen. Giordano Bruno visiting the English court saw her in this posture, of one looking out to sea, and called the *diva Elizabetta* queen of the ocean, Amphitrite, the universal ruler, the One herself.[18] The cult of the sacred virgin-queen, married to her realm, which Bruno embraced with customary zeal, Spenser's greater zeal transformed into the Idea for which his entire allegory is a veil.[19] Britomart leads to Elizabeth, but is not Elizabeth. She presents one crucial image of the queen, but so do Una, Alma,Belphoebe, together with every female deity, personage and place which has anything to be said in its favour throughout the whole poem. Gloriana is the unseen *una dea* who collects all the names and all their attributes up into herself and yet is still beyond them all, like Apuleius' Isis. Spenser's invocations address her in the tone with which the Platonist may approach God, as the apprentice of Reality; asking as a poor copyist of a merely mimetic art to be allowed to paint the Idea of Elizabeth's virtue of Chastity: 'That I in colourd showes may shadow it' (III. Proem, 3). His words will stain and darken what they represent. His voice in relation to her is childlike, but its claims are vast and hubristic. Spenser stands to Queen Elizabeth as a tiny figure on the skirts of his own poem. She is the poem. As his 'dred Soveraine' (3) the terrible aspect of her divinity is always disagreeably present to him. The warrior-queen or silent, veiled politician takes on from time to time the aspect of the Terrible Mother; the poet's voice is generally careful with this archetype, though at times defiant or furtively critical.

It is crucial to be aware that Spenser's poem recognises the distinction between the Idea of Gloriana and certain actualities with regard to Elizabeth. Covert allusions to the texture of court life may be felt in Spenser's reflections on life in Lucifera's self-regarding palace, the House of Pride, with its hidden dungeons and rotten foundations which would not bear a surveyor's scrutiny (though the official candidate for the role is, of course, Elizabeth's rival queen, Mary Stuart). To get up Philotime's chain in the Cave of Mammon, huge crowds of those ambitious for place shove and elbow each other, like the souls of the unscrupulous damned:

Some thought to raise themselves to high degree,
　　By riches and unrighteous reward,
Some by close shouldring, some by flateree;
Others through friends, others for base regard;
And all by wrong wayes for themselves prepard.
Those that were up themselves, kept others low,
Those that were low themselves, held others hard,
Ne sufferd them to rise or greater grow,
But every one did strive his fellow downe to throwe.
　　　　　　　　　　　　　　　　　　(II. vii. 47)

Like vicious children, the courtiers seem to fight and struggle as it were behind Gloriana's back: we see the manic spite on their silent faces as they hold each other down and we seem to catch echoes of the whispering behind the courteous etiquette; purses are quietly opened and mouths unctuously smile. Spenser had been at the court and observed its manners in detail. The queen of such a court has a ruthless, moody face: the 'Queene of love, & Prince of peace' as Spenser calls Elizabeth in Book IV (Proem, 4) behaves as temperamentally as the Old Testament Jahweh. In the second half of the poem, published in 1596, Spenser as the friend of the belligerent, ostracised Raleigh, losing real hope of preferment, mutinies against his own best interests, stands to his full height at the edge of his poem and shouts up pieces of good advice at Gloriana: 'reade this lesson often' (IV. Proem, 5). Queen Elizabeth is at once praised as a god amongst men and her court stigmatised as fallen, 'runne out of square' (V. i. 7), 'corrupted sore' (V. iii. 4) and infected by the thousand tongues of the Blatant Beast, the splenetic voices of false witness. Yet when we stand back from the poem and think of it as a whole, such moments of dark preoccupation with the gaps between Idea and reality represent a microscopic proportion of the entire effect. They are the minimal but essential shadows in Gloriana's broad sunlight. The poem's disappointment in the failure of Idealism as pragmatically untenable only reinforces its dedication to the vision the poem can sustain of the 'fourth Mayd' (VI. x. 25), whose place in the celestial dance on Mount Acidale is known without doubt by Colin, the poet within the poem, to be that of 'another Grace' (26).

BRITOMART TO FLORIMELL

In the Book of Temperance, Sir Guyon had to spend twelve long and laborious cantos learning to overcome the temptations of nature, accompanied by a singularly doleful Palmer whose function was to teach him to say 'no' to many of his desires. Guyon's final temptation took place in a delectable garden in which naked nymphs cavorted in a pool through six stanzas of semi-pornographic poetry (II. xii. 63-8), showing to him and leaving to our imaginations 'many sights, that courage cold could reare' (68). There he had encountered a sinister androgynous figure at the gate; a Circean female with a poisonous drink of wine which she 'scruzd' (56) between slender fingers so that the grape juice slowly ran down between her fingers into the cup; and the enchantress Acrasia bathed in post-coital sweat, enjoying her handsome prey as he slept (78-9). Sir Guyon and the Palmer netted this sister of Arachne for safety's sake at the centre of her world of sensual bliss, devastating, and then sharply removing themselves from, the garden of sexual fantasy. Guyon's task had been to learn the art of repression so as to walk the Aristotelian tightrope balance between extremes of behaviour—a gruelling and deeply unrewarding quest. Book III takes us and Guyon into a completely different world.[20] Hardly has he advanced six stanzas into this new world than the Knight of Temperance is unhorsed by an unknown knight (i. 6), which strikes him as an embarrassment and us as food for thought. It seems that Guyon's painstaking efforts to make his horse walk and not run in the moral dressage of Temperance (II. 1. 7)—the horse of passion, of course—who has been educated in the art of governing lust for gold, and women, and even laughter, has learnt nothing particularly useful throughout the long palaver of Book II. The poet consoles the comically prostrate knight with the thought that the 'speare enchaunted was, which layd thee on the greene' (III. i. 7).

This is the book of the colour green. its 'Legend...of Chastitie' is a story of fruitfulness, its hero a girl, its enchantment the secret law of nature which is expressed in allowable human desire. At its centre is the Garden of Adonis, recycling shed lives into renewed forms and sacrificing the male seed to the magic of recreation by the female. Guyon's

knowledge is insignificant in a world where order is understood
as the organic rhythms and flowing patternings of the natural
cycle rather than as a system of weights and measures. In this
pastoral world the Palmer's beady eye is correct in its perception
that Britomart's power is likely to be lethal to his well-trained
pupil, 'For death sate on the point of that enchaunted speare' (i.
9). The uncontrollable goodness of Britomart stands for an
instinct which bloodily sacrifices the male principle and yet
remains herself holy and intact; Guyon nearly undergoes the fate
of Marinell and Adonis in ritual slaughter but becomes a comic
victim instead. Even Arthur's customary interruption at around
canto viii as *deus ex machina* (which happens in every other
book) does not occur here. Its world of feminine powers and
subconscious life does not need, and would not tolerate, his
manipulations. Its material is primal and chthonic, linked to the
underworld, and extending onto and into the matrix of the sea.
Its symbolism concerns generation, continuity and home-
coming in trees' deep networks of roots, women giving birth,
flowers springing into life on the margin of the sea, twin seeking
twin, the garden-world of Eros at the centre. In Book III
Spenser locates the most powerful and terrible mystery of the
whole *Faerie Queene,* founding a pastoral world which is not
casually Arcadian, for it mingles blood and soil, the earth as
simultaneous womb and burial chamber. And it addresses itself
to a female readership.[21]

It is Britomart's legend, and her genealogy (linking her to
Queen Elizabeth) is crucial to the heroine's individual story, the
political meanings of the poem and to its deepest paradoxes.
Genealogies, staple ingredients of epic poems, tend to have a
drearily obligatory air and to be taken at a dash by the poet as a
necessary digression from the story. But Britomart's genealogy *is*
the real story. It is a tree, reminding us of the human tree, which
bled, in Book I (ii. 30-1), of the Tree of Knowledge in Eden
which yielded the catastrophe of its fruit into Eve's hand, and of
the Tree of Life itself. The tree of British genealogy will be
rooted, Merlin tells her, in Britomart's love-pain, and she must
suffer deeply for the tree to put down deep roots. Spenser
revises God's stigmatising of Eve in the curse of labour pains: 'in
sorrow thou shalt bring forth children' (Genesis 3:16).
Britomart's love-longing, expressed in her quest for Arthegall, is

the equivalent of prolonged but innocent and fruitful labour pain. Womanhood in the person of Britomart has done nothing to atone for; as stainless virgin-mother, she has creative power to be a source for a final Elizabethan peace. Superficially, this reminds us of the power of Mary, the second Eve, but the resemblance is superficial, for the Brito-martial warrior-maiden has nothing of the meek passivity of the heroine of the Gospels:

> For so must all things excellent begin,
>   And eke enrooted deepe must be that Tree,
>   Whose big embodied braunches shall not lin,
>   Till they to heavens hight forth stretched bee.
>   For from thy wombe a famous Progenie
>   Shall spring, out of the auncient *Troian* blood,
>   Which shall revive the sleeping memorie
>   Of those same antique Peres, the heavens brood,
> Which *Greeke* and *Asian* rulers stained with their blood.
>
> (III. iii. 22)

Never has a genealogical tree seemed less abstract and theoretical, more heavily composed of matter, 'embodied' thus. Britomart is the earth as Celtic Britain's landscape is the earth, into which the network of roots must grasp for fruitfulness to occur. The huge energy of growth from cell to complex form is suggested by the poetry: the cost to the human individual of engendering great processes in time. The central word of the central line is 'womb'—the principle of growth mitigating the mutual destruction through history of Britain's vagrant tribes. The feminine is presented as the reconciler of opposites: of heaven and earth, past and present, origin and destiny.

Between Britomart and Elizabeth I lie many losses, principally the subjection of the original Celtic race in Britain to the invading Saxons. Spenser sees the Tudor solution to the English civil wars as having lain dormant until it could be 'kindled in the fruitfull Ile/Of Mona' (III. iii. 48), exiled in that last outpost of Celtic Druidism, Anglesey. As female is to male, the suggestion is, so Celtic ('fruitful Ile') is to Saxon. Androgynous political reconciliation will be effected in the Tudor concord, claiming a line of descent through Llewelyn and the indigenous Welsh dynasty, and therefore bringing the 'female' element of the nation into a fuller equivalence with the 'male'. The blood-

stained old regime gives way to a newly defined 'white' kind of
power:

> Thenceforth eternall union shall be made
> Betweene the nations different afore,
> And sacred Peace shall lovingly perswade
> The warlike minds, to learn her goodly lore,
> And civile arms to exercise no more:
> Then shall a royall virgin raine, which shall
> Stretch her white rod over the *Belgicke* shore
>
> (III. iii. 49)

Britomart is a type of Elizabeth I, who marries the contending
houses of York and Lancaster in her person. Feminine 'white'
power is a strenuously achieved and rigorously preserved self-
regulating power. The 'white rod' means the 'rod with ye Dove'
which the sovereign is handed at the coronation ceremony,
signifying responsibility to exercise rule with justice and
mercy.[22] The dove as symbol of peace is a central symbol of
Spenser's conception of feminised rule, bearing associations of
fertile warmth (the turtle-dove as emblem of fidelity), chaste
'white' love, and the cosmic link between heaven and earth
(Noah's dove and the dove of the Holy Spirit, which is feminine
in the Hebrew, *Ruach Hakodesh*).[23] Spenser's genealogical tree,
rooted in nothing more elevated than the love-pangs of a young
girl, is seen as ultimately able to reach 'heavens hight', in a power
which is as generative as that of 'the spirit of God [which]
moved upon the face of the waters' (Genesis 1:2).

The image of the 'royall Mayd' in Book III, then, is an image
of power, understood as a *concordia discors*[24] and exemplified in
the emblem of the *Venus virgo*. But Britomart is distinctly felt by
most readers to exist as a person rather than as a walking
concept. This complicates the power theme, for we are
constantly reacting to her as a teeming personality, full of
instincts and initiatives that are not always comprehensible. The
idea of the coincidence of opposites, when it is translated into
the language of a recognisably human personality that comes
near to being 'realistic' in texture, may reveal itself in the
appearance of someone self-contradictory or paradoxical.
Because Britomart is interesting in this way (like so many of the

characters of Book III), the Book not only produces a conception of feminised power but also questions and puts it to the test. Further levels of complication are added when we remember that the Book has a mythic dimension. The warrior-woman playing her active part in the great tournament of history is a political figure; but she also acts within the structure of a framing fertility myth, and all her actions relate to this dimension. Britomart's nature strikes at the personages who come her way with the power of the grass-blade spearing through soil, or the seed that will become a tree, or the growing force of the child who will become a mother and in her turn bear a child. The hard armour protecting the sensuously described and vulnerable 'soft silken skin' (III. i. 65) beneath it offers a cryptic paradox to the imagination of a reader. The complexity of the poetic meaning is suggested by the relationship between the voices of the protagonists and the narrative voice, particularly in the images it chooses. Britomart explains her unladylike posture and attire to the inquisitive Guyon as they ride along together. Her idom is a bluff and hearty reproduction of the soldier's manner:

> Fair Sir, I let you weet, that from the howre
> I taken was from nourses tender pap,
> I have been trained up in warlike stowre,
> To tossen speare and shield, and to affrap
> The warlike rider to his most mishap;
> Sithence I loathed to have my life to lead,
> As Ladies wont, in pleasures wanton lap,
> To finger the fine needle, and nyce thread;
> My lever were with point of foemans speare be dead.
>
> (III. ii. 6)

The male idom is so easily impersonated by Britomart as to imply pastiche. But Spenser's transvestite woman is not deliberately feigning a role as alien to her true nature as, say, Shakespeare's Viola when she finds that she has swaggered convincingly enough to provoke a duel she is unprepared to fight in *Twelfth Night*. The vigour of Britomart's soldierly archaisms—'To tossen speare', 'affrap'—is not sham; soon she will all but kill Marinell. This language has become second nature to her—second, but not first. We can feel this in the

robust sense of humour which fortifies the alexandrine. She
would rather be dead than sit stitching indoors. The 'point' of
the enemy's spear entering her frame to finish her off stands in
ironic contrast to the finicky world in which you do not 'hold'
things but you 'finger' them laboriously pricking at cloth with a
needle's point. The long boredom of the indoor lady's world is
conveyed in Spenser's neatly stressed balance of disgusted
epithets: '*fine* needle', '*nyce* thread'. There is almost nothing
there at all. Britomart's swashbuckling utterances in favour of
hurling missiles, actively 'hunt[ing] perils and adventures' in
which she expresses 'delight' speaks for the residual childish
energy latent in evey adult, male or female. Who in her right
mind, she suggests, would choose to sit at home sewing a
sampler when she could be out of doors looking for trouble? No
one in Spenser's poetic world is content to stay at home and 'sit
in pleasures wanton lap'.

But Britomart speaks only part of the truth. She moves from
her adopted behaviour to her deeper motives, the love of
Arthegall which causes her quest. When Guyon praises
Arthegall, the narrative voice goes on to comment on 'The
royall Mayd's' private response to hearing him well spoken of:

> The loving mother, that nine monethes did beare
> In the deare closet of her painefull side,
> Her tender babe, it seeing safe appeare,
> Doth not so much rejoyce, as she rejoyced theare.
>
> (III. ii. 11)

We are shocked by the beauty of this simile, in context. A
thought in the mind of a martial maid involved in a warring male
world is focused in the image of a mother's pregnancy, labour
and delivery of her baby. The simile has been vaguely thought of
as erotic,[25] but this is quite wrong. It is not a sexual image but a
gendered one, conveying Spenser's sympathy ('deare' closet) and
identification ('painefull' side) with experiences peculiar to
womankind. The simile imaginatively encompasses the full nine
months' growth of the child in the womb, sharing in its
painfulness for the mother as her child swells up against the ribs,
and then her birth-pangs. He dwells, too, on the hazardousness
of the child's route out into the daylight world. The mother's

face seems caught at the joyous moment of delivery, or deliverance, from waiting and fear: 'it seeing *safe* appear' (my emphasis). This emotional and biological realism reinforces the tragi-comic implications of the image; both the anxious mother and the journeying baby represent almost helpless questors, subject to chance or fate, who obtain deliverance into knowledge of one another. As such they may stand as archetypes of the many questors of *The Faerie Queene*, tracing a labyrinth of paths in search of union with some person or conception; seeking, in other words, to be born or to give birth to some reconceived idea of the self. More specifically, the image is applied to Britomart's hidden and private individual experience, mediated by the insight of the narrator. This creative supplying of metaphors for wordless and intuitive states of mind is characteristic of Spenser's art. Here the image of growth in a mother's womb is an image of a mental process: the 'deare closet' is the mind in a state of longing, seeking to bring forth a new reality. We say that we 'conceive' or 'gestate' thoughts, or that we 'bring them forth' in words or gestures; Spenser's treatment of the feminine principle tends to brings such buried metaphors alive, so as to create an original mythology of the inner world.

At the same time, the simile links both to the political allegory and to the great fertility theme of Book III. Elizabeth the warrior-queen (herself, according to the genealogy of the Book, a child of Britomart) is organically linked to the fertility of nature. The state is her child; her authority is a kind of begetting. This relationship between the figure of a sacramental virgin and the fertile cycle of nature roots Book III in the fertility cults of the ancient Greek and Egyptian world, the earth-mother goddesses—Cybele, Isis, Ceres—with their ecstatic cults which were often also blood-cults, associated with the ritual shedding of hymeneal, menstrual or life's blood itself, and involving the ritual sacrifice of a sacred animal or (in later and less physically gruesome versions) allusion to such sacrifice,[26] and ritual initiation through it. Thus man, or woman, bloodily participates in the terrible secrets of Mother Earth's cycle of autumnal death and vernal resurrection. Spenser's Britomart has been presented as sacred virgin and as holding an inner and secret principle of motherhood, in the tender image of childbirth of canto iii. Nothing of this seemed threatening on this deeper, elemental level. But in canto iv, the virgin-mother announces it, unaware of the significance of her actions. She divulges the chthonic power of the female, entering in to the alternative female cosmos for which there are no known laws and where Arthurian power cannot reach. On the sea's edge, she plunges her spear into Marinell's left side, and leaves him for dead, his life bleeding away into a sand that, surreally, is strewn with 'pearles and pretious stones', its gravel mixed with gold ore (iv. 18). The gentle girl, whose just acts make her an embodied emblem of *Iustitia,* commits ferocious violence. No reason is given for Britomart's attack on Marinell. On a surface level she seems to play the man's game of taking exception to a person just because he is in her way. Making no effort to reason with the newcomer and discern his nature, Britomart puts on an angry mood, produces her spear and meets his challenge with the curt 'Fly they that need to fly;/Words fearen babes' (iv. 15). The mortal damage she does Marinell is not explained. Yet we feel that it is not meaningless. Its cruelty is obscurely rooted in that process of fertility and regeneration to which Britomart's maidenhood alludes. It binds her actively to the cycle of nature herself, the mysterious processes of dissolution and rebirth in whose throes all human, animal and vegetative nature is annually delivered and to whose structure Book III is committed. Marinell's fall is described in terms of a blood-sacrifice, the slaughter of a sacred animal at a pagan fertility festival:

> Like as the sacred Oxe, that carelesse stands,
>   With gilden hornes, and flowry girlonds crownd,
> Proud of his dying honor and dear bands,
> Whiles th'altars fume with frankincense arownd,
> All suddenly with mortall stroke astownd,
> Doth groveling fall, and with his streaming gore
> Distaines the pillours, and the holy grownd,
>   And the faire flowres, that decked him afore;
> So fell proud *Marinell* upon the pretious shore.
>
> The martiall Mayd stayd not him to lament,
>   But forward rode...
>
>   (III. iv. 17-18)

The connotations, though with the animal world, are not

subhuman but rather mysterious, and holy. The shoreline is a sacred place, like a temple. But Britomart seems to blank out her consciousness of her actions and their construction, wiping her mind of them, as if—like the gory death of the ox in the simile which so shocks the reader's emotions—its memory would pollute her and disturb her single-minded purpose. She hardly seems to act in a human, or humane, way at all here but to move by instinctual co-operation in a pattern for which she is not responsible. The narrator now drops her as abruptly as she has dropped Marinell, taking the story to the bereaved mother, the water-nymph, Cymoent, and her efforts to revive her son. He has finished with her for the moment because she has performed her most vital function in wounding Marinell. On the shoreline between land and sea—the point of transition and initiation—Britomart enacts the terrible role of priest-murderer and goes off blithely and (in a literal sense) sublimely ignorant that she has participated in more than a routine pugilistic encounter. The key image is of the slaughtered 'sacred Oxe', whose suggestions are duplicated by Timias's wounding in the thigh in canto v, and culminate in the Garden of Adonis in canto vi.

The ancient Greek sacrifice of an ox involved a curious ambiguity, for unlike the pig and the ram (rooting up seed and trampling the vine), the sheep and the working ox were seen as friends to man.[27] Spenser shows us a picture of harmless and noble creature being destroyed; sentience in the moment of its extreme pain. There is no suffering creature in *The Faerie Queene* for which Spenser fails to show pity. Even if the sufferer is conceived of as unworthy, Spenser's negative capability seems so automatic that it invariably asserts and invites a relationship of compassion. This is the feminine ethos. Yet here the feminine principle has caused a grotesquely ironic pain: the blood of Marinell seeps into the beach as the sacrificial ox at the *Bouphonia* ritual,[28] decked in flowers, anointed with perfumes, horns gilded, in his animal innocence became the substance of a blood-bath, The poet emphasises the horror of the spilt blood. It pours out a stain on the temple and saturates the flowers which had garlanded the holy ox. Spenser's version relates the sacrifice as experienced by the animal itself, standing proudly casual and then 'astownd…groveling', as if the victim of some obscene joke. We are revolted as well as bewildered; and emotionally part company with Britomart, and Elizabeth.

The Renaissance understood well the significance of the *Bouphonia* and *Adonia* as fertility cults, and the links between them. Blood soaking into flowers is an image which leads simultaneously down into Hades and the death of the old year, and up into the renewed growth of another spring. The Countess of Pembroke's *Ivychurche* shows Venus's horror at finding Adonis gored, 'Dismembered, wounded, with his owne blood all to besprikled'[29] and translates his death as 'the absence of the sunne for the sixe wintrie moneths' and his genital wound as the earth's winter barrenness.[30] Marinell, like Adonis, lies gored in his prime, in his own blood, transitional between worlds. Loved both by Proserpina (the lower world) and Venus (the upper) he inhabits a threshold of experience, midway between opposites, and the point of their conjunction. The logic of *The Faerie Queene* would dictate that we should move, therefore, to the opposite experience of the *una dea* at this point, veering away from the ruthless, death-dealing aspect of Mother Nature, and that we should simultaneously follow the downward course of the shed blood, seeing into the underworld itself. Thus the very structure of the poem may be understood as a sequence of *coincidentiae oppositorum.* From the female agent of bloodshed we move to the bereaved mother of the victim. Imperceptibly, we cross the border between the Adonis and Ceres myths. We vacate the land and enter the sea-world.

Cymoent, Marinell's mother, is identified by the poet as the child of the sea (iv. 19), the feminine matrix from which all creatures take their origin. We first travel inland to find her at the edge of fresh water:

> whereas she playd
> Amongst her watry sisters by a pond
> Gathering sweet daffadillyes, to have made
> Gay girlonds, from the Sun their forheads faire to shade.
>
> (III. iv. 29)

Throughout Book III, pure pastoral turns, and turns again, into pastoral elegy, as here: the music of this scene of innocent spring idyll is burdened by the message *Et in Arcadia ego.* Spenser's poem makes constant acknowledgement of the facts that generate pastoral elegy: early, random death, spring's brevity. But whereas *The Shepheardes Calender* had swept from the exultant gesture of 'Aprill's' 'Strowe me the ground with Daffadowndillies' (140) to 'November's' vision of the nymphs' funereal garlands of cypress and the Muses' exchange of laurel for 'bitter Eldre braunches seare' with their sour tang (145-7), *The Faerie Queene* unites the two opposite experiences, of jubilee and mourning, within the same image. The garlands of 'sweet daffadillyes' woven by Cymoent's nymphs recall the garlanded ox in stanza 17, its flowers filthy with blood. But the dark knowledge we bring to the image of Cymoent amongst the living yellow of the daffodil-world does not absolutely undermine the validity of her play. The sensuous qualities of the imagery are felt almost on our skin as we read: cold, smooth English flowers upon the warm foreheads of the water nymphs. The daffodil is traditionally associated with Proserpina, the daughter of Ceres, whose abduction to the underworld was partially retrieved by her mother's pilgimage. The story of loss, anger and affliction is in both cases understood as a myth of home-coming and renewal. Cymoent casts the woven daffodils from her in the hostility of grief, but the flowers will rise again from the same bulb, and the flower of humanity will equally obtain renewal. In the *Orphic Hymns,* Demeter is referred to as 'the first to yoke the ploughing ox' (*To Eleusinian Demeter,* 8), linking both the season of ploughing and of harvesting, of blossom and of fruit. Spenser's drawing on these areas of female classical mythology represents not a denial of pain but a way of approaching mortal suffering which both responds to and transcends it. Cymoent, the mother-figure of an androgynous Marinell (Adonis/Proserpina, marginal between land and sea), travels a journey not unlike that of Ceres. The beaconing yellow faces of the daffodils signal the eventual success of her quest, without denying their own transience or her enduring pain.

It is not the fact that Spenser draws on classical mythology of this sort for patterns of meaning that distinguishes his imaginative world, for such allusive art is the staple of Elizabethan poetry; rather, his uniqueness lies in the eccentric, imaginative way he blends the stories into one another, without exposing any edges or outlines between them, so as to figure his philosophical commitment to the One as a hallucinating mingling of an apparent infinity of stories. The Adonis myth meets and becomes the Ceres myth. Like his compounding of genders into the androgynous motif which dominates the poem (see pp. 44–9 above), so he compounds all mythologies into one, emphasising his vision of totality by presenting the world as a fluid plenitude, capable of infinite metamorphosis. In Book III the direction of this metamorphosis is all towards the feminine, as if Spenser strove to play out reality under a specific kind of light which affects the appearance of all individuals in a consistently radical way. Thus, for instance, Marinell is Adonis feminised more fully by contact with the Proserpina myth. The feminine is an autonomous world, with its own laws and perspective, which 'sea-changes' all who enter it. And thus too the descent to the underworld is not a mining into the bowels of the earth but a flight into the strange, unguessable world under the sea, Cymoent's underwater bower. Dolphins, the ancient holy symbols of nature's and the gods' friendship to man, intelligent and warm-blooded in the cold sea,[31] draw Cymoent's chariot to visit her maimed son. Their smooth passage raises no foam, for 'As swift as swallowes, on the waves they went' (iv. 33). This glorious image of swimming as flight in air reinforces the redemptive theme: air and water are naturally opposed. But the dolphins' bodies upon their liquid element seem to 'fly' with the athletic grace of the birds which must migrate in autumn, faithfully to return with spring. There is a sense in which all the travels by all the questors in Book III are migratory in this sense: they travel in order to trace the journey home, and home-coming is universal and identical for all. In Plato's *Phaedrus* the homing soul seeks the One Source from which it came; whichever god the individual soul follows, the home is the same place for all by its very nature 'a reality without colour or shape, intangible but utterly real' (247C). Immortal souls cyclically exit from the vault of the heavens to contemplate creation, but recurrently and eternally 'go home' (247D).

Britomart and Cymoent are on the face of it as opposed as air must be to water, girl-aggressor to mother-victim, the swallow that flies to the dolphin that swims. When Britomart came to the sea she named it her enemy, feeling the mother-element as a threat both to her control and existence itself:

Huge sea of sorrow, and tempestuous griefe,
  Wherein my feeble barke is tossed long,
  Far from the hoped haven of reliefe,
  Why do thy cruell billowes beat so strong,
  And thy moyst mountaines each on others throng,
  Threatning to swallow up my fearfull life?
                                    (III. iv. 8)

Within the terms of Spenser's epic, this recoil is a powerfully *male* response, echoing his personal horror of the 'long stormes and tempests sad assay' in which the boat of life is 'tossed sore' in the *Amoretti* (LXIII). Safety, rest and home from the tumult of the sea-world are sought in the fourth Elizabeth who provides haven to the not very heroic male hero of the sonnet-sequence. Britomart's predominant image is an analagous one of homelessness. In her incompletely androgynous state, she can only perceive the sea as another kind of land: 'moyst mountaines' which pile in a grotesquely heaving landscape. She knows of no laws according to which its churning surfaces move, and therefore of no power within herself to order her passage in or on it. The moon which regulates the tides, daily and monthly is not consciously recognised by her, though it is profoundly related (as Diana, Lucina) to her nature as maiden and future mother. But around Britomart's speech of hostility to the sea are set allusions to the theme of birth through her nature which paradoxically ally her with her victim, Cymoent. At her most lost and rootless, she is only a breath away from reclamation and home-coming. Seeking Arthegall:

So forth she rode without repose or rest,
  Searching all lands and each remotest part...
                                    (III. iv. 6)

Claudian had written of Ceres' desperate search for her daughter in *De Raptu Proserpinae*: *'quantasque per oras/ sollicito genetrix erraverit anxia cursu'* (I. xxxiii. 28–9).[32] Milton would write of the same tragedy 'which cost Ceres all that pain/ To seek her through the world' (*Paradise Lost*, IV. 271-2). Britomart generates the bloodshed which sends Cymoent into the womb of the sea with her wounded offspring. But despite their implacable opposition, both Britomart and Cymoent in playing the role of Ceres (and Psyche, Apuleius' female seeker) co-operate in a single process, as dolphins mime swallows, as shed blood breeds renewed life. Marinell is taken by Cymoent into her underwater bower, to be reborn:

> Deepe in the bottom of the sea, her bowre
> Is built of hollow billowes heaped hye,
> Like to thicke cloudes, that threat a stormy showre,
> And vauted all within, like to the sky,
> In which the Gods do dwell eternally...
>
> (III. iv. 43)

The world of the sea is now shown from within, as a great recess whose composition seems to the reader full of threat, its architecture disturbing and self-contradictory (a vault made of water is perpetually about to collapse on its inmates). Its verbal music is eery: 'hollow billowes' are made of vowel-assonance so close that meaning is undermined, sounds collapsing in as if on a vacuum. The poet's distortion of his own lyric gift seems to express a primal male terror of the female principle as a kind of open grave ('vauted') ready to close and swallow the boy-child back into itself. Spenser recognises but does not endorse this fear. The poem is an unfolding structure of developing understanding; through reading it, we are asked (in the Letter to Raleigh) to grow in wisdom; and the protagonists make gradual progress towards ripening too. Through their attitudes to the sea, and their behaviour in relation to it, the characters open themselves to our judgement. It is important that this does not only occur in relation to the male characters' terror of the sea's instability but also to the female characters' responses, whether of recoil or mesmerised absorption. As Marinell is borne down into his mother's bower, he is making a regressive return to the womb, an area of his own psyche from which he must emerge or stifle in a breathless atmosphere which copies, but is not, 'the sky' where 'the Gods do dwell'. But, equally, Britomart's horrified certainty that the sea is an area of sterility and destruc-tion only is judged as an immature response to that sea of love-longing she holds within her, which 'in these troubled bowels raignes, and rageth rife' (iv. 8). Spenser's presentation of the sea has the absolutely paradoxical quality of archetypal symbolism.

The place of death is also a place of healing: Cymoent can call on the aid of Tryphon, brother of Aesculapius the Egyptian healer-god, so deeply associated with the Eleusinian Mysteries.[33] The realm of Proteus, the treacherous shape-changer, is also the place of transformation, characterising the mutable world as a great round of action in which life (Britomart) breeds death (Marinell), which again breeds life. The sea is like the alchemical crucible, or Hermetic bowl of *gnosis* (see pp. 214–15 below), reforming original conceptions in fresh and vital patterns. Spenser's sea retrieves and delivers, as the sea of Shakespeare's *Pericles* delivers the body of Thaisa to the resurrecting magic of the Asclepian physician, Cerimon (see pp. 140–1 below), and as the magus-poet Milton draws Lycidas from 'the bottom of the monstrous world' (158). In each case the process of ripening, both spiritual and physical, is imagined as a cycle of loss and gain in individual terms and, in cosmic terms as a universal recycling. In terms of the total anatomy of *the Faerie Queene*, Book III has been very aptly called 'the book of the womb'[34] which gives birth to character with counterparts, which then generate other parallel figures, likenesses or doubles. Each seeks the secret of personal fruitfulness in passing across our line of vision, mingling with other selves in a lace of quests. For most characters, the 'other self' belongs to the opposite gender, but this is not always so, like Chrysogone's twins born of the sun, Amoret (fostered by Venus) and Belphoebe (by Diana). This multitude of shadow-sisters and shadow-brothers who are the cast of the poem are presented as potentially endless variations on the human theme. At the centre of the Book is the Garden of Adonis through which all beings must pass, the point of source and return. Here, the 'enclosed garden' represents the womb itself, thronged with possibilities, relating all the disparate personalities of the poem, from Britomart to Florimell. This location, which is at once universal source and ending, presided over by Venus, yields the clue as to how to connect all the permutations of character into a single vision. The One of Platonism, understood as feminine, may be mysteriously entered into by all who desire fruitful union with a beloved. It can only be entered by minds which can contemplate the existence of a radical world independent of patriarchal structures. At the centre of the Book the poet seals off an autonomous garden-world, provided with a gate for initiation.

To emphasise the centrality and priority of the Garden of
Adonis and its mysteries, it is flanked symmetrically   by
underwater garden-worlds, the Adonaic bower of Cymoent in
Book IV and, in Book VIII, the underwater bower in which
Proteus imprisons Florimell. The figure of Florimell is the
feminine counterpart of Marinell. She is woman as victim, prey,
fleeing from the male as from a rapist but magnetically drawing
the iron-hearted rapist along with her by a delicate beauty whose
power is experienced by the male as temptation. All Florimell
can do is to flee. She is conceived as that sensitive, entirely gentle
aspect of the feminine which by its very nature has no defence,
but in order to maintain its particular virtue must lie open to
every act of brutality. It is a complex but crucial conception.
Spenser has, as it were, inverted Psyche's quest, so that it
expresses itself as pure flight.[35] The tone taken by the narrative
voice in relation to her is not only tender but awed: Florimell is
experienced not as weakness but as power. Her unself-
protecting beauty eternally realises itself only to vanish with
active quietism; the straining eye of the reader cannot grasp it.
Her power indefinably equals and outdoes that of Britomart
through steadfast abstention from coercive action; it draws the
reader by immaculate absence of exerted will power. In
Florimell, earthly beauty is at the consummate point where it
shades into the divine.[36] Where Britomart exemplifies the
feminine as exerting a power which is, at least in part, political,
in a world where swift confrontations are unavoidable, Florimell
expresses the feminine principle as unable to fight because it
cannot and will not compromise itself to hurt or even resist.
Though she appears at first sight so conventional—the
distressed damsel in urgent need of knightly rescue—Florimell is
a more radical and subversive figure than Britomart, inhabiting
more deeply the alternative female world imagined by Spenser's
poem.

Eternally fugitive, Florimell is also an embodiment of fidelity
which, in the lair of Proteus the shape-changer, will not consent
to change faith. In the midst of her passionate flight from a
world she so deeply fears, she emits an extraordinary energy
which links her with the sacrifice of Marinell/Adonis. The
poetry associated with her is as numinous as that associated with

the hermaphroditic Nature, Venus and with Britomart's unhelmeting (see pp. 50–2 above). Britomart's first glimpse of her opposite Florimell comes in the first canto, where a lady whose white face seemed 'cleare as Christall stone' and whose dress was of gold rode desperately through the forest on 'a milk-white Palfrey' (III. i. 15). Already she seems composed of a tissue almost too fine to abide the pressure of the coarse material world. Her clear, milky whiteness shows her to be the soul of chastity, and connects her with the candid Una of Book I. But unlike Una she is in motion, and her motion is always away from us:

> Still as she fled, her eye she backward threw,
> As fearing evill, that persewd her fast;
> And her faire yellow locks behind her flew,
> Loosely disperst with puffe of every blast:
> All as a blazing starre doth farre outcast
> His hearie beames, and flaming lockes dispred,
> At sight whereof the people stand aghast...
>
> (III. i. 16)

Extreme timidity assumes the character of meteoric flight. Her fair hair streams behind her as if it burst into flame like a comet's wake. It is this detail which transforms her image into one of dynamic energy, inspiring fear in watcher and reader. Humanity comes to a standstill before an irruption of divine meaning in the cosmos. As in the case of Britomart's unhelmeting (see pp. 50–2 above) the ordinary event casts light at spectators who then become victims of the divine and poetic riddle. Britomart's hair appears like the night sky in summer, 'creasted all with lines of firie light' (IV. i. 13); Florimell's hair cuts an individual path across Britomart's line of vision as comets descend the heavens outside any known orbit. In each case the individual woman stands opposed to 'the people's' common view. The frightened consensus of society faced with such prodigies is that the abnormal constitutes a threat (comets are traditionally bad omens). Spenser adopts the rare usage, noted by Heninger,[37] of the comet as a good sign. The illustrious disaster of Florimell expresses itself as the full force of cosmic beauty—in Platonist terms, the Idea of beauty as manifest as it can ever be in the sublunary world. Spenser's lyric power here removes all tactile quality from the beauty of a woman's hair; it turns her into a message from the cosmos itself, whose language the poet can transcribe but not translate. The people will continue to 'stand aghast'.

Spenser images the human incapacity to read such divine meassages in terms of the predatory attitude of the male towards the female. Florimell is pursued by an example of human bestiality, in the form of a 'griesly Foster' so hungry to get hold of her that he is spurring his horse with enough cruelty to make 'from his gorie sides the bloud...gush' (i. 17). The bleeding animal prefigures the slaughtered ox of canto iv, the lanced side of Marinell, the goring of Timias and the mysterious Garden of Adonis in which love eternally flowers at the centre. In pursuit of the forester goes Arthur, who tracks Florimell through Book III as a species of emanation of Gloriana. Like the Platonic emanations of the Divine, Florimell's light-emitting, elusive nature seeks return to the perfect Light of its source. The instinct to follow Florimell is experienced as in itself good, but the poet offers in this chase an allegory of the fundamental antipathy between body and soul. Florimell's pursuers correctly perceive her as infinitely desirable. They need her, but because in the world of matter we must see through merely material eyes and communicate through the rough, callused senses, her beauty is misunderstood as a form of *materia* rather than the light of *spiritus* glowing into the mortal world. Therefore the seekers grasp at Florimell with earthly hands, use and exploit her like the forester and like the fisherman in canto viii, in whose boat Florimell finds herself adrift at sea. These monster-men are not figures antithetical to ourselves but an allegory of a universally fallen condition. The predatory self wants what is beautiful and bright but expects to have it as appetite wants food: the forester and fisherman, like the satyrs, seeing Florimell, automatically burn to man-handle her, not concerned as to whether she is hurt or stained and unable to discern the fact that she cannot be held in this way. Man the rapist is placed as an emblem of fallen humanity against the woman victim whose nature images the divine. The problem is seen as tragically innate in the human condition, where the soul is, in Ficino's phrase, 'weighted down by the burden of a most troublesome body',[38] or in that of Hermes Trismegistus, clothed in 'this cloak of darkness, this web of ignorance...this living death, this conscious corpse, this tomb you carry about with you'.[39] Ficino had set out both the problems and meaning of human concupiscence, and its solution in his *Commentary on Plato's 'Symposium'* (as in Spenser's *Faerie Queene*) gives this theory vivid and compassionate life:

> Plunged into the abyss of the body as though into the river of forgetfulness, oblivious at the moment of itself, the soul is seized by sensuality and lust as though by a tyrant and his bullies. But when the body has matured, and the instruments of sense have been purged through learning, it recovers itself a little, then its natural light shines out, and it searches out the order of natural things...This kind of appetite and desire is true love, and under its leadership the one half-man seeks the other half, because the natural light, which is one half of the soul, tries to kindle again in the soul that once neglected light which we have said is the other half.[40]

Both in Ficino and in Spenser the Fall is viewed rather with fellow-feeling than with disgust, and each expresses a guarded optimism that man will be able to 'grow out of' his animalism as he ripens from his initial fall into the narcissism of insatiable appetite. In Ficino, the 'half-man' seeks 'the other half'; in Spenser, the half-man seeks the fulness of his original being in woman. Each stresses immaturity and the need for growth either through learning or love. Even when he is describing man at his lowest and least regenerate, Spenser makes him pathetic and ridiculous rather than absolutely vicious. The 'griesly Foster' gores the horse's sides with his spurs, because he knows no better:

> Large were his limbes, and terrible his looke,
> And in his clownish hand a sharp bore speare he shooke.
>
> (III. i. 17)

The 'clownish hand' on the phallic spear suggests the rustic stupidity of the senses which, correctly identifying the beautiful, only know how to communicate with it by hunting it down and swallowing it into 'this cloak of darkness, this web of ignorance'.

This theme of man the mortal rapist, woman the immortal prey, is sustained throughout the Book. In the fisherman's boat in canto viii, Florimell is borne by the tide under a clement, balmy air (21). She has escaped from the witch's beast 'likest to an *Hyena*.../ That feeds on womens flesh, as others feede on gras' (vii. 22) with its horrifying suggestion of man's carnivorous appetite tearing its human food from the carcase of what it has destroyed in the name of 'love'. But Florimell's dilemma is that she can only escape into another version of her original predicament. Threats from land-dwellers are matched by the threats to her nature to be found on the volatile, perilous and always ambiguous element of the sea. She is no more safe in the boat than before, though her person shines there in its quietness like a living light. As the fisherman wakes he sees a physical aura of light with him in the boat:

> when he saw that blazing beauties beame,
> Which with rare light his bote did beautifie,
> He marveild more, and thought he yet did dreame
> Not well awakt, or that some extasie
> Assotted had his seruse, or dazed was his eie.
>
> (III. viii. 22)

In a Platonist *ekstasis*, the fisherman awakens from the dream-state into visionary reality. But he does not know how to respond to this reality. He stares. We see the coarse look of decision come over his face. His fixed stare 'marke[s] her snowy skin' (24). This word-play carries a judgement on his way of looking, out of eyes which carry a polluting willingness to deface the cool, pale beauty of the victim, having first 'marked' it as a target. Spenser characterises him as an old man, the old Adam of our race, whose 'drie withered stocke' is soon kindled. The poet does not spare us the unpleasantly arousing details: the fisherman tries to thrust 'his rough hand/Where ill became him' (25), and 'ne cared to spill/Her garments gay with scales of fish' (26) as he throws her down and fouls her dress. Florimell's deliverence by Proteus is into another form of captivity, in an underwater Hades which parallels Marinell's detention in his mother's underwater bower. The Adonis myth and the Proserpina figure become symmetrically static: neither figure is to be released in the course of Book III, enacting the long winter burial of the floral world.

It is only when Florimell has become so distant in the poem's time that she is hardly an echo at all, at the end of Book IV, that Spenser enacts her return. Marinell's mother, Cymoent, secures her release, connecting the Adonis myth again with the Ceres/Proserpina story in a miniature Eleusis which figures not just a seasonal healing and redemption but, within the poem's vision, a complete and eternal union of counterparts. Marinell revives:

> As withered weed through cruell winters tine,
> That feeles the warmth of sunny beames reflection,
> Lifts up his head, that did before decline
> And gins to spread his leafe before the faire sunshine.
>
> (IV. xii. 34)

Marinell 'lifts up his head' humanly, reborn with Florimell like the sea-born Venus; it is an image of purging through love, revived power to grow, out of immersion in the saline, astringent waters of the sea.[41] Marinell also 'liftes up his head' inhumanly, for within the context of the poem we see that he is not only like but also *is* the 'withered weed' which parches throughout winter, reduced to minimal existence as the tough root in the underworld, from which it can expand ('spread his leafe') in the warmth of an annual miracle. The poetry celebrates the dormant potentialities which man holds in common with nature, and mimes in its very structure the 'cruell winters tine' which protracts this dormancy, by retarding the budding-together of Marinell and Florimell until the end of Book IV. The English winter is so long that spring is not expected; then it comes. Just as Spenser endows the animal world with a sentience which invites and requires our sympathy, so also his poetry confers upon the world of vegetation an almost animistic capacity to feel delight and undergo sorrow. Both man and flower lift their heads in the same emotional world, reflecting one another's lives as they reflect those of the gods, sharing meaning between them. This aspect of Spenser's feminine vision recalls the kind of pantheism which Bruno expounds in *The Expulsion of the Triumphant Beast,* the Egyptian natural religion which says '*Natura est deus in rebus*' (p. 235) and is exemplified in 'the Sun in the Crocus, in the narcissus, in the heliotrope' (p. 236). Under the feminine Wisdom of Sophia, Bruno's

integration of the universe so as to value all possibles expresses
itself thus:

> Everything, then, no matter how minimal, is under infinitely great
> Providence; all minutiae, no matter how very lowly, in the order of
> the whole and of the universe, are most important
> *(Expulsion of the Triumphant Beast*, p. 137)

In the Brunian universe, each microscopic detail expresses an
individual meaning which relates it to a flow of meaning through
every other detail; each speck of the cosmos is a holy place, each
pore breathes with the same spirit of actively intercommunicat-
ing love, and both high and low speak an identical language of
patterned meanings. What Bruno expressed as a philosophy,
Spenser enacts as the organic world of his poem under the rule
of the *una dea*, a matrix of being in which all minutiae respond
to the same recreative law through which is felt 'the warmth of
sunny beames reflection'.

Yet we cannot fail to notice that, in terms of the Florimell-
Marinell motif, the image we take away from Book III is not of
this surfaced, elucidating light. It is of bloodshed, loss and light
drowned in water. Florimell's threatened catastrophe is figured
in the tapestry of Jupiter's rapes of mortal maidens in canto xi
(the House of Busyrane): Leda, raped 'in daffadillies sleeping'
(32), motifs recalling the rape of Proserpina; Daphne becoming a
laurel tree in flight from Apollo's rape; Hyacinthus extinct as a
person, remade as the flower of the *Metamorphoses* (37). Shape-
changing—metamorphosis violently downwards on the chain of
being—is the material of the plot. Proteus in canto viii plays on
the stability of Florimell's identity. The preservation of such
integrity as hers is achieved at a cost, conveyed to us through
poignant images from the natural world. Florimell resembles the
beautiful creatures of earth and sky which have to flee before
carnivorous animals, predatory man and his 'tame' pets. The
male is the huntsman, the female the prey. The price of her value
to the male is the shedding of her blood:

> Like as a fearefull Partridge, that is fled
> From the sharpe Hauke, which her attached near,
> And fals to ground, to seeke for succour theare,

Whereas the hungry Spaniels she does spy,
With greedy jawes her readie for to teare...
(III. viii. 33)

Florimell's double danger is enacted in the partridge's failure to
find safety in either available element, air or earth. The hawk's
jabbing beak gives place to the spaniel's efficient teeth. She is
meat for both. Behind the spaniel is implied the existence of
man the huntsman who has 'tamed' its instincts. Florimell's
sacrifice to the protean artfulness of the male appetite cannot be
thought of as meaningful unless it can also be shown that there
is some other, opposite kind of hunter within the dark forests of
Book III of the poem whose power makes sacrifice redemptive.

DIANA AND VENUS

In the great house in Derbyshire, Hardwick Hall, which was
being built by Elizabeth, Countess of Shrewsbury, at the time
The Faerie Queene was being published, we have a chance to
enter physically into the heretical alternative world-system
mythologised in *The Faerie Queene* and narrated in paint, stone,
cloth and wood in the art and architecture of Queen Elizabeth's
England. A building may be taken to stand as a living text,
especially one preserved from an age like the Renaissance when
the visual arts were to an extreme degree conceived as literary,
and literature as intensely visual. Elizabeth of Hardwick was in
her seventies when she built this monument to her own power,
out of wealth accumulated from four marriages. The building
celebrates an ethos of power, drawing attention to the cosmic
completeness of its conception of power by its Palladian symmetries and by features such as the astrolabe, tapestries recording
whole epic narratives and complete runs of detailed emblem-
patterns. The shock of the building, however, is not its scale and
detail but in its translation of an entire pantheon of traditional
motifs into the feminine gender. All the emblems are female, not
just the demure and mild-mannered virtues (which are few) but
especially, and challengingly, the ruling virtues. The degree of
heresy implied is extraordinary. There are no male gods, or
God. Sol is personified as a woman,[41] in defiant contradiction to

the combined authority of ancient Israel, Egypt, Asia, Greece and Rome that the sun is male, and king, and God. Hardwick Hall celebrates the moon-queen and the sun-queen, and personifies the female as judge and law-giver in innumerable threatening emblems of *Iustitia,* arrogant, severe and royal. In prominent friezes and tapestries, Actaeon is very visibly in dire straits before the ruling Diana. Behind the local Elizabeth is felt the presence of the greater Queen Elizabeth, not least in the portrait of the countess with the fashionable red-gold hair, the female Sol ruling the concentric universe with both warmth and rigour. Linked to this matriarchal assertion of the female as power is a continuous allusion to the garden-world of growing things, rooted in recognisably English soil, where tapestried stones, mushrooms, worms and crickets inhabit garden-plots of lovingly stitched cloth. This garden world expresses a variant form of power, the generative pattern of the natural world over which the great deities—Venus and Diana—preside and which they exist to protect. Bruno's 'minutiae', Spenser's vegetation, are paralleled here in a mythology of power benignly rooted in the English earth, whose lowly creatures are raised in significance, and the simple fruits of the earth—hazelnut, pea-pod, marrow—are praised as holy, through the artist's care to depict them.

A Hardwick tapestry represents an image of the divine hand reaching out of the clouds enacting Omnipotence's providential gesture of sovereignty over the world below, a gesture both of judgement and of safe-keeping. But the hand, we perceive with a slight shock, is not the strong right hand of the Father: it is a slender, female hand. Spenser extends such a hand over the events of Book III, in the form of the twinned but opposite figures of the goddesses Diana and Venus, who preside over the whole in such a way as to ensure the ultimate safety and fruitfulness of Florimell within a rapaciously fallen world. Diana is the virgin huntress whose protégée in the Book is the warrior-maiden Belphoebe. The huntress opposes the hunter as Diana did Actaeon, turning his own hounds against their master as penalty for his unlawful entrance into the free forest-world, which is both her domain and the territory of Spenser's poem. She is virgin as forests are—wild, uncivilised, living according to a personal code. Her 'terrible' and even murderous aspect relates to her function as protector of all femininity, from ancient times invoked by women in childbirth, as Lucina, but having no connection with the trammels of marriage, which is foreign to her. It relates also to her role as guardian of the animals, particularly the cubs and young of all species, including human children. Sacred inland waters—lakes, marshes, streams, rivers—were in her care. Spenser's Diana is authentically pagan, refusing assimilation to the modest Madonna of Christianity.[43] Her powerful hand is suspended over the violations attempted by the intruders into the primal forest world of Book III, so that each male figure is potentially Actaeon. Diana often effected the metamorphoses of human maidens into vegetation alluded to on the tapestry of divine rapes (see p. 76 above). Thus her power participates in the great round of decay and recreation in Book III. And as at Syracuse she had been worshipped as Artemis Arethusa, her emblem being the dolphin, her nature could be understood as transcending the forest world and extending beyond its margin (the beach which bounds the mainland) to include the sea-waters.

Meeting her in *The Faerie Queene*, Book III, comes her own opposite, Venus. The two great female oppositions meet, and talk, and disagree, and part. But the fact of their communication at the magnificent centrepiece of the Book demonstrates Spenser's calling together of the dynamic oppositions within the female conception of divinity and power, combining them in the plenitude of an inclusive meaning. We glimpse the fact of the existence of these opposites within one another and obtain clues to meanings throughout the Book. As Venus approaches Diana, sexuality approaches virgin rigour, passionate and untouchable privacy is met by the passionate claim to see and touch. But the austere inwardness of Diana somehow mirrors the fulness and abundance of Venus. Diana's forest is also a forest of sexuality, in which the satyrs orgy and dance and in which Hellenore is declared their May queen, shading her face with Diana's laurel (x. 44), and couples with one of those bestially potent creatures under the jealous eye of Malbecco: 'Nine times he heard him come aloft ere day'. The voluntarily deflowered Hellenore given over to this savage appetite is perhaps more pitiable than her virginal opposite Florimell penned in Venus' element, the sea. They are versions of one another, though opposite, as by tradition there were two Helens of Troy, the 'unreal' one who was the sexual source of Troy's disaster, and the 'real' innocent Helen, apart in Egypt immune from stain.[44] Thus Venus and Diana imply one another, as each part of *The Faerie Queene* implies the whole of the rest.

In canto vi, Venus enters the forest to seek her errant son, Cupid. Thus she comes upon Diana whilst engaged in a search for a lost part of herself. The goddesses taunt each other in as coarsely human and comic a manner as Shakespeare's Venus in *Venus and Adonis*. They are recognisably of the same family, as are their entourage:

> Some of them washing with the liquid dew
> From off their dainty limbes the dusty sweat
>
> (III. vi. 17)

Nymphs of Diana who 'sweat' bring the divinity down to meet our human clay; but to wash sweat off with 'liquid dew' inspires that clay with sensuous lyricism which lifts earth towards the heavens. The portrait of Diana which follows is as sensual as if it were being copied in the moment of writing from a living model:

> She having hong upon a bough on high
>   Her bow and painted quiver, had unlaste
>   Her silver buskins from her nimble thigh,
>   And her lancke loynes ungirt, and brests unbraste,
>   After her heat the breathing cold to taste;
>   Her golden lockes, that late in tresses bright
>   Embreaded were for hindring of her haste,
>   Now loose about her shoulders hong undight…
>
> (III. vi. 18)

The reader of the poem pries into that most secret, vulnerable and dangerous place—of naked Chastity—as her thighs, loins and breasts are exposed; the reader becomes an Actaeon, delighted at the revelation but also tensely intrusive into the scene of a passionately guarded shyness. In enjoying the erotic set-piece, he also violates a taboo. Though Diana closely resembles Venus in her nakedness, when in the next stanza she sees that she is seen, she reasserts her own nature, in a very human gesture:

> Soone her garments loose
> Upgath'ring, in her bosome she comprized
> Well as she might, and to the Goddesse rose,
> Whiles all her Nymphes did like a girlond her enclose.
>
> (III. vi. 19)

The powerful goddess is caught by Venus—and by poetic voyeurism—disadvantaged and gauche. Eyes can 'feed' in Spenser, as Mammon's do on his gold (II. vii. 4) or Guyon's on the cavorting naked nymphs in the Bower of Bliss (II. xii. 63-4). The eye of the senses is a potentially lethal instrument of destruction, rape or contamination. To protect the goddess from such eyes as ours, the nymphs of Diana fold round her 'like a girlond' in the magnificent lyricism of the concluding line. Girls and flowers are perceived as one in beauty (flesh like silky petals) and one in perfection (the ring of the garland, the circle of eternity). Evanescence is also suggested: girls like flowers may be plucked, torn and scattered. Diana in her insecure enclosure looks for a moment humanly vulnerable, before her invulnerability is re-established.

Britomart, Florimell and Belphoebe—'Her yellow lockes... About her shoulders loosely shed' (II. iii. 30)—are all linked to the goddess Diana at this moment of revelation, through imagery of flowing golden hair. Paradoxically, they are assimilated (together with Diana) to the goddess Venus, for yellow is Venus' colour.[45] The Book's central synthesis is the pacification of Diana the fighter by Venus the lover (vi. 25). In Venus' secret Garden of Love, Venus and Adonis enjoy one another at the source and end of creation, where the seeds of all species are regenerated and recycled. As against the sterile sexual fantasy which gratifies the inhabitants of the Bower of Bliss, pleasure in the Garden of Adonis is experienced as the fruitfulness of joyous sexual love born and ripening in time with the seasonal rhythms of the natural world. Its prelude is, fittingly, a birth, and—more specifically—a virgin-birth and a twin-birth, the story of Chrysogone's conception and delivery of her daughters, Belphoebe and Amoret, which opens the central canto. The relationship of mother to twin daughters is that of the One to the *coincidentia oppositorum*, Belphoebe being a human Diana, the huntress of the sun, and Amoret the protégée of Venus and the narrative's means of entry into the Garden of Adonis where she is nurtured. 'Amoret' means 'little love'; Spenser's sonnets to Elizabeth Boyle were entitled *Amoretti*, and the poetry associated with Amoret seems to declare an emotional and personal partiality which distinguishes its tone from the awe generated by the more superb Belphoebe. Such partiality does not imply preference, for the poetry of canto vi everywhere stresses that there is no choice to be made between Venus and Diana, Amoret and Belphoebe, Elizabeth Boyle and Queen Elizabeth I. Book III celebrates wholeness. But it insists that the *una dea* can never be known in the singular; like Apuleius' Isis whose nature contains all qualities, figured in her garments 'of fine silke yelding divers colours, sometime white, sometime yelow, sometime rosie, sometime flamy, and somtime (which troubled my spirit sore) darke and obscure' (*Golden Asse*, 259). Thus, though it is Amoret whose future leads us into the vision of the Garden of Adonis, Belphoebe has been linked since Book II with the same processes of creation into which Amoret will be initiated in the womblike Garden of her second, single birth: her daintie paps' amorously described as 'like young fruit in May' which 'little gan to swell' (II. iii. 29) and her pubic hair (in an image blushfully described in Hamilton's annotation as 'startling') florally embellished:

> As through the flouring forrest rash she fled,
> In her rude haires sweet flowres themselves did lap,
> And flourishing fresh leaves and blossomes did enwrap.
> (II. iii. 30)

Here the poet is taking the idea of the virgin-queen as 'the flower of chastity' rather literally; Gloriana might well have felt taken aback looking into this image of herself as *Venus virgo* in the person of a scantily clad May queen to whose disclosed private parts raw nature makes such a demonstrative overture of fellow feeling. The point is that while it is Amoret whose 'steadfast womanliness'[46] alone can wear the lost girdle of Florimell, and flower within that zone, the poetry makes striking insistence on the fertility of all true forms of chastity, even to the point of displaying its 'rude haires' wreathed with 'sweet flowres' to public view.

The twin-theme is central to the present study as an ancient motif through which tradition states its sense of the original union of mortal with immortal, male with female, self and other. It represents the double vision of identity which seems universal amongst human cultures, the ambiguous intuition that we both 'are' and 'are not' one another. In contemplating the natural prodigy of the twin-birth the mind studies the simultaneous mirroring of the one source in different features. Spenser doubles the miraculous associations of twinning by linking it to the Virgin Birth and concentrating on the person and role of the mother, Chrysogone, one of the most beautiful of Spenser's characters yet one of the most fleeting and impersonal. The narrator says of Belphoebe that 'Her berth was of the wombe of Morning dew' (III. vi. 3), suggesting a fusion of the natural world with human nature, place with person, mother with Mother Earth, which delicately introduces the major theme of canto vi. Chrysogone, whose name means 'bringing forth gold', submits to strange alchemy. In the heat of the day, she bathes in the forest, lies down to sleep 'all naked bare displayd':

> The sunne-beames bright upon her body playd,
> Being through former bathing mollifide,
> And pierst into her wombe, where they embayd
> With so sweet sence and secret power unspide,
> That in her pregnant flesh they shortly fructifide.
>   (III. vi. 7)

This warmly sensuous description of Chrysogone's impregnation by the rays of the sunlight—'Great father he of generation' (vi. 9) prefiguring Adonis, 'the Father of all formes' (47)—with the poetry's unashamed anatomical candour, showing the open, abandoned languor of the sleeping girl's body, calls up less the image of the abstract and business-like Virgin Birth than archaic Hellenic images of the intercourse between Mother Earth and Father Sky, or Zeus' descents to mortal maidens (rapes woven into canto xi's erotic tapestries). Spenser makes the sun-rays penetrate deep and forcibly into the darkness of her body ('pierst'), with a power as 'secret' as the mystery of the origin of life itself. But though this is technically a rape, it is never other than benign, a glow of the creative life-force into the person of humanity so as to leave her 'fructifide'. In a myth of regeneration comparable to the vegetation myth of Marinell/Adonis and Florimell/Flora, Chrysogone provides the living matter in which the sun inspires form, with a gentleness close to that with which Zephyrus breathes the warm gale of spring-time into the waiting nature of Flora. There is allusion, too, to the Christian annunciation and Virgin Birth, particularly in the image of Chrysogone 'In this wild forrest wandring all alone' (vi. 5) and her fear of the constructions society might put on her husbandless condition. But there is no Joseph, no inn and no saving boy-child. Spenser's heresy is like that of Shakespeare in the Last Plays, in delivering miraculous and redemptive girl-children.

But if Chrysogone represents this meeting-place of heaven and earth, she also figures a predicament to which *The Faerie Queene* recurrently alludes with concern. This is the predicament of the weak, helpless and lonely, in the persons of women or children: those for whom society has no place, persons denied status and lacking the qualifications which gain admittance to the safe-keeping of the respectable comunity. The poem records the existence of this unheroic class of wanderers in Gloriana's England: vagrants, the uprooted, the orphaned. In Book II, the most severe of books, another such lost and helpless woman is introduced in the person of Amavia, literally 'the path of love', whose suicide orphans her child. For many like her, the path of love leads to the grave. Sir Guyon cannot refrain from weeping for her, though this is no doubt in flat contradiction to the unlovable virtue of Temperance. Digging open 'the great earthes wombe', Guyon and the Palmer bury Amavia and Mortdant and 'bid them sleepe in everlasting peace' there (II. i. 60). This leaves as sole survivor the baby with the bloody hands, to whom Sir Guyon says 'with bitter teares':

> Ah lucklesse babe, borne under cruell starre,
> And in dead parents balefull ashes bred,
> Full little weenest thou, what sorrowes are
> Left thee for portion of thy livelihed,
> Poore Orphane in the wide world scattered,
> As budding braunch rent from the native tree,
> And thrown forth, till it be withered:

Such is the state of men: thus enter wee
Into this life with woe, and end with miseree.
(II. ii. 2)

This is not in the virile traditions of Temperance, which seems committed on the whole to a poker-faced stoicism. But Guyon is not rebuked either by the narrative voice or by his companion. In a lovingly observed detail, the baby, taken up into the warrior's arms 'Gan smyle on them, that rather ought to weepe' (ii. 7). Our sense of the original sin which the baby is supposed to represent is contradicted by this picture of an original joyous innocence at the core of newborn life. The allegory would seem to want us to blame Amavia, but not only is this impossible in the light of the protective pity Spenser's poem constantly stirs in us at her gentleness and affection but also (as Robert Reid has shown in a sensitive and learned article)[47] she seems to represent a genuine tragic virtue. Spenser reverses the accepted Augustinian hierarchy of the soul in which male *spiritus* is higher and better than female *anima* and both are preferable to the weak fleshly *corpus* (the baby). The feminine indicts the masculine, by turning her loving power to his redemption. Guyon rightly puts women and children first in his lament over a young life which does not know how 'scattered' it is from its outset. For a moment the poetry rises to the level of pastoral elegy. The child is in bud upon the 'braunch of his native tree', the nurturing mother. His time of life is spring; but his condition is autumn, in a wilderness. Upon this immense landscape of desolation, the tree of life is seen as a victim of the broken pastoral of the fallen world, simultaneously budding and withering through no fault of its own. In Spenser's poem, the One is seen as broken into multiplicity; the personal cost of this philosophical abstraction is figured in the one baby 'in the wide world scattered', dispersed from source as an emblem (Guyon maintains) of the essential rootlessness of human nature.

It is this principle of 'scattering' which Spenser again evokes in the figure of Chrysogone in Book III, but here the themes of loss and loneliness are retold within a redemptive context and contained within a tragi-comic matrix. This is the Book of Love, where what happened to Amavia would never be allowed to happen. Whereas the Book of Temperance kills Amavia and she cannot be revived, the Book of Love visits on Chrysogone an experience of nightmare horror which, as if in a benign dream, is resolved below the level of consciousness. Shocked to find herself pregnant, Chrysogone 'Wondered to see her belly so upblone/Which still increased' (vi. 9) and seeks anonymity in the forest. A sense of her mounting horror is conveyed in the grotesque verb 'upblone', but underlying this is a suggestion of divine inspiration that blows or breathes into human nature, bearing natural fruit. The importance of the theme of 'scattering' in this central Book is reinforced by the narrative interpolation immediately following (vi. 11) of Venus' loss of and search for the errant Cupid through court, city, country and forest. As in alchemical processes, disintegration and incoherence must occur before the work ('Bringing forth gold') can be accomplished. Dismembering and loss imply an Isis endeavour for reunification. Chrysogone gives birth to the twins, Belphoebe and Amoret:

> Unwares she them conceiv'd, unwares she bore:
> She bore withouten paine, that she conceived
> Withouten pleasure...

>   (III vi. 27)

God's vindictive curse on womankind is thus evaded in the feminine universe:

> Unto the woman he said, I will greatly multiply thy sorrow and thy conception; in sorrow thou shalt bring forth children; and thy desire shall be to thy husband, and he shall rule over thee.
>   (Genesis 3:16)

There is no husband; there are no labour pains, no multiplication tables of sorrow to daunt her, but rather a birth of new selves from the unconscious psyche, 'Unwares...unwares', delivering the twin oppositions of the female nature into the light of day. A reader of *The Faerie Queene* may seriously doubt whether Spenser was at heart a Christian at all.[48]

The Garden of Adonis episode may be read as a statement of an alternative faith. It is a vision of universal return to the great fund of matter which is home to all species, to be recycled and reformulated. Everything that happens in Book III before this episode points forward to it; everything that will subsequently happen points backward to it. Thus it is a place of gathering, collection of disparities, recollection, adverse to the principle of 'scattering' exemplified by Amavia's child. The Garden is also an emblem of the creative mind in the act of *poiesis,* 'making'. The poet's imagination conceives and germinates ideas in a state of union with itself, as Venus breeds through Adonis, as Psyche fuses with Cupid. The creating mind is stocked with an extraordinary range and diversity of forms, eager for utterance, 'That seemd the Ocean could not containe them there' (vi. 35). This theme is all the more subtly used when we consider the 'containment' of Marinell and Florimell on the sea-bed, and their inevitable release. The garden-womb, the ocean-womb and the mind-womb reflect one another, incorporating the creative principle as a female power, in which the poet is privileged to participate, as *creatix* as well as *creator.*

The structure of the Garden is also archetypally female, according to the pattern favoured by Spenser, a series of concentric circles (see pp. 40–1 above). We constantly move inwards towards the core of the experience. In this way the reader's penetration of the place is like a sequence of initiations into its mysteries. We move always more deeply towards 'the middest of that Paradise' (vi. 43), towards the Mountain of Venus. This is on one level anatomical, the *mons Veneris* reached as the consummation of the physical act of love. For Spenser as for Milton, sexual 'shame' is 'guilty' (*Paradise Lost, IV. 313*), and the naked female body is presented as sacred, a landscape of the higher love, even, or especially, when it is aroused by desire. The myrtle trees:

> like a girlond compassed the hight,
> And from their fruitfull sides sweet gum did drop,
> That all the ground with precious deaw bedight...
> (III. vi. 43)

The aromatic moisture running down the bark of the trees suggests the fluids expressed from the vagina in physical desire. Modifying adjectives direct the mind's eye through the lascivious connotations of this imagery to its mysterious role in the pattern of creation and recreation: the 'sides' of the trees remind us of the 'side' of a pregnant woman; the dew is 'precious'. Secrets of futurity held within the Garden intimate a value beyond the sexually gratifying, though inclusive of it. The flowers growing towards the centre of the Garden are flowers of death and metamorphosis: hyacinth, narcissus, amaranthus (vi. 45). The common name for the purple amaranthus was 'Love-lies-a-bleeding', which gives a vivid clue to the deepest meaning of the bower in which Venus enjoys Adonis. The flowery ground looks, for a moment, blood-soaked. Phoebus' beloved, Hyacinthus, Narcissus, and the dead Amintas (possibly a compliment to Sir Philip Sidney killed at war in the Netherlands) are images of sacrificed male youth, taking us back to Marinell/Adonis, who was mysteriously sacrificed in his sexual prime. The flowers that spring from blood lead back to the ancient fertility myths as related by Ovid. But 'Amaranthus' leads beyond the mortal casualities of the temporal world: its Greek root means 'unfading', a defeat for mutability by the eternally recurrent coition of Venus and Adonis. In asserting this possibility of dealing a death-blow to Time, by acting within time, Spenser rises to a massively universalising poetry:

> some say, in secret he does ly,
> Lapped in flowres and pretious spycery,
> By her hid from the world, and from the skill
> Of *Stygian* Gods, which doe her love envy;
> But she her selfe, when ever that she will,
> Possesseth him, and of his sweetnesse takes her fill.
>
> But sooth it seemes they say: for he may not
> For ever die, and ever buried bee
> In baleful night, where all things are forgot;
> All be he subject to mortalitie,
> Yet is eterne in mutabilitie,
> And by succession made perpetuall,
> Transformed oft, and chaunged diverslie:
> For him the Father of all formes they call;
> Therefore needs mote he live, that living gives to all.
>
> (III. vi.46–7)

Spenser's poem is like a living mnemonic, speaking memorably against the Stygian forgetfulness which is presented here as an underlying darkness constantly preying upwards into the world of memory. Memory, for the Renaissance and for Spenser, is the faculty which in binding past and present tenses together fixes the individual mind within the continuum of human and divine knowledge, uniquely and indispensibly ensuring our humanity. It is the preliminary to all knowledge, and the mother of poetry itself, as Mnemosyne was mother to the Muses.[49] In this passionate assertion against the powers of oblivion which 'bury' meaning, Spenser centralises the verb 'to be'—'Yet is eterne'—at the core of the stanza. The effect created is of the force of language to contradict the nihilistic raids of the underworld. Words assert truth but also (because they draw on memory and reinforce it through stress, rhythm and sense) they create their own reality. In the grammar of contradiction ('All be...Yet is') the poet gainsays the curse in Genesis, that man is made of dust and will shortly return to his objectionable origins. He substitutes a myth of the eternal recycling of matter through Love, which bears close relationship to the Hermetic doctrine of the cyclical patterning of creation, where Hermes explains that 'the Kosmos is ever being made' (*A Discourse of Hermes Trismegistus,* 2, *Hermetica,* p. 175) and that bodies through 'dissolution...are reinstated' (*Ibid.,* 4, p. 177). The conjunction of Venus and Adonis, the great mother and 'Father of all formes', repeats the theme of the female hermaphrodite alluded to in the hermaphroditic Venus of Book IV, Nature of the Mutabilitie Cantos, and Britomart within the more human sphere. Venus and Adonis in the act of coition make up an androgyne within the feminine gender. Venus is spoke of in the active voice, Adonis in the passive; Venus represents the transforming spirit, Adonis the transformed matter. She descends upon the acquiescent male in a direct reversal of the rape motif exemplified in the behaviour of the '*Stygian* gods'; thus Venus 'Possesseth him', 'takes her fill' of Adonis, at the discretion of her own lively appetite.

It is only through submission to a love that is female *and* active, Spenser suggests, that the male—excluded by his biological make-up from the power to procreate—can deal with that obsession of Spenser's poetry, mutability. It is only 'by succession' that the male is 'made perpetuall'. He is dealing with the problem which has beset the male-centred society from its very origins: how man can bear children. The Garden of Adonis is thronged (in the abstract) with potentialities, but in the concrete with babies, all clamouring to be born. Plato treats it as a known fact of life that young men grow up with an instinct to breed: 'as soon as he comes of due age he desires to procreate and to have children' (*Symposium*, 209), but he regards the best kind of children as intellectual and abstract, for they take longer to wear out. Shakespeare repeats the theme in the *Sonnets*, urging the friend to beget heirs, and turning himself inside out in the sequence by trying to bear himself the immortal child of poetry. Property laws are founded on the male desire for self-perpetuation; entails, wills and legal codices, together with the idea of 'legitimate' children; art-works and religious creeds seek to perpetuate the male image of himself beyond the individual life. I think we should read the Garden of Adonis episode in the light of these factors, as Spenser's individual, heretical solution to the problem of the essentially uncreative, or positively destructive, nature of the male. It is also a deeply personal reaction to his own plight as male narrator-questor. The poem has constantly circled the problem of mutability, inscribing its fears as if on a palimpsest, on which the same preoccupation multiplies itself in different images. But at such moments as the vision of the love-making of Venus and Adonis, the narrator-questor seems to reach a point of intense clarification, which is equally an illumination to the reader. It is not through the denial of male aggression and rapacity that this illumination is reached but through the yielding of coercive power to the female, together with the language by which it finds expression. Thus in Spenser, Venus 'Possesseth' Adonis. Such possession by a male of a female would be understood as morally dubious. Inverting the relationship however reverses its valuation. Venus is love: to be 'possessed' by love is not to be taken as property but recreated as one's self, 'Transformed oft, and chaunged diverslie'. At this great central section, we are experiencing a redemption of language itself through association with the feminine. The malign element in male sexuality is shown as potentially capable of restraint through this voluntary yielding to the female. The phallic 'wild Bore' whose tusk gored Adonis is imprisoned by Venus in a rocky cave (vi. 48), an image of safe containment ensuring potency and fruitfulness, within the canto of reconciliation.

The reconciliation in the Garden of Adonis is not single but double and quadruple. It multiplies itself to imply the union of all variables at the concise centre of human experience. Venus' wanderings, like Ceres', were caused by the loss of a child. In seeking for a son she came by a foster-daughter, Amoret. In drawing the daughter into her garden, she is reunited with the son she sought. Thus the girl-child mediates the dislocated experiences both of men and of gods. The presence of Cupid and Psyche in the Garden, to act as Amoret's foster-parents, is a serious illumination regarding this theme of psychic unity, which even the Goddess of Love herself lacks and must pursue. It alludes, of course, to Apuleius' *Golden Asse*, but from the perspective of the completed tragi-comic structure of that story rather than to the unfolding tragic experiences of Psyche. Spenser's Cupid in the intervals of 'ransacking' the world of human nature, returns 'home' not to Venus (the older generation of divinities) but to his wife Psyche (the younger generation of humanity):

> And his true love faire *Psyche* with him playes,
> Faire *Psyche* to him lately reconcyld,
> After long troubles and unmeet upbrayes,
> With which his mother *Venus* had revyled,
> And eke himselfe her cruelly exyld:
> But now in stedfast love and happy state
> She with him lives, and hath him born a chyld,
> *Pleasure*, that doth both gods and men aggrate,
> *Pleasure*, the daughter of *Cupid* and *Psyche* late.
>
> Hither great *Venus* brought this infant faire,
> The younger daughter of *Chrysogonee*,
> And unto *Psyche* with great trust and care
> Committed her, yfostered to bee,
> And trained up in true feminitee...
> (III. vi. 50–1)

The emphasis here is on the fruit of pain rather than on pain itself. The healed soul (Psyche) bears a child. Imagery of child-birth is almost overpowering in the extract, for each figure is seen as somebody's child: Venus' son, Psyche's daughter,

Chrysogone's daughter. In Venus' acceptance of Psyche as her own daughter, we see the female principle itself participating in the universal atonement of reconciliation. In Apuleius' story, Venus, splenetic and unforgiving, visits riddling problems on the burdened Psyche for stealing her son's devotion and for wounding him with scalding oil from the lamp by which she tried to see him. She cruelly disowns Psyche's child as illegitimate, and strikes her:

> Then she began to laugh againe, saying: Behold she thinketh (that by reason of her great belly which she hath gotten by playing the hoore) to move me to pitie, and to make me a grandmother to her child: Am not I happy that in the flourishinge time of all mine age shalbe called a grandmother, and the sonne of a vile harlotte shalbe accompted the Nephew of Venus? How be it I am a foole to terme him by the name of a sonne, since as the marriage was made betweene unequall persons, in the fieldes, without witnesses, and not by the consent of their parentes, wherfore the marriage is illegitimate, and the childe (that shalbe borne) a bastarde, if we fortune to suffer thee to live so longe till thou be delivered.
>
> When Venus had spoken these woordes she leaped upon the face of poore Psiches, and (tearing her apparell) toke her violently by the heare, and dashed her head upon the ground.
>
> (*Golden Asse*, 128-9)

Apuleius' Venus is viciously possessive and without scruple. She cannot be appeased nor her mind changed. She has to be forced to accept Psyche as her legitimate daughter-in-law by the higher power, Jupiter, and does so mutely and no doubt grudgingly. Psyche's pregnancy excites a jealous legalism in her, as though love were debased by contact with merely human nature. Apuleius' Venus stands for conservative hierarchy and degree. She sneers at Psyche's mortal pretentions. Jupiter has to reassure her that the child she has condemned as a 'bastard' was conceived in 'mortall marriage...juste, lawful and legitimate' (137), to which the irate goddess makes no reply. In Adlington's translation, Venus assumed that the child will be a boy, 'the Nephew of Venus', and the narrator finishing the tale does not specify gender, simply remarking as a postscript that 'she was delivered of a childe, whom we call Pleasure' (137). Spenser's Venus is only transiently irascible and is not seen to bear grievances towards 'unequall persons'. Spenser's emphasis is on Venus the reconciler and the reconciled rather than the destroyer. Most importantly of all, Spenser insists on a female gender for Psyche's child Pleasure, and doubles this by having Amoret brought up in her company twinned 'in true feminitee'. Characteristically, Spenser's adaptation of the myth is a recreation of its values and personages in terms of the feminine, and in a language proper to this re-gendered, regenerated ideal. Amoret ripens in the feminine Garden so as to encounter the world of art to which she must accommodate herself outside that Garden.

ART AND AMORET

'Ripeness is all' both in Shakespeare's *King Lear* and in Spenser's *Faerie Queene*. But ripening implies change, and change (especially shape-changing) for Spenser is always suspect. The legend of Psyche accurately exemplifies this potentiality of threat, with its association with the butterfly's serial metamorphoses, miming the life of wholly different species. Such shape-changing has a nightmarish quality, close to the protean magic of Archimago, whose manufacture of a duplicate Una in the Duessa of Book I, together with his own shape-changing performances, so beguiles the Red Crosse Knight from the straight and narrow. In Book III there is a fabricated Florimell, a puppet 'snowy Lady', faked-up by a witch from snow and wax and treated with mercury (viii. 6-7). The result is really a 'carkasse dead' (7) but looks convincing enough. Such fabrications are germane to the volatile world of Spenser's art, with its exhausting unreliability. It is a danger latent in the art of narrative poetry itself, which can seldom be still but constantly seeks to unfold and develop. Spenser's painfully self-conscious alertness to the dangers of his own art are signalled everywhere. His objection to himself is a Platonist one. He fears that the scattering of delusions in the world of the senses may be mirrored and multiplied in the world of the poem. The poem then becomes an elaborate dissimulation, a version of the riddles set to Psyche with the addition of mendacious clues and solutions.

Spenser's aliveness to the dangers of his art is clear in Book II. Mammon's coat exemplifies the filthy art of the underworld:

> A worke of rich entayle, and curious mould,
> Woven with antickes and wild Imagery...
>   (II. vii. 4)

The tale-telling brilliance of the 'wild imagery' he wears on his own surface is not unlike the narrative and allusive extravagance of Spenser's own art. To get the gold for such precious work-manship as Mammon's, Sir Guyon knows that men had to violate the Golden Age itself, a time of equal distribution and temperate living in the interests of the whole community:

> Then gan a cursed hand the quiet wombe
>   Of his great Grandmother with steele to wound,
>   And the hid treasures in her sacred tombe,
>   With Sacriledge to dig. Therein he found
>   Fountaines of gold...
>   (II. vii. 17)

The nature of the Fall is clarified here. Technological exploitation of the mineral wealth of the underworld is viewed as a sexual crime and an act of matricide. Technological art is rape. Whereas in the fertility myths the underworld rises against the feminine principle in the upper world, here the converse is seen. The male principle in the upper world rapes the underlying earth to exploit the feminine wealth contained there and convert it to his own use. The earth is seen both as a seed-bed or growing-place, and a resting-place for what has been. Man's art is the violation of a taboo, reinforced by the emotive phrase 'her quiet wombe'. Spenser suggests a terrible regressiveness in human behaviour, which would rather go back forcibly along the birth-tunnel into unnatural darkness from generation to generation than move forwards to breed new life for the future. The Mammon-fantasist feeds his eyes on an art which is founded in the abuse and exploitation of the feminine. This theme recurs massively in the Bower Bliss episode:[50] Spenser's art distrusts art in the proliferation of 'curious imageree' (II. xii. 60), 'rare device' (54) or 'work of admirable wit' (44). The sterile garden of art breeds nothing but the male rapacity of 'greedy eyes' (64).

Spenser, therefore, is not simply confronting the problem of the potentially immoral and self-defeating nature of art itself but more specifically a moral problem unavoidably attaching to the *gender* of the artist. His raw material is or includes woman and the mother-planet; his difficulty is how to avoid the exploitation of such material, a problem as intransigent as that of original sin, to which it contributes as an essential factor. The poet is responsible for inventing everything in his poem, including that imagery he chooses to condemn. The tempting world of the Bower of Bliss is not, properly speaking, Acrasia's invention, for she is a fiction like all the rest of his personages. Mammon's 'wild imagery' and the Bower of Bliss's 'curious imagery', 'rare device', fake themselves onto the page through the poet's fantasy; the ransacked bower is therefore the equivalent of the scribbled-over or torn-up poem. In attempting the role of creator-creatrix of his poem, Spenser everywhere concedes the doubt that he may be acting merely as its fabricator, the Archimago or Busyrane of the poetic world. This is a particular anxiety in relation to the theme of the feminine, for in laying the feminine open to the voyeuristic eye of the reader, the image-creator may be arousing a concupiscence he can neither allay nor control. The 'quiet wombe' of a treasured privacy may thus be susceptible of wounding by the explorations of the poet bent on telling hidden truths, just as sacrilegiously as by Mammon and his fellow gold-hunters. Such a danger would be felt with peculiar force in the Book of Chastity, for chastity is founded on the unviolated privacy of its protagonist. The chaste woman in Spenserian terms is free, self-controlling, autonomous. But the poet's urge is always towards exposure, the tearing off of veils or the offering of clues as to what might lie beneath. If he abstains from unclothing this privacy, his very abstention may have a furtively arousing quality. The extraordinary success Spenser achieves in guarding the women of his story and the values they represent is exemplified particularly in his treatment of the veiled figures associated with androgynous image of Venus and Britomart (see pp. 48–52 above). His chaste terror of offence against his own best principles is exemplified by his study of erotic works of art within the work of art itself, in Book III, a preoccupation which is felt from the very beginning of the Book as he contemplates the Tapestry of Venus and Adonis at the Castle Joyous (i. 34–8), to its end, the Tapestries of Cupid in canto xi and the Mask of Cupid in canto xii. Here also Spenser studies the dark figures of the artist-magician in the person of Busyrane, whose trade of exploitation is pursued by dipping his pen in the blood of a still-living girl, a profession more murderous than anything attempted by Marlowe's Faustus.

Spenser enters the Palace of Art under the protection of the nearly invulnerable company of Britomart. As Florimell is held under the sea by Proteus (another archtype of the artist), so Amoret is held by Busyrane, 'her small wast girt round with yron bands' (xii. 30). The artist-enchanter is identified with a rapist in the Tapestries of Cupid, which celebrate the artful metamorphoses of Jupiter in his rapes of mortal maidens. These images of metamorphosis are ironically praised by the narrative-voice as it leads us round the art-gallery, jovially commenting on each sordid representation with approval:

> Then was he turnd into a snowy Swan,
>   To win faire *Leda* to his lovely trade:
>   O wondrous skill, and sweet wit of the man,
>   That her in daffadillies sleeping made
>   From scorching heat her daintie limbes to shade:
>   Whiles the proud Bird ruffling his fethers wyde,
>   And brushing his faire brest, did her invade;
>   She slept, yet twixt her eyelids closely spyde,
> How towards her he rusht, and smiled at his pryde.
>
> (III. xi. 32)

Several 'artists' are involved in this rape: the one who designed the tapestry so artfully, and 'made' Leda lie in the daffodils with a look so slyly welcoming, and 'made' her do so as if he might personally be able to enjoy her; second, Jupiter, the artist who pretends so convincingly and outrageously to be a swan; third, Leda herself, for according to the tapestry's conception, she is avidly but deviously ready to entertain the 'invasion' of the phallic bird. Her crafty smile flickers from between half-closed but all-seeing lids. Finally, there is Spenser himself, the primary artist, who invented the whole scene and must be responsible for placing it before our eyes as a sequence of mental pictures and for the interpretations his language suggests. He personally lays

Leda down amongst the cool, marginal daffodils, sacramentally associated in his poem with Proserpina, and with Cymoent, and Florimell. 'O wondrous skill, and sweet wit of the man!' It is as if the narrative voice turned against itself. The tale-teller blames his own corrupted vision for bringing forth this insidious image of woman lusting after her own rape. With dexterity the artist manipulates a sinister craft. His only saving grace is that he bitterly sees himself do so, and is able to signal to a reader through irony that she or he must question the complacent authority of the narrative persona, implicated as it is in the world it criticises.

The artist is conceived of as a figure of power. This is a power which both Britomart and Amoret must confront, for different reasons. Britomart, the androgynous warrior-girl in male clothes, active on the battle-field of a man's world but needing to maintain the feminine as the most essential source of her virtue, is on a difficult borderline of behaviour. She could if she wished learn for herself the kind of power that Busyrane wields, accepting and exploiting all the codes and conventions of the fathers. *'Be bold'*, the inscription over the door proclaims, *'Be not too bold'*, says another, and this is the significant imperative (xi. 54). Britomart must preserve the stability of her nature against the temptations to become part of the world of power. She must in some important way understand the secret of abstinence from the enchanting power-games of Busyrane's world. In the case of total collaboration on her part, her power to see through its fraud would be lost. She would become, through collusion, just as much a victim as Amoret through her guileless innocence. In both cases the real question is not primarily one of chastity's fear of yielding in marriage—as Roche suggests, the 'female fear of sexual love'[51]—though this is certainly an important meaning, but rather a problem germane to female experience in a male world of making distinctions between illusion and reality. Both Britomart and Amoret have to learn the difficult knack of suspending their belief in the power of male art. Busyrane can only violate Amoret because she credits him with the power to do so. Insight and power are profoundly linked, as the Masque of Cupid demonstrates. Britomart hears 'an hideous storme', 'dreadfull thunder', 'earthquake' within the house itself (xii. 2) and naturally concludes that this furore implies some real catastrophe. But then:

> All suddenly a stormy whirlwind blew
> Throughout the house, that clapped every dore,
> With which that yron wicket open flew,
> As it with mighty levers had bene tore:
> And forth issewd, as on the ready flore
> Of some Theatre, a grave personage,
> That in his hand a branch of laurell bore,
> With comely haveour and count'nance sage,
> Yclad in costly garments, fit for tragicke Stage.
>
> (III. xii. 3)

The cosmic catastrophe is, therefore, just that of a play: and an awful play too, at which only doors would 'clap' (the witty pun in the second line maintains) for a human audience certainly would not. The laurel-crowned Prologue enters upon a scene which mocks him as an embodied bathos. The storm in a teacup feared by Britomart was nothing more than sound-effects producible by stage gadgetry. The masquers are led by Fancy, 'a lovely boy' (7), likened to Jupiter's homosexual conquests; he is followed by a pageant of the infirmities attendant on love, sterile, incongruous or bestial. The unreality of the pageant is manifest to us, and to Britomart, at whose entrance into the actors' room they vanish into nothing: less so to Amoret, who is so convinced of the power of the enchanter.

At the centre of Book III was a sealed garden; at the end, the chambers of a house. Both enclosures suggest spaces of the mind. But the House of Busyrane (from Busiris, the tyrannous Pharaoh) is remote from the garden-world of Amoret's tenderly fostered beginnings. It is a disturbing ending to the Book of Love, far from pastoral safety, inconclusive, without bearings. And, too, it is a questioned ending, for there are two variants, that of the 1590 edition which unites Amoret and Scudamore, and the later one which cancels this. I shall use the beautiful original, with its cancelled clue to final meaning. In the inner chamber of the House of Busyrane, Britomart discovers Amoret chained to a brazen pillar. Her breast is cut open, her heart exposed and transfixed by the shaft of an arrow. The narrative voice tells this shocking detail, taking care to dissociate itself from the sadism for which he supplies all the images:

> And her before the vile Enchaunter sate,
>   Figuring straunge characters of his art,
> With living bloud he those characters wrate,
>   Dreadfully dropping from her dying hart,
>   Seeming transfixed with a cruell dart,
> And all preforce to make her him to love.
> Ah who can love the worker of her smart?
> A thousand charmes he formerly did prove;
>   Yet thousand charmes could not her stedfast heart remove.
>
> (III. xii. 31)

The hands of Amoret are 'bounden fast'; the hands of the artist are busily active. His work is demonic, a version of that unnatural black magic so feared by Ficino as likely to be accidentally triggered by the natural philosopher as he intercepts stellar effluences in the hope of turning them to good use. All the occultists writing of Hermetic magic at the time of Spenser show awareness of the problem of distinction between the legitimate and illegitimate versions of their art. And all write in the awareness of the intimate links between the magic of occult philosophy and the magic of art and poetry.[52] Because Spenser's 'vile Enchaunter' is tampering with the vital life-force and turning it to his own obscure but certainly diabolical purposes, we recognise him as a black magician. Because he is engaged in making literature out of Amoret's life-blood, we further recognise him as magician-poet.

It is not only the passive and gentle archetype of woman who is endangered by Busyrane's profession, but potentially all women. He draws blood from Britomart's breast (33) before she is able to force him to use his magic powers to heal Amoret's wound, the steel falling softly out as if of its own accord (38), and her body closing over. Inevitably the theme of a bleeding wound evokes the motif of Adonis and the fertility cycle which shapes the Book; in a ghostly way both Marinell and Florimell are called to the surface. The seven-month period of Amoret's captivity evokes the winter sleep of Proserpina. But this episode has a more troubled, self-doubtful atmosphere than these sacrificial images. Its feeling is of distressed wakefulness, unreality and pointless suffering, which are associated with art in its antipathy to nature. Questions are raised but not answered by Spenser at this crucial moment. Busyrane is writing in a book within the Book, a poem within a poem (36). But we are not told what he is writing. Neither are we given any sense that the sacrifice of virgin blood to the pen of the scribe is worth anything at all. The activity is presented as that of an inexplicable madman, totally absorbed in his meaningless occupation: 'Figuring straunge characters of his art'. Whereas Marinell's blood is given back to circulate in the living cosmos, Amoret's is being written out in dead letters on a page. Spenser creates a perspective in which we see poetry as being spelt out at the expense of the feminine principle to which it is dedicated: written in the heart's blood of the beloved. This dark side of the artist opposes the creative white magic exemplified in Merlin; it is crueller than Pluto to Proserpina.

We may also think of the blood spilt by Amoret here as suggesting the hymeneal blood which her virginity fears to spill in marriage with Scudamore. The reality of sexual fear is emphasised in stanza 36, in which Britomart makes Busyrane reverse his spells by reading out the contents of the book and its 'bloody lines' of verse. She too feels dread at what she hears, and there is no suggestion that Amoret's fears are disproportionate or unjustified. The book of fantasy is terrifyingly real. Only when it is fully brought to the light and read out—read away—can its victim be free. It is here that Spenser expresses hope for a white magic in poetry, which can work through the poet's steadfast identification with the feminine, in alchemical conjunction. The black scribe is countered by the white maiden, Britomart, brought to the exercise of white artistic magic by the white scribe, Spenser. It is only by his faith in the androgyny of poetry that the male artist can redeem and regenerate his art.

This faith in the possibility of a poetically effective Hermetic androgyny is endorsed by the powerful imagery which consummated the Book in its first edition, of the union of Amoret and Scudamore, brought about by Britomart. The emphasis is on Amoret's power of voluntary yielding:

> she faire Lady overcommen quight
> Of huge affection, did in pleasure melt,
> And in sweet ravishment pourd out her spright.

> No word they spake, nor earthly thing they felt,
> But like two senceles stocks in long embracement dwelt.
>
> (III. xii. 45a)

The replacement passages supplied for the second edition (presumably in the interests of narrative development) are entirely inferior. For here the two bodies become one, but as they join they empty of spirit, as in Hermetic *mors osculi* (see pp. 4–5 above). The consummated spirit absents itself, through the channel of the senses, vacating the body for an opposite—perhaps a mirror—reality. As in the *gnosis* enjoyed by Milton's lovers in the Eden of *Paradise Lost,* perception of time is abolished; epiphany is experienced as a momentary, eternal intuition of reality. Apologists for the poem who stress its Christian basis are fond of claiming that the imagery of this passage relates to Spenser's desire to celebrate holy matrimony. But there are no certificated emotions here. The source is more obviously the *Asclepius* of Hermes Trismegistus and his bisexual God:

> and not God alone, but all kinds of beings, whether endowed with soul or soulless... in that conjunction of the two sexes, or, to speak more truly, that fusion of them into one, which may be rightly named Eros, or Aphrodite, or both at once, there is a deeper meaning than man can comprehend.
>
> (*Asclepius* III. 21).

This 'deeper meaning' is expressed but not explained in the lyric beauty of Spenser's celebration of their 'long embracement'. His phrase 'sweet ravishment' is very touching in the context of all that has gone before, for it turns the recurrent image of erotic coercion associated with woman as Man's prey into an image of a female power to lose herself in ecstasy. Amoret's vigilance yields to unearthly trance. The imagery is associated with melting, pouring herself out, to be developed in the culminating symbolism of the hermaphrodite. The narrative persona directs itself to the reader, to indicate how we should begin to picture the embrace:

> Had ye them seene, ye would have surely thought,
> That they had beene that faire *Hermaphrodite,*

Which that rich *Romane* of white marble wrought,
And in his costly Bath cause to bee site:
So seemed those two, as growne together quite,
That *Britomart* halfe envying their blesse,
Was much empassiond in her gentle sprite,
And to herselfe oft wisht like happinesse,
In vaine she wisht, that fate n'ould let her yet possesse.
(III. xii. 46a)

The wistful beauty of this image, together with its clearly classical and pagan insistence ('that rich *Romane*'), is not accounted for in terms of the pieties of man and wife as 'one flesh' in marriage. With Britomart we stand outside and apart from their exclusive bliss, viewing it as if it were an object of art, a 'costly' artifact 'wrought' of 'white marble'. The imagery is in fact loaded with potentially suspect connotations, which are then redeemed by the white Hermetic artistry that can go on to consider them as 'growne together quite', an organic, natural image. Amoret and Scudamore, returning to each other as if the divided halves of the Platonic hermaphrodite had at last found one another, are nature's work of art. They melt into one another's nature—Herm/Aphrodite—until there are no raw edges left, but a sense of almost chemical wholeness. The image of the white marble statue bathed in liquid suggests the alchemical *conjunctio* or the solidifying of the philosopher's stone in the crucible of his art, together with the transforming solution of mercury (*hermes*).

Finally, the image of 'white' stone of the hermaphrodite points forwards to Britomart's much later dream in the Temple of Isis (V. vii. 3-24). Here Britomart, dreaming of her love-longings for Arthegall, is identified both with Psyche in her terror of Cupid which made her try to 'see' him and precipitated her wanderings—and also one with Isis, the white lunar goddess, the collector, unifier, recreator, who is known by many names and resolves all that is problematic in her status as *Magna Mater*. The Priests of Isis explain to Britomart that her dream of the devouring crocodile, displaying a sexual terror akin to that of Amoret at the House of Busyrane, is to be assimilated as a portent of the turbulent history through which Britomart will be able to breed the royal line that culminates in Elizabeth I.

Osiris mutilated and scattered—the body politic dismembered by fratricidal civil war—will be collected together by the recreative power of Isis, her country's mother.[53] Thus Britomart, though revealing in bursts of illumination (the unhelmetings), a mirroring within herself of the Hermetic bisexual God, always remains a process, never complete within the poem. Fate, or the poet, 'n'ould let her yet possesse' that state of impassioned bliss in union with her twinned opposite which has to be cancelled even for Amoret, in the interest of narrative development. In order to act, Britomart must be imperfect, stirred by need. She, like us, is extraneous to the union of Amoret and Scudamore, a bystander only, 'envying their blesse'. Such perfection as theirs would call her outside the dimension of time and space. She lives within history, an active artist of life whose search is (like that of Isis seeking Osiris) to recompose the disparities of history into a final possibility of healing. She leads to Gloriana, and Gloriana gestures outside the poem to the queen herself.

We are returned to the four Elizabeths. The queen, like a Titan, dominates the entire work. The work must ultimately fail her, as art in Spenser's creed does consistently fail, through its multitudinous images which elaborate a simple reality, to render truth:

> But living art may not least part expresse,
> Nor life-resembling pencill it can paint,
> All were it *Zeuxis* or *Praxiteles:*
> His daedale hand would faile, and greatly faint,
> And her perfections with his error taint...
> (III. Exordium, 2)

Spenser writes of art's handicaps in the most awe-inspiring and magical poetry. He inscribes his doubts with 'daedale hand', sharing with Daedalus an expertise unknown to the usurping Icarus. This 'daedale hand' with absolute certainty of touch brings to life before our eyes the ancient dead and all their dreams. In these lines of artistic self-deprecation, Zeuxis the painter and Praxiteles the sculptor are aroused into contemporary life. As Paulina brings the semblance of a statue to life in Shakespeare's *Winter's Tale,* Spenser's art motions the seeming-dead artists of classical antiquity to reveal themselves, as if they were to be seen through an open doorway working in an adjoining room. Spenser returns us to source, but doubly, by giving re-naissance through his pen not only to the wisdom of the fathers but also to the mother-spirit of the ancient world. His denial that a 'life-resembling pencill' can paint the glory of his vision of Elizabeth I, and the triad of Elizabeths who give the queen a context, is subtle and elegant. For Spenser's art is not representational. Neither was the 'daedale hand' that painted and modeled in the Greek world. Zeuxis, Praxiteles and Spenser inscribe a reality of dream, vision, mystery: the essences rather than the particulars. Art fails. But in the moment of its acknowledgement of this failure its 'daedale hand' reveals the eternal secret of Eleusis.

3

Shakespeare

HAMNET AND JUDITH

Boy-and-girl twins are the *coincidentia oppositorum* in person, simultaneous selves of opposed gender, attached to source at a fused root of being. As an experiment in human nature, they have seemed in many cultures to inhabit a borderline of proximity to the divine. Miraculous births such as that of Artemis (Diana) and her twin, Apollo, have been read as special articulations of divinity, deeply associated with the art of poetry. In their duality, such twins encompass wholeness, the range of human possibility in miniature, suggesting a tantalising condition of blessedness to which man in the singular fruitlessly aspires. To be the parent of such twins is to view the Spenserian 'faire Hermaphrodite' at source. To experience the death of one of the twins is to encounter the sharp pain of knowing intimately nature's refusal of the choicest imagery of human hopes. It is at once the severing of Plato's all-round spherical people and the universal fall into mortality, mutability and incompletion. The metaphor may be extended (as Shakespeare extends it) to represent in the cutting of male from female twin the devastation of the bond between boy and mother as he is weaned by the men's world.

Shakespeare was the father of boy-and-girl twins, who were born and baptised in 1585, two years after his first child, Susannah. The children were named after his married friends Hamnet and Judith Sadler. Eleven and a half years later the boy-twin died: he was buried at Stratford in the August of 1596. Judith outlived her brother by sixty-six years; she survived to grow old while her companion remained an eternal child. We have so little definitive information about Shakespeare's life and personality, and have suffered from so many centuries of

105

hearsay, guesswork and impertinent biographical interpretations of the Sonnets, that what little information we possess is rightly treated with cirumspection.[1] But as the psychoanalytic school of Shakespearean criticism (to whom my reading must be indebted) has sensitively shown, certain vital preoccupations animate his entire career as a playwright, notably 'the feminine sources of masculine identity',[2] the consequences of male severing from those sources, and a final recreation of 'the bond of trust'[3] in the feminine principle. Related to this theme in his plays is the death or loss of the boy-twin; the separation of a child of either sex from its mother; the raid of the fathers upon the mother-world, with the consequent violent distortion and bereavement of character, leading in the late plays to exploration of the possibilities of atonement. It seems apt in such circumstances as these to take the liberty of remembering that the theme of boy-and-girl twinning, so crucial to Shakespeare's art, had a paradigm in life. The roots of metaphor may well have drawn energy from a literal narrative of birth and loss.

In twinning characters within his plays, both in a simply biological and in a broader, metaphoric sense, Shakespeare therefore enters into themes which we have both identified as Spenserian and recognised as a preoccupation of Renaissance Platonising art: concern with integration of being, fusing earth and heaven, man and woman, soul and soul. More so than Spenser, Shakespeare centralises family as the basic and crucial unit of human society within which integration may take place. But the patriarchal basis of the family is absolutely challenged and queried. Aristotle's *Politics* showed the father's governing role in the family as the foundation of civil rule, historically and morally (1252B, 1259B), a position which became classic and conventional in succeeding political theories[4] and which the Renaissance tended to take on trust. The ideal within this model would be the king as *pater patriae* and the father of a family as *rex familiae*. Against this ideal, personal experience might suggest to many that paternal rule might not always be in practice the perfect model for human relationships, whether private or public. The king-father (or father-king) under Shakespeare's analysis—imaged, for instance, in Thesus and Oberon in *A Midsummer Night's Dream*, in Lear in *King Lear*, and in Leontes in *The Winter's Tale*—is seen as potentially able, or even liable, to represent a force disruptive of order, for order (Cordelia's 'bond' of nature, violated by Lear in his nihilistic attachment to self, which owes 'Nothing' to the feminine principle [I. i. 92, 95]) is understood as based on the union of the twin genders of human nature. Milton, too, in *Paradise Lost* sees sexual union as the 'true source' of all virtue, especially civic virtue (IV. 750-62). It is the cordial feminine within Lear's own character, the girl-child of his nature, with which he needs to unite.[5] Thus the quest which for Spenser was figured in romance terms as the search of maiden for man, united in the 'long embracement' of a state comparable with 'that faire Hermaphrodite' of sexual fulfilment (III. xii. 45a, 46a), finds expression in Shakespeare's plays both in these terms (the search of the young for sexual fruition) and in a Hermetic twinning across the borders of the generations.

This theme represents a double denial of the established hierarchy of power. In the beautiful reconciliation scene of *King Lear,* which looks forward to the tragi-comic resolutions of *Pericles* and *The Winter's Tale* but comes fatally early in its own play, Cordelia asks her father's blessing:

> O! look upon me, Sir,
> And hold your hand in benediction o'er me.
> No, Sir, you must not kneel.
> *(King Lear,* IV. vii. 57-9)

The elder kneels to the younger, male yields to female. Through that voluntary humiliation, each is raised to equal and mutual stature. Male authority assumes the character of an Old Testament unregenerate without its completion in the New. This pattern is repeated, even more radically, from Lear's dispossession of 'my sometime daughter' (I. i. 122) to Leontes' repudiation of his baby girl: 'This brat is none of mine' (*Winter's Tale,* II. iii. 92). Paulina tells and shows him that the baby is his own; she can be read 'Although the print be little' as a 'copy of the father' (II. iii. 98, 99). But the baby writes him out more perfectly than he has it in himself to be. She represents a higher wisdom, akin to Bruno's *Sophia,*[6] new-born and languageless as she is. The moral and its spirit are scriptural. We remember Christ drawing to him 'a little child' and explaining to his disciples its status as the 'greatest in the kingdom of heaven' (Matthew 18:1). Shakespeare develops this scriptural message according to the language of a gender reverenced less explicitly by the Bible than by the spirit of the Hellenic religions. Matthew's account of the heavenly hierarchy assumes a boy-child as its focus of meaning:

> And Jesus called a little child unto him, and set him in the midst of them.
> And said, Verily I say unto you, Except ye be converted, and become as little children, ye shall not enter into the kingdom of heaven.
>
> (Matthew 18:2-3)

Shakespeare's final statements about power and value reverse the status quo more extremely than this. It is as if the poet called a little child and 'set *her* in the midst of them'. The girl-child in little print rewrites the traditions of the state in the feminine language.

Such a revised world is not presented in the Last Plays as a real hope or feasible possibility on the level of practical external implementation; it is hardly even imaginable. The Last Plays concern another world of dream, myth, art,[7] expressive of an oblique relationship between what we feel might or ought to be and what we know or fear to be in actuality. As Spenser's 'faire Hermaphrodite' is sculpted white stone rather than breathing human flesh and blood, so Shakespeare's Hermetic feminine secret animates herself in *The Winter's Tale* as the semblance of a statue of a woman rather than in the guise of any less complicated reality. The feminine ideal and the art-world are mysteriously akin, a reconciling mythology perceived just round the corner from realism, in the self-cohering world of dream and symbolism. The theatre draws attention to itself as a world of art, as Spenser's narrative self-consciously presents the world of Faerie as an allegory of, but not identical with, the landscape of human nature. Milton's Eden of perfect *gnosis*, where it is possible to be 'Imparadised in one another's arms' (IV. 506) is in some sense sealed in an analogous way, since it is recorded as prior to our reality.

Insofar as the dream-world of perfect union with the feminine approaches the condition of our reality, this involves the incorporation of death and mutability (Shakespeare), fall and partial separation (Milton) or the cancellation of the perfect symbol in order that the imperfect narrative may continue (Spenser; see pp. 101–3 above). As Shakespeare's comedy develops towards tragi-comedy, it becomes clearer that the realisation of art's dream of unity involves a sacrifice. That sacrifice often involves the irredeemable loss to the male of some vital aspect of himself, in the form of a figure which doubles for him. Leontes' achievement of reunion with the slandered Hermione and the exiled Perdita cannot retrieve from his grave the sacrificed boy-child. Value remains and is collected in the surviving girl-child, but the dark consequence of error in the perishing of the boy innocent cannot obtain atonement. Related to this theme is the motif of loss, or imagined death, by water, beginning in *The Comedy of Errors* and developing in *Twelfth Night* in relation to the twin-theme. The development of this and related threatening symbolisms, attaching an element of permanently Osirian sacrifice to the apparently inclusively restorative Isis-world of tragi-comedy, distinguishes Shakespearean use of the genre from that of his contemporaries, whose convention is summed up in Guarini's stricture that tragi-comedy involves 'the danger, not the death'.[8] This professed incapacity on the part of Shakespeare's tragi-comedy to effect a fully comic healing has been interpreted as a wish to bring the world of dream into a closer union with 'life's meaningful issues'.[9] Bearing in mind the cyclical seasonal patternings of the Last Plays, it may also be understood as a metaphoric statement of the eternal proximity of the realm of Plutonian winter to the spring-to-autumn cycle which Ceres and Proserpina reclaim for mankind. The plays allude to the Eleusinian cult, and its truth to nature. The underworld exists, the Last Plays seem to suggest, in man himself as he moves to adulthood, away from the mother-world. He sheds the innocence of his original self as Leontes sheds Mamillius. The outlived young self peels away. The boy-twin dies.

Earlier versions of Shakespeare's tragi-comic vision of the antagonistic mother- and father-worlds may be discerned in two plays, *A Midsummer Night's Dream* and *Twelfth Night*, the former dated around the middle years of the 1590s, the latter about 1600. Both these plays, but more especially *Twelfth Night*, derive in part from the root-sources of Shakespeare's Last Plays, the Greek romances of the early Christian era (*Apollonius of Tyre, Chaereas and Callirhoe, Aethiopica*), with their emphasis on the love-quest, the crucial role of the heroine, ritual death or loss of consciousness and rebirth.[10] Both plays belong to a sequence of comedies which, though they were being written concurrently with the history plays, incorporate experience assiduously omitted by the histories. Shakespeare's history plays concern a male world in eternal feud with itself, where woman plays a negligible or debased role; the colour of that world is blood-red. The comedies are set apart as an exploration of the feminine world; their colour is the green of pastoral,[11] and of an Arden which is equally the title of the forest in *As You Like It*, the real forest near Shakespeare's birthplace whose despoliation was lamented by Drayton in *Polyolbion*,[12] and the maiden name of Shakespeare's mother, Mary Arden. Whereas so many of the histories and tragedies seem to be struggling with the problems of patrilinear legitimacy and inheritance, the comedies search out the links between man and mother-country, mother-tongue, seeking to bring to light the legitimate Arden-inheritance, so darkly veiled behind the Shakespeare surname. They seem to search out ways for man to come back into fruitful relationship with the green world of his origins, finding a sanctuary that is neither regressive nor narcissistic. In a sense, the means of comedy are more difficult and perplexed than the means of history. There is no possibility of Agincourt. The enemy cannot be eliminated, for he follows demandingly at the characters' own heels like his own shadow. Shakespeare identifies this shadow-self as male repudiation of the feminine. The negative, self-defending male ego is shown in a state of perpetually escalating tantrum—whether feigning passivity like Orsino languorously awaiting the next feed, or raging like Malvolio self-deprived of the diet of 'cakes and ale'. The comedy does not claim the power to educate such egos nor can its structure necessarily contain them. Malvolio rants out of the comedy: 'I'll be revenged on the whole pack of you' (*Twelfth Night*, V. i. 377). Orsino mercurially switches allegiance from Olivia to his 'fancy's queen', Viola (387), in an unreassuringly blithe manner. Coppelia Kahn has memorably shown how Shakespeare's plays explore the self-defeating male need for violent differentiation from the initial union with the mother, in a society that prizes masculinity at the expense of humane values, which it takes the liberty of labelling and scorning as 'female' and thence effeminate.[13] This theme is played out in all genres, bloodily and terribly in history and tragedy, but more hopefully in comedy, which seeks in the darkness of human identity to read the braille of clues and intuitions imprinted on the deepest self, as to how to redress the lost balance of gender. That is one reason why Shakespearean comedy (and thence tragi-comedy) presents itself so consciously as the world of a dream-art, within the year's cycle—the twelfth day of Christmas, the eve of midsummer; dates out of time, eternally and timelessly recurrent for all generations.[14] At such times of change-over—the old year entering the new, the new year at its meridian—the solstice gives pause for renovating dreams, suggesting the possibility of transition based on remembrances evoked of the way to the green world as it was originally known.

The playwright's imagination impersonates everyone, both male and female, as Plato noted with disapproval (*Republic*, 395 d-e). Spenser's narrative art may have been protean in its sympathies but was not by its very nature committed to automatic identification with and animation of all given possibles. Given Shakespeare's material, as playwright he is in this sense himself geministic, hermaphroditic. Through impersonation he 'becomes' the twins of *Twelfth Night*, combining the two sexes within the hermaphroditic Viola/ Cesario with an intense conviction. As messenger between man and woman, she plays the role of a Hermes and shares with that figure a fluid instability of character that is potentially able to unite with either sex (not only Herm/Aphrodite or Love, but also Herm/Athene or Wisdom), the ingenuity of that divine infant prodigy who was able to deceive Zeus himself from the cradle, the tale-telling skill (both Hermes and Viola are able to fabricate stories at need) and the musicality which is echoed in the very name 'Viola' and its variations 'Olivia' and 'Malvolio'. Hermes, as the *Homeric Hymn to Hermes* tells us, was the inventor of the seven-stringed, tortoise-shell lyre, on which:

he tried improvisations, such as young men do
at the time of feasts when they taunt and mock each other.
He sang of Zeus Kronides and fair-sandaled Maia,
and how they once dallied in the bond of love,
recounting in detail his own glorious birth.
(*Homeric Hymn to Hermes*, 55–9)

To quote this brief passage about Hermes may also recall for us
some of the gifts and attributes that characterise Viola. She is a
presence within a play which is a kind of 'feast when they taunt
and mock each other'. She is aware of and exploits her own
powers of musical improvisation, asking the captain to help her
to disguise herself so that she can serve Orsino, 'for I can
sing,/And speak to him in many sorts of music' (I. ii. 57–8). This
art of singing, she informs Olivia, might be exercised in a choice
fashion if she were to:

Make me a willow cabin at your gate,
And call upon my soul within the house;
Write loyal cantons of contemned love,
And sing them loud even in the dead of night...
(*Twelfth Night*, I. v. 272–5)

This delightfully confirms her likeness to the crafty Hermes
defined in the *Hymn* as:

a bringer of dreams,
a watcher by night and a gate-keeper...
(*Homeric Hymn to Hermes*, 14–15)

Viola presents a fantasy of herself as Olivia's dream-bringer,
night-watcher and gate-keeper. Her imagined nocturnal
ministrations, so threatening to the eardrums of the listener,
conveying a light-fingered, light-hearted attitude to the agreed
borderlines between fantasy and reality, beautifully suggest the
Homeric Hermes' disrespect for dull fact and his deep-rooted
association with the imagination. The life of Hermes is a dream
of unlimited freedom. Walls and arms cannot hold him. In the
Hymn his mother speaks sternly to this amoral 'weaver of
schemes' (155), all seraphic innocence and guileful charm from

his very cradle. He dissolves away like an artful child from the grasp of anyone wishing to hold him:

> And Hermes, the son of Zeus,
> slipped through the keyhole of the dwelling sideways,
> like autumnal breeze in outer form, or airy mist.
>
> (*Homeric Hymn to Hermes*, 145–7)

This lyrical image of Hermes' insubstantiality presents him almost in the form of music itself: thin air. As Olivia reaches out with her emotions to catch hold of Viola, the comic plot spirits her/him away. We observe Orsino making baffled, oblique advances towards a friendship whose identity he cannot conceive: 'Give me some music', he demands (II. iv. 1), and in the next line demands to be given Cesario, as though Cesario/Viola were somehow in person the 'light airs and recollected terms' of Orsino's desire (5). And his equation is a truthful one: Viola is the music her nature makes. But what the gods may do with ease and elegance, human nature finds more vexing, constrained by what the *Hermetica* calls 'the garment in which you have clothed yourself' which 'grips you to itself and holds you down' (p. 173), existence in the world of time, place, matter and desire. Viola only transiently impersonates Hermes: the clothes don't fit.

Shakespeare makes clear the fact that the Hermetic gift of impersonation is tolerable and feasible only in the art-world, under the spell of the artist, and not in the reality it mimes. The compass of Viola/Cesario's freedom is small, its duration brief. But for a time she does operate as the visible counterpart of the poet within *Twelfth Night*, bearing the message of form between the discordant, inactive poles of male and female. Orsino and Oliva begin with 'O'—nothing—and without their quicksilver messenger might remain in a state of original emptiness and impotence, like contraries in alchemy lacking the catalyst of Mercury. Olivia's association with the olive branch of peace links her with Venus the reconciler, but at the beginning of the play she is not yet emergent from the 'eye-offending brine' (I. i. 30) of grief for a lost brother. She stays safely within the matrix of the microcosmic seas. It is only Viola who can genuinely represent the 'sea-born Venus': we see her as born onto the seacoast in Scene 2. It is her role to touch Olivia's nature into the motion of Eros. As *coincidentia oppositorum* the 'bisexual' Viola—like Spenser's Venus-figures—is associated with change, impulse, a dynamic arousal of human nature's possibilities. Orsino withers in his indoor, unweaned world, babbling melodiously to himself, while the real music all but slips 'out through the keyhole of the dwelling sideways'. As in Paracelsus, mercury (*argentum vivum*) acts as transforming *anima mundi* and *spiritus mundi*.[15] Alchemy is essentially the healer's art, as it is the playwright's. Orsino's love-sickness is cured by the mercurial Viola. She herself is refined by the art of her transformation into a double-gendered identity, rather as alchemy explains as happening with the alchemist's treatment of mercury:

> its body must be separated from the ore and purified by fire. It achieves its third form when it has gone through fire and is a molten metal ... The practice of medicine is a work of art.
>
> (Paracelsus, p. 168)

In Viola's case, the fire is the fire of Love. Transformation, as in the alchemist's experiment, both purifies and compounds its agents in new forms of energy.

The Renaissance Hermes, and the Renaissance Mercury (Hermes) of alchemy lead automatically to the Renaissance Hermes Trismegistus and the *Hermetica*. The theme is touched by the sagest fool in the play, Feste. He is baiting Malvolio by disputing the state of the light:

> *Mal.* I am not mad, Sir Topas. I say to you, this house is dark.
> *Clo.* Madman, thou errest. I say there is no darkness but ignorance, in which thou art more puzzled than the Egyptians in their fog.
>
> (*Twelfth Night*, IV. ii. 41–5)

The Clown as comic magus of the play airily dismisses his fog-bound predecessors, the Hermetic Egyptians. Malvolio's dogmatic singularity imprisons him in his own loneliness, for he lacks the power to coalesce, which is so vital to the lives of the other characters: play, change, mercurial laughter. Viola's bisexual role figures this capacity of the world from which Malvolio excludes himself, to make fluid and thence to recast reality in new forms of perception and union. Yet she too suffers pain of self-division in her liberating disguise. In this sadness, 'pining in thought' like the double she invents to communicate her distress obliquely to Orsino (II. iv. 113), she is representative of all the characters. She expresses a mutual and universal longing, but also the secret of its healing. It is not just Viola who is potentially bisexual but all the major characters associated with her: she is lovable both as man and woman. As her nature flows between Orsino and Olivia, it activates and impels their desire. She functions as Eros in awakening them to what Giordano Bruno called the 'heroic frenzy' of the love-search. The lover for Bruno is like Actaeon, violating an inner secret which must transform and devour him as his own prey until he is 'renewed for a divine course'.[16] The important component of the myth, for Bruno, is its allegorisation of an individual's relationship with himself rather than any external relationship. In comparable terms the myth of Actaeon is written deeply into *Twelfth Night*, from its very beginning. Orsino rhapsodises on Olivia as the nude Diana, who has taught him to pun so painfully on the hunting of 'the heart' and 'the hart':

> O, when mine eyes did see Olivia first,
> Methought she purg'd the air of pestilence;
> That instant was I turn'd into a hart,
> And my desires, like fell and cruel hounds,
> E'er since pursue me.
>
> (*Twelfth Night*, I. i. 19–23)

Bruno in *The Heroic Frenzies* explains that Actaeon represents 'the intellect intent upon the capture of divine wisdom and the comprehension of divine beauty' (p. 226). The dogs of desire eat up the old self in order to release the new. Beauty is converted into the substance of the self. Actaeon, in this constructive and, in the largest sense, comic interpretation of the myth, becomes the contemplative mind able to perceive the divine beauty within itself. Without attributing to Orsino's delightful state of mental lassitude the solemn dignity of Bruno's conception of the *vita contemplativa*, it is possible to see that certain parallel

patterns exist in the reading of the Actaeon story: the divine
feminine understood as part of the self, the gradual union of
opposites through a scale of likenesses rather than differences.
Orsino's genuine heroic frenzy is reached stealthily through a
series of twinnings: a man loves a 'boy' who becomes a girl.
Olivia works back along the same route: a woman loves a 'boy'
who becomes a girl who introduces a twin brother. Thus the
frantic twinning of *Twelfth Night* comes into clearer focus as
part of the motion of Eros towards arousal, transformation and
reidentification of character in a solution of mercury. The
complex system of near-anagrams and sound patterns which
name the characters as part of each other and part of the
whole—Viola/Sebastian, Sebastian/Antonio, Viola/Olivia,
Viola/Orsino, Olivia/Orsino, Viola/Malvolio—constantly refer
us back to the matrix of the One in the many. This proliferation
of likenesses evokes the Hermetic insistence on the keen
resemblances between man, God and cosmos, each made in the
one image (*Pimander*, 12–13a), its glorification of sexuality as a
way of pouring the miscellaneousness of human identity back
into original form (*Asclepius*, 21–22a) and its high valuation of
music as a unique way of understanding God's wholeness:

> the ordered system in which each and all by the supreme Artist's
> skill are wrought together into a single whole yields a divinely
> musical harmony, sweet and true beyond all melodious sounds.
>
> (*Hermetica*, I. 13, p. 311)

Shakespeare's play makes such a music upon the 'viol' of its
central heroine's nature. Its delicate comic patterns point
towards the redemptive feminine vision of *The Winter's Tale*
and the Last Plays.

When he wrote *Twelfth Night*, Shakespeare's own boy-twin,
Hamnet, had been in his grave for perhaps five years. Had he
lived, he would have been about sixteen years old, the equivocal
age of transition which Viola can impersonate when she takes on
the male gender disguise as Cesario. The play's twins are
intermittently associated with a father-figure who is not
intrinsic to the play's action but seems vital to its deepest
meanings. The boy-girl Viola invents a sister to cover for her
'dead' brother's loss to her and to act as a mask for her real

gender. Orsino is lovingly concerned:

> *Duke*. But died thy sister of her love, my boy?
> *Viola*. I am all the daughters of my father's house,
> And all the brothers too; and yet I know not.
> Sir, shall I to this lady?
>
> (*Twelfth Night*, II. iv. 120–3)

Viola uses the art of story-telling as a veil for reality. Her prototype, the original Hermes, was too expert with words to need to tell explicit lies. The passionate inwardness of her speech is also governed and controlled. It moves towards the stasis of a pause as she meditates on the possibility of the survival of her literal brother: 'and yet I know not.' It is as if the playwright could speak his impossible hope through her and her situation. Viola has spoken of herself as a metaphorical 'daughter' which we know to be accurate, though Orsino does not, and then as if she were the 'brother' of that 'daughter', which we know to be inaccurate. She has not told a lie, but neither has she communicated a truth. But behind the riddle seems to lie a paradox. We do experience Viola, both through how she looks and through what she says, as somehow both daughter and brother: the shadowy but powerful father-figure is a real presence in the background of his children's lives, drawing the two genders of his separated children together. Throughout the play there is a sense of this shadowy father striving to reanimate the boy-twin in and through his sister. The male playwright strives to give birth, through a redemptive art, to a boy who can be seen to live again in the inclusive nature of the surviving girl, and then, by assocation with the mother-archetype of water, be given second birth.

Shakespeare's comedies often resolve themselves, as Richard Wheeler has noted, through the actions of a strong, wise and loving woman who protects the comic genre and closes it against its more violent implications.[17] Examples are Rosalind in *As You Like It* and Portia in *The Merchant of Venice*. These comedies place an absolute hope in a figure standing for the person of a nurturing mother, and they do so as if by a forceful act of will, for Shakespeare shows in all genres a deep awareness of the difficulty for men of making this trust, the ease with which she may be slandered, misconceived and abused. In the tragi-comedies such human figures are not enough. They have to be surrounded and reinforced by archetypal symbolism of the feminine—the great seas of *Pericles*, *The Winter's Tale*, *The Tempest*, the mother-deities who enclose humanity in a dream of final love and reconciliation. Shakespeare's poetic development may be seen as a struggle towards the possibility of the assertion of this dream, in which the universe may be imagined as standing in relation to humanity as mother to son, and where the hero's journey is understood as being a redefined epic away from the warrior-culture of the patriarchy into clarifying knowledge of the mother-world. This hope is portrayed as a world of dream and mythic symbol, a transforming world of art in which the dead can be redeemed, the stigmatised released.[18] In *Twelfth Night* we see the poet gesturing towards this magically compensating universe of art, which never deludes itself that it *is* the world of life, but for that very reason gives us a haunting sense of its own validity. In the reunion of Viola and Sebastian, the emphasis is on death by water:

> *Seb.* Do I stand there? I never had a brother;
> Nor can there be that deity in my nature,
> Of here and every where. I had a sister,
> Whom the blind waves and surges have devour'd:
> Of charity, what kin are you to me?
> What countryman? what name? what parentage?
> *Vio.* Of Messaline: Sebastian was my father;
> Such a Sebastian was my brother too,
> So went he suited to his watery tomb.
> (*Twelfth Night*, V. i. 224–32)

The meeting is intensely poignant and lyrical. The characters have left the safe dimension of time and space behind them and have to find their way back. They have seen the self mirrored on the external universe—'Do I stand there?'—and so their speech must take the form of endless questions, for their previous reality has been wholly dissolved. What the twins say has a curious quality of anonymity about it, like dream-speech. What they deny is paradoxically affirmed by the poetry. Sebastian refuses to believe that there can be 'that deity in my nature,/ Of here and every where'. Yet his own lyricism, combined with the riddling tendency of the whole play to erase the boundary-lines of common sense and common experience, reading 'brother' into 'sister', name into name, the many into the All, strongly suggests the existence of the universal in the particular, the *una dea* perhaps, 'of here and every where'. Viola and Sebastian give one another ritual burial by committing their past selves to the sea, she to the 'blind waves and surges', he to his 'watery tomb'. They then give one another a kind of ritual rebirth by referring to their father, who died when Viola was thirteen years old. No explicit reference is made to their mother. On the surface level, 'parentage' applies exclusively to Sebastian the father, and the line descends to Sebastian the son. But the feminine principle, symbolised by the sea, is sensed throughout as agent of birth and restoration. At the end of the play Viola can take her stand free from 'masculine usurp'd attire' (248), suggesting not so much a return to the status quo as the fulfilment of and release from the initiation into fully human being.

Twelfth Night, then, effects its recovery of the lost boy-twin by inhabiting a marginal world between perspectives and realities, the meeting of shore with sea, male and female elements, in an inclusive vision. This is Cymoent's and Marinell's world in Spenser's *Faerie Queene*, (see pp. 64ff. above) an area of transition at the water's edge associated with the Proserpina story, reworked by both Spenser and Shakespeare by a gender-reversal. Like Marinell, Sebastian suffers detention in a kind of underworld; like Marinell, he is sea-born. Delicately, Shakespeare prefigures the Eleusinian theme in the tragi-comedies with their great generative myths of rebirth. These are statements about the relationship between absolute power and extreme frailty; the territorially prowling male and the apparent stillness of the feminine. The tide of power in these plays will require an absolute submission of the law of the fathers to the law of the mothers.[19] We should not minimise the difficulty involved for the male maker of a play in performing that proxy abdication, tantamount to Prospero's surrender of his magic art. It took Shakespeare almost the whole of his writing life to make that surrender the central topic of a sequence of plays which would be his final statement. In *A Midsummer Night's Dream* we may see him at an intermediate stage in the movement towards this renunciation in favour of the female. Here, too, we find the meeting of shore with sea-line, figured in the yellow sands of Titania's remembrance; and here is the struggle between the world of the fathers and the world of the mothers for possession of the boy-child. In this most lunar of Shakespeare's plays, the mother-goddess shows the validity of her right, but the father-god still gets the spoils.

ISIS AND CERES

When Isis, the moon-goddess, appears to Apuleius's Lucius in the dream-vision of Book 11 of *The Golden Asse*, she associates herself with salvation from storm at sea by requesting Lucius, if he wishes to be released from his cumbersome and humiliating asinine disguise, to present himself at the ceremony which takes place 'after the tempestes of the Sea be ceased' (p. 260). In an unforgettable image, she appears to him in the form of the full moon 'as though she leaped out of the Sea' (p. 257). This vision of moon and sea entered deeply into Shakespeare's as into the Renaissance imagination. Apuleius gave him as material for *A Midsummer Night's Dream* not just the ass's head, which fits Bottom so very comfortably, but also the form in which to envision a benign, teasing, all-inclusive mother-goddess surrounding the universe in an ultimately comic form. Apuleius' Isis wears the moon and stars upon her garment; she is an image of power and protection raised to cosmic capacity and scope, declaring herself the providential friend of humanity: 'I am she that is the natural mother of all thinges...Queene of heaven' (pp. 259–60). Apuleius' work is a comedy of transformation, within which the hero is grotesquely trapped and in which release does not come until the very end, standing in the radiance of a moonlit world in which the characters of *A Midsummer Night's Dream* also search and struggle. It is a world of serious dreaming which became central to the mythographers' account of the alternative feminine reality (Cartari, *Imagini*, p. 121), feeding into English dream-literature along with works like Francesco Colonna's *Hypnerotomachia. The Strife of Love in a Dream* and Macrobius' Neoplatonic *Commentary* on Cicero's *Somnium Scipionis*, nourishing imaginative commitment to a radical subconscious dimension of dream, free of the masculine laws which shape the daylight world of linear history, where time circles in a timeless pattern generated by the moon's cyclical rhythm of repetition. Here art belongs, taking its forms and energies from the fund of the subconscious, allowing the artist to speculate on the nature of art's special, precious but always devious and equivocal reality. *A Midsummer Night's Dream*, in considering the character of the dream-world, and equally in linking this with art's illusions and truth-tellings (the-play-within-a-play) moves towards the absorbing themes of the tragi-comedies. Like the *Hypnerotomachia*, *A Midsummer Night's Dream* deals in 'a singular woorkemanship of sundrie representations and counterfeits'[20] and invites us to lose ourselves in the 'intricate Labyrinth' (p. 63) of a world whose marvellous forms are shared both by art and dream.

Because the dream-world is by its very nature lunar, Shakespeare relates it to the lunar cult of the virgin queen, and we clearly glimpse in this most directly Spenserian of Shakespeare's plays, the image of Gloriana, who is the Isis (but not the Ceres) of *A Midsummer Night's Dream*. The play utterly transcends the boundaries of contemporary allusion, however. Many generations have wanted to stand in its moonlight and see themselves transformed. This is a vision expanding to include other realms of being than the merely human and life-size, other kinds of power than the male politics of the daylight world. The human lovers move within the parentheses enforced on them by the existence of layered strata of forms of being. The men, Lysander and Demetrius, are fickle and susceptible of change. They are game hunted through someone else's dream. Outside them, austerely governing the body politic, are the Heroes, Theseus and Hippolyta, the Amazon Queen, her silver bow a crescent mirroring the bow of Diana the huntress and the new moon whose arrival she eagerly awaits. Beyond the world of 'Heroes', where human authority and knowledge have reached the very edge of their limitations, lies the nocturnal world of Titania and Oberon. They are powers within and over nature, Titania[21] being linked with Diana and Hecate, the moon in her aspect of 'waning', going under the earth, and thence with Proserpina, the lost daughter of Ceres and the dark Queen of the Underworld. Beyond all these reigns, in a quiet of contemplation which is much more than self-absorption, is the pale moon described in Oberon's celebrated speech to Puck. The moon is the farthermost limit into the divine or supernatural world which the audience of the play and the observers within it can perceive. She journeys across the heavens at the boundaries of mortal eyesight, not accessible to the passion with which sublunary creation is instinct, but nevertheless linked back to us through her shining upon the mortal planet:

> That very time I saw (but thou couldst not),
> Flying between the cold moon and the earth,
> Cupid all arm'd: a certain aim he took
> At a fair vestal, throned by the west,
> And loos'd his love-shaft smartly from his bow
> As it should pierce a hundred thousand hearts.
> But I might see young Cupid's fiery shaft
> Quench'd in the chaste beams of the watery moon;
> And the imperial votress passed on,
> In maiden meditation, fancy-free.
> (*A Midsummer Night's Dream*, II.i. 155–64)

If we remember that in 1595 Elizabeth I, to whom allusion is made, was an elderly person of increasingly peremptory and capricious temperament, ornate in dress and her face a pure cosmetic artifact, Shakespeare's allusion to her as a 'maiden' might seem painfully inauthentic. Yet, there is a redemptive quality to the guiding metaphor which transforms the apparent lie into a self-recognising paradox. Shakespeare emphasises Cupid's age: he is 'young' Cupid (almost a tautology), and this insistence on his not very advanced years automatically places into relief the old age of the 'imperial votress' moving unselfconsciously across her realm. A 'hundred thousand' would have been felled by the power of his single arrow. The only exemption is an old women—not beyond sexual desire, but, in her freedom of dreaming, transcending it. Cupid is young (Venus' immature and uncivilised offspring) beside the moon, which is as ancient as creation itself, and belongs to the genesis of all things. Yet the moon is as young as Cupid, or younger, when we remember that she is reborn from month to month. As

Dull and Holofernes learnedly agreed in *Love's Labour's Lost*, the moon is an infant never more than a month old (IV. ii. 36–44). Shakespeare's image is a lyrical presentation of the possibility of eternal self-renewal, associated with an inviolable quality which is not—despite the fact that Oberon wishes to think of her as a 'cold moon'—frigid or sterile. Her other-worldliness is not the remoteness of a planet considered as an impersonal bundle of matter in physics but the remoteness of thoughtfulness. Her 'maiden meditation, fancy-free' speaks of a liberty to conceive thoughts: her course of contemplation is an image of human inwardness, the thinking mind, resembling the creative imagination, itself pursuing its course of unseen motion.

Diana, the virgin goddess, embodies no principle of chastity disconnected from the continuum of created life, but exerts as Comes had shown in *Mythologiae* (p.91) as Lucina a direct influence on the flux of desire, generation and procreation in the world below. All the events in the play take place within the transforming medium of moonlight, and the tendency of those events is from singleness to union, in the case of both the Heroes and the human beings, and from discord to harmony in the case of the fairy protagonists. As Oberon's moon conceives her thoughts within her solitude, so she brings the natural world to fruition. Theseus threatens Hermia with the punishment of remaining

> a barren sister all your life,
> Chanting faint hymns to the cold fruitless moon.
> (*A Midsummer Night's Dream*, I. i. 72–3)

But the play's unfolding demonstrates that the moon of Shakespeare's vision is not fruitless but life-giving: it victimises in order to release. Its movement is towards reconciliation and synthesis. Theseus is usually taken as the model of the just ruler in *A Midsummer Night's Dream*,[22] a mask for Elizabeth and an upholder of a law whose austerities are rather endorsed than questioned by the dream which intervenes at the centre of the play. But this view is questionable. Theseus' power as the embodied voice of the man-made law, the subduer of the mighty Amazon, is undermined and contradicted throughout the play. He and his court reassemble and patronise the artisans at the end, returning to the status quo, because the playwright is pragmatic: the day-to-day world does run according to this system, and perhaps Theseus' is the best available version of the system. But Shakespeare's play has asserted the primacy of another kind of (feminine) law over the makeshift categories devised by men, to keep themselves under some sort of control. When Theseus condemns Hermia to the life of a 'barren sister', under the 'cold fruitless moon', he hardly knows to whom or of what he speaks. He talks in the dark.

The image of Hermia 'chanting' by night in a faint voice yields an impression of loneliness and exclusion, the smallness of an unseen girl's voice heard from a distance, as if muffled by the prevailing night. There is no force or clarity in it. But Hermia, despite the burlesque to which she is consigned in the wood, does not conform to this image. Her name relates her to the Hermetic mysteries of the cult of the goddess Isis, popularised through Apuleius' *The Golden Asse*. She links heaven and earth, just as in *The Golden Asse*, Hermes/'Mercurie' is an intermediary between Isis and her realms, 'the messenger of the Goddesse infernall and supernall' (p. 264). In a play about being scattered and then being collected, Hermia's name points back to the mystery cult centred around Isis' search for the scattered remains of her brother and lover, Osiris. Finding them, Isis is joined to Osiris. He mirrors her as her brother; he joins her as beloved. Hermia is from the beginning of Shakespeare's play in touch with the great controlling mysteries of existence—matters of life and death—in a way that is foreign to Theseus, spokesman of the establishment. His threat to make her a 'barren sister' shows us the Isis in Hermia, where twinning and identity, rather than opposition in sex, are important. She will find her 'brother'. Theseus' low opinion of the moon as not only 'cold' but 'fruitless' shows minimal understanding of the lunar cycles: the moon works the tides and seasons, and its cold light is benign to the warm, sentient human beings who yield to it.

Finally, the image of Hermia as a nun is an irony unguessed by the speaker, for here he identifies Hermia with a 'votaress', a key word in this play of reflected identities. Hermia is passing out of reach, like the 'imperial votress' of the heavens described by Oberon. In being a priestess of Isis she is also a manifestation of the goddess. The mind's eye as one remembers this word looks out into the night sky. But simultaneously it must look down to the darkness that is under the earth, the aching area of void and loss when Diana has waned to Hecate, and disappeared below the horizon—the grave where Proserpina came to grief. This play, through its evocation of the lunar mystery-religions, and the votaresses of these religions, takes in both the upper, celestial world and the underworld. It forces us to relate and reconcile them, within the limits of what comic art may attempt, and in doing so leads outside the limits of the man-made world. Male society is indicted by this vision, and only tolerated because there is not very much that can be done to alter it. The patriarchal is built on a structure of theft and deceit, and it will continue to be so, beneath the impassive moon, and above the threatening abyss of the underworld. The source of the discord within *A Midsummer Night's Dream* is the quarrel between the fairies Titania and Oberon over possession of a small child. Like Proserpina and Dis of classical myth, they reign over the lower world. Oberon wants the little Indian boy back to be his 'henchman' (II. i. 121) and thinks this a small request to grant and easy to gratify. Titania's reply is essential to the play's debate over the primacy of male and female principles:

> Set your heart at rest:
> The fairy land buys not the child of me.
> His mother was a votress of my order;
> And in the spiced Indian air, by night,
> Full often hath she gossip'd by my side;
> And sat with me on Neptune's yellow sands,
> Marking th'embarked traders on the flood:
> When we have laugh'd to see the sails conceive
> And grow big-bellied with the wanton wind;
> Which she, with pretty and with swimming gait
> Following (her womb then rich with my young squire),
> Would imitate, and sail upon the land
> To fetch me trifles, and return again
> As from a voyage rich with merchandise.
> But she, being mortal, of that boy did die;
> And for her sake do I rear up her boy;
> And for her sake I will not part with him.
> (*A Midsummer Night's Dream*, II. i. 121-37)

This passage is mysteriously close to the heart of the play's meaning, most especially in the line which tells of the death of Titania's friend—the shock of 'But she, being mortal, of that boy did die'. This line opens up a dark abyss in the comic structure, within which no meaning or sense can be discerned, an opening into the underworld, across which one must quietly step without comment, to the next line, and the lyrical continuum of the play's comic mode. This inconsistency, the mortal moment, feels troubling because it so obscurely offers a clue to meaning, affecting all the issues on which the controversy between Oberon and Titania rests. If the boy's mother was loved by Titania, and died in childbirth, then clearly Titania's was the valid claim on him, since it was motivated by a love-bond. But the play's action detaches the boy from her and passes him over to Oberon, which critics of the play have approved as a healthy initiation of the child into the adult male world from the suffocating or repressive female one.[23] The matriarchal world is taken to be a condition of perpetual infancy. Oberon wants the boy as a 'henchman'—to serve him—and more as a thing to be acquired, or an object of barter, out of jealousy, than for any personal motives.

This male jealousy—like the envy Spenser noticed in men's attitudes to women's greatness, and like that destructive jealousy which Shakespeare in the tragedy of *Othello* and the tragi-comedy of *The Winter's Tale* shows as murderous and fallen—seems invalidated by the power of the poetry in which Titania evokes her dead friend. The baby's mother was herself a 'votaress', like Hermia and like Diana, and, like them, a point of mediation between mortal and immortal worlds. Titania dramatises a moment in a friendship which, natural, human and playful as it was, was also impossible. It was amity between a mortal and an immortal, on equal terms—gossiping, laughing, playing—upon the narrow margin between sea and land, experienced late in that transition between states of being which is the nine-month period of human pregnancy. The joy of that friendship was at the same time marked with danger. The ships in full sail 'on the flood' were mimed by the pregnant woman, 'rich...rich' with her own dangerous cargo, from the apparent safety of the shore. But just as merchant ships might be wrecked at sea, so the unnamed woman fails to survive her labour. She is never mentioned again. The friendship between mortal and immortal, bound by identity of gender, seems to have failed by its very conditions.

In a play concerning the ultimate benignity of lunar experience, it is curious that the moon as Lucina, whose influence shortens labour, eases pain and ensures safe delivery, was so notably absent during the birth of the changeling child. Titania speaks of sitting with her friend 'by night' on the shore. We must think of this loss as occurring, then, when the moon has waned and disappeared beneath the horizon. Beneath the horizon is the grave. A clue to the power and suggestiveness of this 'mortal' line may be that, in directing our attention down to the underworld, it leads from a myth of the moon as Diana down to the point at which that myth touches and activates another myth of rebirth, that of Ceres and Proserpina. In alluding momentarily to the anonymity of the boy's mother's grave, *A Midsummer Night's Dream* touches upon the myth of hope in loss which would become the symbolic basis for Shakespeare's most mature plays, his tragi-comedies.

Simultaneously, this cluster of images—the pregnant woman 'feigning' the outside world, full of enjoyment and unaware of danger—may suggest an image of the artist himself, creative, imitative and mortal. The friendship between Titania and her votaress, paralleling that described by Helena as a 'union in partition' which made herself and Hermia from their earliest years 'incorporate' (III. ii. 210, 208), is a sacramental union of like with like. Oberon crows with triumph over his exaction of the changeling child from his queen, during the delusion of her dream, but there is no endorsement of his action or attitude. The means of possession are manipulation and deceit, law of conquest rather than law of right. The Hermetic figure within this play, unlike the feminine Hermes impersonated by Viola in *Twelfth Night*, is the trickster Puck, errant and comically malign as Venus' child Cupid himself, but under the final control of the male author of power. When Oberon reclaims his rule, and Theseus leads the characters into the reasserted status quo of the final Act, the issue of the changeling child is laid aside, the mother forgotten, as the play closes around the artisans' comedy it contains. But a reader may not forget nor really forgive the misappropriation of the boy-child by the law of the fathers, nor is the haunting music of Titania's elegy contradicted by a preferable ethic or emotion. For Shakespeare has called forth for this fraction of a moment in the play the great fertility-magic of the Ceres mystery, and all its sanctities, and having evoked such powerful energies, cannot disperse them. I have associated Titania with Diana as Hecate, and with Hecate as the Queen of the Underworld, Proserpina, but in the great speech for her dead friend's sake, the association is deeply with Ceres/Demeter, the mother of harvest and of civilisation in the ancient world, and emotive beyond the power of her daughter. This association is echoed in the name of Demetrius and reinforced by the blight Titania casts upon 'the green corn' (II. i. 94) and on 'The childing autumn' (112), which echoes the grief-sticken goddess's curse on the earth at the loss of her daughter:

> Onto the much-nourishing earth she brought a year
> most dreadful and harsh for men; no seed
> in the earth sprouted, for fair-wreathed Demeter concealed it.
> In vain the oxen drew many curved plows over the fields,
> and in vain did much white barley fall into the ground.
> (*Homeric Hymn to Demeter*, 305–9)

The rage of the corn-goddess can be appeased only by the intervention of Zeus to reinstate justice on her behalf. The Greeks stress the power of Demeter and what is and must be due to her. Translated into the English world of Faerie, Titania suggests this theme without assuming its eminence. Only a genuinely tragi-comic structure can be a strong enough framework to bear the weight of the Ceres/Proserpina myth towards which *A Midsummer Night's Dream* tends. In *Pericles* and *The Winter's Tale* Shakespeare would evolve a form capable of opening that dark place where human consciousness encounters the blight of 'a year/most dreadful and harsh for men', and sustaining that vision of the grave within man's mind and the grave within the nourishing earth, he would enlarge the comic matrix to a scale immense enough to enclose, dissolve and redefine its tragic experience. The transfiguring rituals which make Eleusis the most holy and mysterious place in the classical world are reborn in dramatic form on the English stage. The Athens of *A Midsummer Night's Dream* hints at such a development but centres its classicism rather in Apuleius than Eleusis. The blind human lovers in the forest are in the dark about their experiences, rather as Apuleius' Psyche[24] is about Cupid, her 'unknowen husbande' (p. 105): after their communal dream they open their eyes but the message of illumination has flowed away down to the unconscious world. They have not grown in conscious perception. By contrast, the world of Shakespeare's later 'Greek plays' is wholly concerned with the expansion of a memorable vision of sacred things, shared between characters and audience.

MARINA AND ELEUSIS

In Spenser's *Faerie Queene* The Book of Chastity, with its new female hero, led out of the inland pastoral landscape of forest and plain, to the shore and the sea. Shakespeare too in his Last Plays, with their profoundly Greek outlook and ethos, takes his drama off the known map to a sea-world classically presented as agent of storm, ruin and change and, paradoxically, as the source of unifying, generative music. Archetypally, the sea is female. It represents the amniotic waters of birth and the fluid world of matter which man must re-enter in death, returning to source.[25] Shakespeare's Last Plays recognise this archetype as female, and it is crucial to our understanding that we do so. Critics who do not respond to this female symbolism in a play like *Pericles*, where the stage represents alternately sea and land throughout, are baffled into weak explanations of the mysticism, mythological structure and political meanings of the play, premising their findings on equations as limp as Howard White's 'The sea stands for chance, the unknown'.[26] Mother Earth and *Mare Mater* reflect one another's nature in different mediums. Renaissance artists were fascinated by the proposition (based on Platonist adaptation of a remark by Pliny)[27] that, while all the Ideas that exist in the Divine Mind are copied upon land, so the types and species which exist on land are mirrored by a parallel (but not identical) collection of types and species within the sea. We recognise these mirroring images of reality because the mind of man itself possesses a complete cosmos, to which it compares the plenitude it encounters in the material world (Plato, *Meno* 85B–86). The important psychic task is therefore that of recognition, bringing our ideas to light. Marvell speaks of the human mind as incorporating a sea within: 'The Mind, that Ocean where each kind/ Does streight its own resemblance find' (*The Garden*, 43–44).[28] Shakespeare's tragi-comedies are also concerned with the nature of perception as recognition and self-recognition, leading to a 'patient' acceptance of material reality and the hope of a transcendent view of a reality beyond matter. Sea and storm are located in the external cosmos, but the hero's journey is in behavioural terms rather humiliating and embarrassing than epic: the realer odyssey is the voyage across the seas within, and as with Homer's Odysseus the place of destination is home in Ithaca, and in Penelope. The sea within is envisaged as hoarding in its subconscious world treasures and horrors dispassionately and incongruously together. Normally, these contents are either not looked at or are experienced as invisible. Shakespeare presents the art-world as our unique means of vision, filtering refracted light down through water:

> *Full fadom five thy father lies;*
> *Of his bones are coral made;*
> *Those are pearls that were his eyes:*
> *Nothing of him that doth fade,*
> *But doth suffer a sea-change*
> *Into something rich and strange.*
> *Sea-nymphs hourly ring his knell:*
> Burthen: *Ding-dong.*
> *Ari.Hark! now I hear them,—Ding-dong, bell.*
> (*The Tempest*, I. ii. 399–407)

It is through music within the play (art within art) that Shakespeare reveals the otherwise unguessable beauty of synthesis which may be achieved by the mind's interior sea. The father in Ariel's song lies transfigured within the mother-element. Marvell in *The Garden* attributes to the meditating mind the capacity to 'create' 'Far other Worlds, and other Seas' (45–48) than those of the recognised material cosmos. In a comparable way, the inner 'seas' of Shakespeare's tragi-comedies disclose tragic loss in a comic illumination. The mind in the dream-state of these plays does not so much remember the images that are drowned in its (or her) seas as recreate them in the form of new, rich and strange, births. To render and elucidate this newly created hieroglyphic world of the 'other seas', Shakespeare creates a richly symbolic and allusive lyrical voice. The visionary experience has its proper dialect.

Chronologically, the first play in this sea-sequence is *Pericles*. The corrupted text of this play, together with its archaic structure and the questioned authorship of major passages, should not lead us to do it less than justice. *Pericles* makes coherent psychological sense as a whole text, not simply in isolated moments of lyricism, and this is so because of, rather than despite, its naïveté and dramatic imperfections. It has a legibility lacking to other plays in the sequence precisely because its codes of meaning are less complicated by cross-currents of emotion and personality. Pericles in the course of the story passes down the Sacred Road to Eleusis. The process he undergoes corresponds to an initiation, or sequence of initiations. The Renaissance was familiar with the general structure of the Lesser and the Greater Mysteries of Eleusis, (see pp. 17–20 above), the former a symbolic representation of Persephone's abduction across the waters of death in the Flower Month (our February); the latter being the autumn festival at which pilgrims followed in the footsteps of the grieving Demeter along the Sacred Road from Athens and entered the Temple. The visionary night at which *mystes* ('having closed eyes') becomes *epoptes* ('enlightened') involves the rebirth of Persephone and the grain seed which is the Eleusinian symbol of rebirth. The harvest is the child conceived in the dark, other world. The resolution of the structure is a concordant balance between the gods above, man at the centre and the dark chthonic powers in the underworld, symbolised in the restoration of daughter to mother.[30] Initiation was open to all men and women, slave and free, provided they came untainted with unexpiated crimes.

Pericles is a king: that is dramatically important and essential to the political meanings of the play. But the hero is also an everyman, or even every-being, on a level with other choiceless victims which inhabit the planet. His experiences are universal. *Pericles* is a play, as Eleusis was a myth, involving the whole community: a community located not solely in Greece, or

England, but across the whole world. Yet we note that the
protagonist's name identifies him deeply with the civic
traditions of Athens, and, particularly in view of the fact that
the playwright changed the name *Apollonius of Tyre* in his
source to *Pericles*, we cannot help remembering the massive
historical figure of the Athenian leader Pericles, who beat off the
city's adversaries and rebuilt the city as a great artistic
monument to its own glory. The Pericles of Shakespeare's play
sails in his namesake's shadow like a miniature man on a paper
boat, at the mercy of the elements. But at the end of the play, by
virtue of this modest status, he expresses a greatness which is
obscurely comparable with that of the rebuilder of Athens, and
more mysterious, but just as Greek: in the spirit of the Delphic
oracle, 'know yourself, know that you know nothing'. As with
Leontes and the Delphic oracle in *The Winter's Tale*,
Shakespeare invokes not the Roman civic sanctities, with their
odour of cold imperial utility, but the Greek originals.
Nominally, the Roman forms of the myths of Diana and Ceres
are given us, as is customary in the Renaissance, but through
them the Greek meanings are yielded: Artemis and Demeter.
Shakespeare evokes the origin within the immediate source.
Pericles, like *The Winter's Tale*, is a political play, but it is not
about how to build the ideal *patria*. Rather it concerns itself
with how to *plant* the potentially self-renewing, organic *polis*.
Political life is referred throughout the play to the feminine
principle. The mythology of power is restructured, around the
mother-and-daughter relationship. Spellbound by this icon, the
political leader is finally released from the law of the fathers.
Solon, Lycurgus, Theseus, are left behind, along with the civic
grandeur of the first Pericles. Through Thaisa and Marina the
terms of political language are restated, and the second
Pericles—ruined and remade in a new image—can 'deliver' this
language as if (in his own phrase) he were a woman in labour
with an eloquence fitting to his tragi-comic experiences. *Pericles*
in Diana's play. Its politics are related to values and sanctities as
simple as the crops we plant and reap, moving through the
patterns of conception, fruitfulness and blight, to a final vision
of *ta hiera*, the holy, seen in personal, civic and religious life.
    The structure of *Pericles* is cyclic, remembering its beginning
in its end. In Act 1 we hear the false music of a misbegotten,

incestuous father–daughter relationship; in Act 5 we overhear the true music of the genuine version, which claims to be the 'music of the spheres'. The play is from its very beginning concerned with the possibilities of human perception and the difficulties of by-passing the duplicities of the senses. Pericles misreads Antiochus' daughter as a spring goddess (I. i. 13ff.), but then accurately and fatally decodes the riddle that reveals the incest between the two. The image revealed is matricidal: 'I feed/On mother's flesh' (I. i. 65–6). Antiochus' inverted sexual activity obscenely travesties the law of nature and the law of Eleusis, with its harmonious passing of nurture forwards across the generations, from mother to child. Pericles unveils the extreme case of mankind's carnivorous hunger, sinning against the whole race in its offence against the forward motion of time. By contrast, Pericles' identification of Marina in the final Act comes of a legitimate reading of the mother in the daughter: 'thou look'st/Like one I lov'd indeed' (V. i. 124–5; and 106–13). The insight achieved in the first Act leads to mystification, and to secrecy, for Pericles swears not to tell anyone of his new knowledge. Like Sophocles' spiritually blind Oedipus, upon the elucidation of the riddle of his own incestuous past, he becomes a stigmatised person, able to take no comfort in the communication of the secrets he has seen:

> the sore eyes see clear
> To stop the air would hurt them. The blind mole casts
> Copp'd hills towards heaven, to tell the earth is throng'd
> By man's oppression; and the poor worm doth die for't.
> (*Pericles*, I. i. 100–3)

Pericles politically buries himself in the terms of his image; he goes underground, beneath the human, to the underworld in which the eyeless mole builds tunnels until, coming up for air, the creature is ruthlessly eliminated. He cannot rub the corrupted imagery of father and daughter off his retina, because 'to tell' is an act of mutiny for which he must die. This insight, like the Lesser Mystery, involves a death. Pericles' status slides. He knows and claims community with all earthbound creatures incapable of making appeal beyond human law. The fact that such a recognition implies spiritual gain—parallel with Lear's

'Take physic, Pomp' (III. iv. 33) in his reversal on the Heath—is not clarified for us explicitly at this point; from this time forward Pericles Prince of Tyre is blown rootlessly before the wind, subject rather than ruler. Yet looking back we can see that Pericles' immediate indentification of himself with the lowest of the low, even to the animal-world in its inferior position on the chain of being directly under man's foot, *is* a powerful gain. It leads directly, though slowly, to the music of the final Act in which Marina enacts her Asclepian art of healing, the 'sacred physic' (V. i. 74) which can awaken Pericles from his accumulated, dehumanising vision of abject universal pain, as Cerimon's art in Act 3 awakened Thaïsa. When Pericles can find and utter the fitting words to approach the daughter who is a 'piece' of himself and a 'piece' of her mother, he is initiated into this final, and Greater, Mystery. The words chosen for this initiation are plain and simple to the point of homeliness, another sign of the identification of the tragi-comic hero with the whole community of suffering and healing, and the participation of the whole race in what the hero loses and finds. There is the recognition of 'this is Marina' (V. i. 199); ritual of initiation, 'Give me fresh garments' (213); the moment of visionary *ekstasis*, 'I am wild in my beholding' (221). Yet the enraptured vision of Marina is not the final stage of Pericles' spiritual journey. The play, like the complex Telesterion at Eleusis, with its many chambers and ante-chambers, reveals rooms beyond rooms. Thresholds of vision are crossed, to arrive at further thresholds. Pericles' 'vision' of Marina leads to his vision of Diana; this in turn leads him to her sanctuary at Ephesus, where the initiation is completed in his 'vision' of his wife. The vision which is the play is not completed until mother and maiden, past and future, meet in indivisible concord.

This concord is understood by the play as the foundation of human civilisation itself, just as the grain-yield guaranteed by Ceres/Demeter to the Ancient World was seen as the basis of 'peace together with the welcome rule of law' (*Orphic Hymn to Eleusinian Demeter*, 19). The vegetation symbolism in *Pericles* is vital to this theme; for the play varies between the rooted world of vegetation on shore and the uprooted world of man committed to the transitions of the sea. Neither of these worlds is safe or trustworthy. The incest which opens the play is not an isolated event in the personal world; it is symptomatic of a state of society as well as a state of mind. Pericles' position as Prince of Tyre is stressed from the outset, together with the relationship of sacramental fealty he shares with his deputy, Helicanus, whose loyal identification with Pericles is tested and never found wanting throughout the play. Helicanus validates this:

> We'll mingle our bloods together in the earth,
> From whence we had our being and our birth.
> *(Pericles*, I. ii. 113–14)

The implied concept is that of 'Mother Earth', the womb in which man and man were twinned at origin and to which they elect to return inseparably. This ideal fealty is seen as rooted in nature and obedient to natural law. Yet Pericles' political power is seen from the first as already maimed. He speaks of himself as a treetop trying to defend its own roots (31–2); Helicanus thinks of his status as being like that of a plant looking up to heaven for nourishment (56–7). Power in their hands is unaggressive. It identifies itself with plant-life rooted in the earth rather than with the predatory animal-kingdom. Pericles' little state is therefore disastrously vulnerable to the power of larger, military neighbours. His ethic is that of 'Patience', from the Latin *patiens*, suffering, implying a feminine and stoical rather than a masculine and military approach to adversity. These are not the ethics of Thermopylae, less still of Marathon. Their Greek roots are buried in the mythology of power conceived as the grain-law of Eleusis. The scene at Tharsus begins to unfold this mysterious theme by presenting Pericles as the bringer of corn to a blighted land.

Cleon describes conditions in the famished and destitute city. Want has perverted human nature into a grotesque abuse of its own fertility. While at Antioch, father and daughter committed a kind of matricide in incest, at Tharsus:

> Those mothers who, to nuzzle up their babes
> Thought nought too curious, are ready now
> To eat those little darlings whom they lov'd.
> *(Pericles*, I. iv. 42–4)

This passage, as Howard White astutely noticed, [31] is directly comparable with Titania's speech on the ruin of the seasons in *A Midsummer Night's Dream* (see pp. 128–9 above), but in mood and tone it is a world away. There the dream dissolves its painful material in the sensuous colour of pastoral: 'the green corn/Hath rotted' (II. i. 98–9) is not as shocking as it is colourful. The lush and temperate climate of Shakespeare's English pastoralism is interrupted by a dream-game of temporary rupture between minor fertility spirits. Despite its echo of Demeter's curse, *A Midsummer Night's Dream* still remains 'a wedding play of Diana reconciled to Venus, as in Spenser III. vi. 25'.[32] By contrast, Shakespeare's Mediterranean pastoral of *Pericles* is a world of sparse and hardy vegetation, living near to subsistence level, in which good dreams are short and constantly challenged by nightmare images of reality. In Tharsus, Demeter's curse seems to engender the terror of the original story to the always imperilled civilisation of the Greeks: 'she would have destroyed the whole race of mortal men/with painful famine' (*Homeric Hymn to Demeter*, 310–11). Mother's 'little darlings' make delicate meat for starving parents. Excess gives way to defect, luxury to a want which undoes the most sacred taboo on which society is founded, the trust from child to mother. To this barbarous undoing of civilisation Pericles, escaping from his own personal blight, brings relief, in a reversal of the Trojan horse motif:

> And these our ships, you happily may think
> Are like the Trojan horse was stuff'd within
> With bloody veins expecting overthrow,
> Are stor'd with corn to make your needy bread...
> (*Pericles*, I. iv. 92–5)

Corn to make bread is the foundation of society. Pericles' adaptation of the Trojan horse motif is anti-Homeric and anti-heroic. Ships seen on the horizon from a city-port may easily be guessed to be warships. But the hero who has acknowledged in this first Act his absolute kinship with human need and helplessness, who has seen and understood tyranny in the form of Antiochus, and felt with 'sore eyes' his likeness to the oppressed victims who share the planet, can only see virtuous action in terms of 'corn to make your needy bread'. Shakespeare's Last Plays ally him with Spenser's glorification of the Elizabethan peace and Milton's espousal of an unmasculine ethic:

> Not sedulous by nature to indite
> Wars, hitherto the only argument
> Heroic deemed...
> (*Paradise Lost*, IX. 27–9)

Pericles is a sustained evasion of action, insofar as action is to be equated with battle-antagonism. This makes the actions he does undertake all the more significant: the bringing in of the corn, his marriage, his response to the birth of his daughter and his reunion with Marina and Thaisa. Each of these acts either impersonates a feminine role (the nurture of the city) or ties the hero to the feminine. Tragi-comedy becomes the vehicle of a categorical denial of Mars and his war-horse, as an out-moded ideal in a corrupted world.

The corrupted world, however, is seen as persistent. Wavelike rhythms of loss and gain, storm and peace, 'wash' Pericles 'from shore to shore' (II. i. 5–6), instructing him in the art of passivity. On the shore of Pentapolis in the second Act, Pericles already has the kind of resignation that is reached only at the close of a Greek tragedy. He reveals himself to the fishermen as having no greater identity than the sum of his afflictions: 'A man thronged up with cold' (II. i. 73). The play's structure is a series of such abdications, centring on the loss of Pericles' wife in childbirth in Act 3. In Gower's phrase, 'A babe is moulded' (III. 11), suggesting the shaping hands around the clay, the timeless journey of each life in the mysterious interior world which preludes her or his discharge into time. Pericles' journey parallels that of his unborn daughter. Helpless upon the dark seas, he is virtually choiceless and resourceless save for the lyric voice of language, with which he is able to shape a ritual meaning for events, measuring the paradox of his experiences in words and attuning himself to acceptance. The birth of Marina from her apparently dying mother is crucial from this point of view. Pericles shapes and harmonises his terrible and self-contradictory experience through the musically tempering power of language. The resolved, composing quality of his mind stands against the choric voices of the sailors in the storm. They speak with, and maintain, the chaos of the universe: 'But sea-room, and the brine and cloudy billow kiss the moon, I care not' (45–6). This image is of the feminine cosmic principles in enraptured disarray, the tide-moving moon and the swelling waters threatening to swamp the world. The sailors' prose is opposed by the music of Pericles' poetry:

> A terrible childbed hast thou had, my dear;
> No light, no fire: th'unfriendly elements
> Forgot thee utterly; nor have I time
> To give thee hallow'd to thy grave, but straight
> Must cast thee, scarcely coffin'd, in the ooze;
> Where, for a monument upon thy bones,
> And e'er-remaining lamps, the belching whale
> And humming water must o'erwhelm thy corpse,
> Lying with simple shells.
>
> (*Pericles*, III. i. 56–64)

This is the music of pastoral elegy, as Orphic as that of *Lycidas* in its composure of the waters of grief, reclaiming through controlled expression the image of what has been lost until it is luminous with visionary light. The disasters imagined in the Last Plays do not, as Rosalie Colie so oddly thought, [33] go beyond the limits of pastoral, for pastoral in its fullest extension as pastoral elegy is able to assume into itself all the grief of all the dismembering experiences humanity can dream of, even to the point of itself declaring the death of pastoral. Spenser's 'All Musick sleepes, where death doth leade the daunce' (November, *Shepheardes Calender*, 105) is a music wide-awake; Milton's lament for the death of Orpheus, 'What could the muse herself that Orpheus bore?' (*Lycidas*, 58) is itself Orphic. The self-reconciling singer is in process of remaking the life that is lost. Pericles 'Must cast' from him through pressure of time that which should be voluntarily and naturally given. There is no grave to receive her, as there is none for Lycidas: 'Ay me! whilst thee the shores and sounding seas/ Wash far away, where'er thy bones are hurled' (154–5)—but this is paradoxical. If there is no grave, there may be no real death; dust may not return to dust. If in imagination Pericles can enter into the sea-world in which Thaïsa is lost, he becomes one with the waters which, the knowing sailor tells him, must be appeased for they 'will not lie till the ship be clear'd of the dead' (III. i. 48–9). Pericles casts away Thaïsa's death and his own (spiritual) death into the sea, trusting to the waters which, the *Orphic Hymns* told the Renaissance, were full of loving presences which 'leap and whirl round the waves,/like glistening dolphins roving the roaring seas' (*To the Nereids*, 7–8). Along with these is the 'belching whale', imagined by Pericles as passing by the drowned body of his wife, recalling the biblical Jonah:

> The waters compassed me about, even to the soul: the depth closed me round about, the weeds were wrapped about my head.
> I went down to the bottoms of the mountains; the earth with her bars was about me for ever: yet hast thou brought up my life from corruption, O LORD my God.
>
> (Jonah 2:4–5)

The classicism of *Pericles* substitutes for Jonah's bizarre realism (the seaweed in the hair, the choking violence of sea-death) the grace and simplicity of the Hellenic vision of purification and benediction in water still and singing: 'Lying with simple shells'. The Orphic theology is not, in essence, tragic.[34] What matters is, as Ficino insisted,[35] the incantatory power of the voice that visited Hades to unite Apollonian and Bacchic oppositions in *concordia discors*. Orphism emphasises suffering and purification, the spirit of patience and tolerance of adversity. Thus Pericles may be said to go down to Hades in imagination in the requiem 'A terrible childbed': a Hades figured in the underworld of water, a Euridyce in the person of Thaisa. He brings his own light there: 'e'er-remaining lamps', his own music of 'humming water', his own artistic vision 'Lying with simple shells'. Platonistically, the seas reflect the image of the All, Pan in Proteus, the one spirit 'Flowing in all things, circular, ever changing form' (*Orphic Hymn to Physis*, 23). By incantation of his beloved and his ritual yielding of her to the waters, Pericles mysteriously unites not only Thaïsa but also himself with the Platonist All. Thaïsa, a fragment of the *una dea* inhabits the waters unseen save through the eye of the imagination, the mind 'that Ocean where each kind/Doth streight its own resemblance find', as Marvell would later express it. In response to Pericles' elegy we feel the strange power of the word to create a visual reality of its own and charge it with meaning and conviction, and perceive the musician-poet as artist in a way that has magical suggestions, near to the divine. This Orphic status for the eternally self-abdicating Pericles was prepared for in the birthday scene at Pentapolis, in which Thaïsa's father congratulated him on his musicianship: 'Sir, you are music's master' (II. v. 30). Act 3 proves to us the validity of the compliment and looks forward to his daughter's acclamation as a scholar and teacher of music at Mytilene. Throughout the tragi-comedies, song and music enact this ritual pattern of pastoral-elegiac atonement and healing from Guiderius' and Arviragus' *'Fear no more the heat o'the sun'*—outdone by Arviragus' earlier unsung music of the elegy 'With fairest flowers' (IV. ii. 218–29)—in *Cymbeline*, and Ariel's *Full fadom five* of *The Tempest*.

The play's beautiful syncretism thus marries Eleusinian and Orphic allusion, and goes on in the same Act (again through the person of Thaïsa) to connect the two themes with a Hermetic theme, that of the Asclepian healer, the artist of white magic, who will become vital in the obscure feminine white magic of *The Winter's Tale* and a central personage in *The Tempest* (where, however, in its alienation from the validating female power, its 'roughness' will be more rigorously questioned). Cerimon, at Ephesus, resurrects Thaïsa from her coffin, to music. In watching this scene the audience is initiated into a secret which Pericles' eyesight cannot penetrate. The resurrection of Thaïsa has a dream-logic. It is predictable, for by this time death and birth have become so close in association as to seem organically one. The structure of *Pericles* is a detailed interweaving of deaths and births, whose complexity is suggested when we consider that Thaïsa, having given birth, is almost immediately sealed into her coffin and cast into the waters of death; transformation occurs, of everything into its opposite; the coffin becomes a womb and the sea of death is converted into the amniotic fluids of birth. As the midwife figure Lychorida (a version of the midwife Hecate so important in the Demeter myth) admitted Thaïsa's baby to the world, so Cerimon of Ephesus (Diana's city) raises Thaïsa into her new cycle of life. Cerimon is pointedly associated with the Egyptian traditions of Hermetic magic. He has heard, he says, of 'an

Egyptian/That had nine hours lien dead,/Who was by good appliance recovered' (III. ii. 86–8). This rumoured individual's nine hours of death had been in reality a nine hours' gestation from which he emerged into new life. As Cerimon exits, having revived Thaïsa, he murmurs, 'Aesculapius guide us!' (114), linking himself both as magus and healer with the Hermetic *Asclepius*, with its elated confidence in man the miracle, the artist, the life-giver. Thaïsa, we know, is not really dead; neither is Hermione in *The Winter's Tale*. Both are dormant, waiting. But then, says the *Hermetica*, properly understood, nothing is really dead. Magic, in Hermetic and Ficinian terms, consists in arousing the spirit that is dormant within the apparently inanimate, working within the laws of nature rather than outside them. The activities of Cerimon in *Pericles*, Paulina in *The Winter's Tale* and Prospero in *The Tempest* should be understood in the light of the teaching of the *Asclepius*, that 'you may well hold man to be a marvel' (23b), for he can create 'statues living and conscious, filled with the breath of life, and doing many mighty works; statues which have foreknowledge' (24a). Cerimon and Paulina exemplify the rapturous humanist dream that inspired Pico's Hermetic pride in 'man the miracle', but tempered by awareness of the scope of human pain and insistence on his reality only within the world of art and dream, guarded or incorporated by the feminine. In *Pericles* the theme is clearly experimental and imperfectly realised. In *The Winter's Tale* the blending of Hermetic and Eleusinian material in the person of Paulina issues in the unprecedented concept of the magus as woman, calling out the life from her likeness, as naturally and 'lawfully' as in giving physical birth.

In the second half of *Pericles*, with the advent of Marina, the Proserpina theme becomes most explicit, and shadow-doubles begin to appear for the major female characters. As Marina becomes the central focus of action, she casts a shadow in the form of the jealous, competing 'twin', Philoten, and Thaïsa is doubled by the dark mother, Dionyza. The motif of rape emerges in Act 4, accompanied by allusions to the musicality of Marina, 'by Cleon train'd/In music's letters' (7–8), suggesting the power of her Orphic inheritance to read the secret hieroglyphic language of the soul, and also of the myths of Philomela and Proserpina. The story of Orpheus had been from

an early time connected with that of Proserpina: each tells of
violent assault by the forces of the underworld, universal
damage to the balance of powers in the world, final harmony and
healing. In Claudian's *De Raptu Proserpinae*, Proserpina is seen
embroidering an exquisite cloth representing the creation and
order of the cosmos:

> You might have thought you heard the seaweed dashed against the
> rocks and heard the murmur of the hissing waves flooding up
> the thirsty sands.
>
> *(De Raptu Proserpinae*, Vol. 2. XXXIII. 257–9)

That art-work's verisimilitude is an index of its sublimity, in a
universe which has emanated from Divinity itself. The cloth is a
present for her mother, Ceres. Likewise, Proserpina wears a
dress upon which the births of moon and sun are eloquently
depicted. This theme of Marina/Proserpina as artist of creation
(and therefore essentially Orphic in character) deepens in
emphasis as the play unfolds her disasters. Act 4 relates repeated
assaults of the dark male principle on Marina's innocence,
assimilating her music to that of 'the night-bird mute/That still
records with moan' (26–7). The night-bird is Philomela, the
nightingale, recording her rape by Tereus, in Ovid's words
'quivering...like a dove, its feathers matted with its own blood,
still trembling and afraid of the greedy talons which held it fast'
(*Metamorphoses*, VI. 529–30). Marina's song heals the nightingale's memory of its violation but is itself threatened by a male
rapacity which Shakespeare, like Spenser, sees as almost
invincibly carnivorous. Just as Ovid's Philomela is imaged as a
dove, so Gower speaks of Marina being to Philoten as dove is to
crow, the white bird of peace and fidelity confronted by the
black carrion bird.

But Marina is, specifically, the 'dove of Paphos' (32), that is,
sacred to Venus; and Marina is like Venus sea-born, a foreigner
to natures compounded solely of earth, and therefore finally
indestructible by them. The text is full of richly allusive
indications of danger and of safety, threat and healing. When
Marina enters (like Perdita in the pastoral Act of *The Winter's
Tale*) *'with a basket of flowers'* (IV. i), Dionyza symbolically de-
flowers her: 'Come, give me your flowers' (26), and pushes her

down to the treacherous marginal area between land and sea, which preluded disaster for Marinell and Florimell in *The Faerie Queene* and death in childbirth for Titania's mortal friend in *A Midsummer Night's Dream*. Like Florimell, Marina 'On the sea-margent' (26) steps out upon this threshold between worlds to become the victim not just of one would-be ravisher but of a sequence. Both are brutally passed from hand to hand, Leonine's attempt at murder being followed by the pirates' seizure, and finally the brothel-keepers' business-like endeavours to 'get her ravish'd or be rid of her' (IV. vi. 5). This pattern of assaults implies a literal fulfilment of her earlier lament that 'This world to me is as a lasting storm/Whirring me from my friends' (IV. i. 19–20), with its suggestion of the ripping sound of wind in the feathers of a bird unable to strive against its conditions with the slender articulations of its wing. Like Pericles, Marina is identified with frail fellow-victims low upon a predatory chain of being. Man is shown as potentially more humane than the world he or she is required to inhabit. The creatures of earth, whether animal or human, share a condition of inexplicable fellow-suffering, and (more painfully) are implicated by necessity in such suffering:

> I never kill'd a mouse, nor hurt a fly;
> I trod upon a worm against my will,
> But I wept for't.
>   (*Pericles*, IV. i. 77–9)

This is the anti-heroic ethos of universal compassion which is everywhere felt in Spenser, and in Bruno, the compassion for all sentient life, however miniscule and undistinguished, in community of suffering (see pp. 63–74 above). It is at the extremest pole from the warrior-code of the male culture. Marina utters what the male culture (personified in Leonine, emblematically the king of the beasts) must scorn as effeminate whimsy. But *Pericles* looks out beyond the scope of the merely human world to bring within the circle of its benediction and regret the animate life which human beings even at their best may compassionate but cannot avoid hurting. Through Love, Ficino and the Platonists were assured, all phenomena from stones to vegetables to animals, men, angels, sought in multitudinous affinity to reascend to their Creator: *amor nodus perpetuus, et copula mundi* (*De amore*, III. iii).[36] *Pericles*, in the person of Marina, tries out the practicality of the system, testing the Idea of universal charity upon the stormy, crowded surface of an earth rooted in suffering. Where *King Lear* had asked in relation to the dead Cordelia a question devastating enough: 'Why should a dog, a horse, a rat, have life,/And thou no breath at all?' (V. iii. 305–6), *Pericles*, that apparently more gauche play of tableaux and happy ending, approaches through Marina the more unpalatable, anti-humanist question, 'Why should a dog...*not* have life?' Tragi-comedy widens rather than limits the scale of moral enquiry.

Marina questions the justice of her relation to the world that is, literally, under her feet. Like the story of Proserpina which also deals with balance and adjustment between upper, middle and nether worlds, Marina's questions represent an encounter with the underworld which occupies most of the fourth Act. Shakespeare's flower-maiden is raped away to Mytilene, the human equivalent of the underworld where the powers of evil work in the Plutonian market-place in which girls are bought and sold. Here the imagery is of sterility, disease and death: 'she made him roast-meat for worms' (IV. ii. 22–3). The inhabitants are feeding the underworld with a banquet of diseased human flesh: Venerean translates to venereal. Proserpina is buried and Ceres' curse blights the land. The brothel scenes gather up mythic suggestions from the previous Acts, presenting them with drily realistic force. Woman is reduced to spitted meat, to be carved up and sold in 'pieces': 'I have bargained for the joint' (129). But the tainted idiom of Mytilene is rich in virtuous innuendo: an ingenious reversal of the normal uses of *double entendre* which points out to us the true direction of Marina's journey, 'to seek my mother' (63). Vegetation imagery proliferates with wonderful suggestiveness. The Bawd calls Marina 'a young foolish sapling' (83–4), and urges Boult to have the 'harvest' of her by advertising her availability (139). She 'grows to the stalk; never pluck'd yet, I can assure you' (IV. vi. 39–40). The obscene intent unpeels from the words; the seed of the corn-goddess has well taken and is mysteriously growing in this black soil towards the predicted 'harvest' in which the fully ripened grain will be yielded by the underworld to the 'herb woman; she that sets seeds and roots' (84–5). We intuit the unseen figure of the mother standing behind that of the daughter, the movement of the spring girl towards the harvest woman until they meet and become one.

Thus Boult discourses of ploughing, ignorant of his own virtuous innuendo. The abuse of language, it is suggested, cannot conceal its hieroglyphic truths. Language itself seems (comically) committed to its own inviolably chaste laws. Base and ugly usages are like the corpse submerged 'full fadom five', revealing unexpectedly subtle and ironic perfection of meaning:

> *Boult.* And if she were a thornier piece of ground than she is, she shall be plough'd.
> *Mar.* Hark, hark, you gods!
>
> (*Pericles*, IV. vi. 144–6)

A piece of ground, piece of earth, piece of virtue, piece of her mother—the play is an Isis collecting the 'pieces' together to accumulate in final unity. Marina may well call upon the gods at this point; Boult has already unconsciously done so. His vile abuse of her in corrupted metaphor as a field to be penetrated by the male and seeded by him unknowingly alludes to Marina's role in the process of ploughing, ripening and harvest on which the play is structured. 'Thorny' ground remembers 'Genesis': 'Thorns also and thistles shall it bring forth to thee' (3:18). Marina is imagined as the wasteland of the fall inviting rough cultivation by the hard-working male. But 'Genesis' continues: 'and thou shalt eat of the herb of the field'. The feminine is habitually associated by Shakespeare with nurture and nourishment—the first gift of milk, the manna of bread.[37] Boult's gross allusion to the ploughing for harvest reminds us that Marina/Proserpina is closing with the identity of Thaïsa/Ceres. Spring declares itself in the wheat of autumn; the desolate ploughed field becomes the yield of abundance. As the daughter takes on the nature of the corn-mother herself, the plot turns. The *peripeteia* ravishes Lysimachus into virtue, by the talismanic white magic of chastity. Much is made, as Marina prepares to leave the 'underworld' of the brothel, of her wish to teach the arts: 'Proclaim that I can sing, weave, sew, and dance' (IV. vi. 182). This is profoundly true to the spirit of Eleusis, the cultivation of the earth standing as the basis for collective social, spiritual and artistic cultivation.[38] Thus in Mytilene Marina 'sings like one immortal' and dances (V. 3-4) like an embodiment of the Pythagorean spheres. Gower's naïve English modifies the splendour of the image into a believable homeliness, enabling us to accept the prodigy. Her art form is woman's work, commonly unsung and unvalued. Though it is true that Marina can talk the voluble academics into silence—surely a great blessing to Mytilene—more stress is placed upon her needlework, which 'composes/Nature's own shape, of bud, bird, branch, or berry' (5-6). The sacred art of realism in a God-made world links her back into the creative cycles of nature, from spring 'bud' to autumn 'berry'. Her reunion with Pericles—the climax of the play—is, on one level, a culmination of the theme of education associated with the feminine principle, education as a birth of what is already within the soul, the Platonic recognition of the *Meno* and *Phaedrus*, and the sacred *dromenon* of Eleusis, revealing to the initiate all he or she ever needs to know. Marina brings the gift of language, a language different in kind from anything we have heard in the course of the play, a dialect of the soul such as Spenser's fourth Elizabeth draws out of him in the *Amoretti*:

> You frame my thoughts and fashion me within,
>   you stop my toung, and teach my hart to speake...
>   (VIII)

Slowly and movingly, Pericles is reborn in an experience that is visionary both to the protagonist and to the audience of the play. All the emphasis at Eleusis was on seeing. The mystery rites were a sacred drama in which the watchers were made aware of the absolute, verified existence of another world whose awful mysteries were:

>   not to be transgressed, violated
> or divulged, because the tongue is restrained by reverence for the gods.
> Whoever on this earth has seen these is blessed,
> but he who has no part in the holy rites has
> another lot as he wastes away in dank darkness.
>   (*Homeric Hymn to Demeter*, 478-82)

The same quality of wonder and awe is generated in the audience by the recognition scene in *Pericles*. The scene is numinous, the hero almost anonymous, as though stripped down to the soul by his losses. Stateless, statusless, without speech, movement or hearing, he is at the edge of the human, about to set forth on the sea of death. He is a living statement of the fact that unalleviated suffering reduces us; it does not ennoble. The soul waits mutely for extinction. As Cerimon, the Hermetic magician, raised Thaïsa to life in Act 3 now Marina's 'sacred physic' (74) enacts Asclepian resurrection. Hermetic themes chime in with Eleusinian. Pericles is like one of the inititates of the *Hermetica* who 'forgets all bodily sensations and all bodily movements, and is still...the beauty of the Good bathes his mind in light, and takes his soul up to itself' (*The Key*, 6, in *Hermetica*, p. 191). In 'the womb of Wisdom' (*A Secret Discourse of Hermes to Tat*, 2, in *Hermetica*, p. 239) the boundaries of Pericles' previous self are broken, opening the threshold of new knowledge. Emptied of sense-impressions, he is capable of *gnosis*. And on another level still, Act 5 represents the final stages of a spiritual alchemy, completing the work that was figured in *King Lear* and shattered there in tragic loss. All these visionary languages have a part in the climax of the tragi-comic dream.

There was no language in which the initiates in the ancient pagan Mysteries could have told their experiences, even had they wished to break their oath of secrecy and incur eternal night. A thing seen may be—literally—unutterable. Shakespeare invents a poetic language to transmit the beauty of what Pericles gradually sees and knows. The single most important symbolic factor in this realisation is its expression in terms of the impersonation and incorporation of the male into the female. Pericles abdicates his gender. The finite limits of the male psyche yield, and he identifies himself with the nature of the female. This is his deliverance. As Spenser's Britomart becomes a herm-aphroditic reflection of the One, by taking to her nature an aspect of the male, so Shakespeare's Pericles leans out to participate in the nature of the woman, and specifically woman as mother:

I am great with woe
And shall deliver weeping. My dearest wife
Was like this maid, and such a one
My daughter might have been: my queen's square brows;
Her stature to an inch; as wand-like straight;
As silver-voic'd; her eyes as jewel-like
And cas'd as richly...

                                        (*Pericles*, V. i. 105–11)

The glory of the speech stems from its source in the initiating
metaphor of childbirth, which gathers into itself the paradox
upon which the whole play has turned. The speaker conceives of
himself as a woman in labour. 'His' labour delivers neither the
tears nor the 'woe' of the first sentence but rather the words
that follow; that is, the speech itself, with its precious ore of
memory. Words are his delivered child. Through the beauty of
their patterning he approaches the reality of the delivered child
who stands on the stage before him, a quickening presence. In
this most moving of images, he takes home at last the lost
feminine 'piece' of himself. The artful and touching paradox of
the 'maternal' father suggests an experience both within and
against nature, but the final connotation is of a process within
Mother Nature as '*Father and mother* of all' (*Orphic Hymn to
Physis*, 18; my italics), like Spenser's ambiguously gendered
'great dame *Nature*' ('Mutabilitie', *Faerie Queene*, vii. 5). The
natural is expressed through the very painfulness of Pericles'
labour of articulation. The pain, as in childbirth, is evacuated,
the word-child delivered. The tragi-comic resolution of the Last
Plays depends on emphasis on deliverance, enacted here through
recurrent word-play involving conception, pregnancy, labour
and delivery of a girl-child.

Pericles' work of words in this Scene, as he gathers Marina
into his understanding, is towards assimilation of what has been
scattered and dismembered. Thus he can credit Marina's
seemingly impossible testimony because he can identify the
mother in the child, seeing that they are one: 'thou look'st/ Like
one I loved indeed' (V. i. 120–5). This process evolves further
when he can see that he and Marina are also one; they are
exchangeable. Again he abdicates his gender, reckoning that if
their sufferings are comparable, 'thou art a man, and I/Have
suffered like a girl' (136–7). The mythic basis of the scene is

adapted into a naturalistic, heartfelt verse which tells universal truths in a personal way. To have a child of the opposite sex, who is a 'piece' of yourself, makes for an extension of self towards its own opposite. Pericles both opposes and in some sense recognisably 'is' the child Marina. The telling over of Marina's story has a ritualistic element. It is a crucial rite in Pericles' initiation, filled with painful intensity for the hearer. Through it Pericles receives a testament which is like the Eleusinian pilgrim's viewing of the 'holy things', the *sacra* in the Temple. Truth is learned by Pericles as we bear children, *in extremis*.

With full recognition comes a state of mind which is close to the accounts by Cicero, Sophocles and Plato of the ecstasy experienced at the Mysteries as producing a clarity of insight, accompanied by wild and enduring joy which ensures for the initiate the cleansing of fear from the whole future. Shakespeare communicates a sense of the nearly unbearable character of such joy, joy as pain, through adaptation of the sea-symbolism upon whose tides the play has always moved. The tide turns, but paradoxically does not cease to threaten:

> O Helicanus, strike me, honour'd sir!
> Give me a gash, put me to present pain,
> Lest this great sea of joys rushing upon me
> O'erbear the shores of my mortality,
> And drown me with their sweetness. O, come hither,
> Thou that beget'st him that did thee beget;
> Thou that wast born at sea, buried at Tharsus,
> And found at sea again. O Helicanus,
> Down on thy knees! thank the holy gods as loud
> As thunder threatens us: this is Marina.
>
> (V. i. 190–9)

The soul turns away from its own illimitable joy to seek the safer limits of the solid shore of tempered utterance: it finds momentary repose in the patterned symmetries of its *credo*, its threefold benediction over a maiden-Christ who has endured nativity, crucifixion, resurrection, but as a human being rather than as ascended God. The terror which is at the heart of his joy is the power of the holy informing this human story. When Pericles calls for 'fresh garments' (213) this climactic phase is

complete, for 'I am wild in my beholding' (221). The verse
disconnects into short rhapsodic utterances. Its 'wildness' is the
ekstasis of the visionary. Out of his mind through the unearthly
power of absolute 'beholding', *mystes* has become *epoptes*. It is
right to see Pericles as mad, out of his senses. He steps over the
edge of sanity and, seeing Marina for what she is, hears a literally
incredible music:

> *Per.*   O heavens bless my girl! But hark, what music?
> ·
>
> *Per.*   [*Music*] But what music?
> *Hel.*   My lord, I hear none.
> *Per.*   None?
>   The music of the spheres! List, my Marina.
>   (V. i. 222, 225–8)

According to the other people on the stage, there is no music.
Lysimachus suggests humouring the old man and suddenly
discovers that he has caught the sound too: 'Music, my Lord? I
hear.' (231). Marina is, suggestively, silent. A stage-direction
instructs that music be played, which may be interpreted in
performance in two ways. Either it represents objectively the
'Most heavenly music' (231) which Pericles claims to hear, in
which case the audience is privileged to share an epiphany from
which the rest of the cast is excluded, or the music is hastily
rigged by the 'sane' and worldly-wise cast to humour the hero,
in which case the audience is still privileged, since the music is
presented as real whether audible to common sense or not. As
Campanella remarked of the impossibility of the human ear
picking up the Platonic-Pythagorean music of the spheres: 'Our
voice is to theirs as an ant's voice is to ours'—theirs would
drown us with thunder.[39] The theatre becomes a miniature
Eleusis in which the audience as 'actively' as Pericles—or as
'patiently'—participates. The music we 'hear' is composed of
the whole action of the play we have witnessed, both its deaths
and births, harmonies and dissonances. The art-world presents
itself as being, by virtue of its very incredibility (about which it
is not really apologetic or defensive), the magical entrance to
'beholding', and thence hearing. In sophisticated Renaissance
musicology, the divine music was understood as being formed of
discord and dissonance, not just of sweet, harmonious sounds.

In this way, everything we have heard in the course of the play adds up to the final music. The false music made by Antiochus on the instrument of his daughter's body in Act 1 is an essential discord on which the tragi-comedic *concordia discors* is based.[40] Ultimately, the music becomes a lullaby to the body, parting it from the soul which awakens in dream. Pericles becomes susceptible to the vision of Diana of Ephesus, which only the audience and Pericles perceive together, the stage being cleared of uninitiated characters. The theatre becomes a communal dream-world encompassing the private dream of our representative.

Through the presiding lunar Diana, 'goddess argentine', Pericles and Marina make their final journey to source and union, in a lyric poetry of tempered exultation:

> Per: This, this: no more. You gods, your present kindness
> Makes my past miseries sports. You shall do well,
> That on the touching of her lips I may
> Melt and no more be seen. O come, be buried
> A second time within these arms.
> Mar.   My heart
> Leaps to be gone into my mother's bosom.
>   [*Kneels to Thaïsa*]
>   (V. iii. 40–5)

At this point of restoration to Marina's mother, the two seekers express themselves in terms of overwhelming desire for loss of identity. Pericles longs to 'melt' and vanish from the world of the senses which veils reality: 'no more be seen'. Marina echoes this in a kindred image, searching 'to be gone'. At the end of the tragi-comic quest, there is no affirmation of the value of individual personality but rather the intimation that there exists a form of mutual being, unconfined by self. The seamless mingling of natures is threefold. Pericles' wish to 'melt' into Thaïsa is instantly balanced by his call to her to 'be buried/A second time' in his arms, reversing the Orphic myth by offering a second 'death' even less real than the semblance of the first. Marina completes the enfolding movement of the triad by evoking the deepest themes the play has traced. Her urge to belong to her own source suggests the 'quickening' of the child in the womb. The verb 'Leap', placed in this emphatic position

on the line, evokes the usage of, for instance, the King James
Bible, when it tells of Elisabeth that 'the babe leaped in her
womb' (Luke 1:41) for joy. The commotion of the unborn
child's body within the womb is interpreted by the enclosing
mother as a statement of joy and as an intention to enter the
future. Marina's heart is a testament to the future and a token of
the past. Timelessly, the life she has it in her to give refers itself
back to the one who gave her life. With this 'quickening' of
union, the circular quest of Shakespeare's Eleusinian play
completes itself in the meeting of spring with harvest, and an
icon of man's power to integrate himself with the feminine and
to give birth from his own nature in an all-but-literal way. In
Pericles' 'melting' to Thaïsa, a strange alchemy of dissolution
and spiritual rebirth occurs, like that of the barren king in
Ripley's *Cantilena*:

> By other meanes I cannot enter Heaven:
> And therefore (that I may be borne agen)
> I'le humbled be into my Mother's breast,
> Dissolve to what I was. And therein rest.[41]

THE TEMPLE OF DEMETER HERMION

To write a play about a girl-child raped away across the sea to
her probable death, a bereaved mother whose name is
Hermione, and a setting in Sicily was to make a number of
suggestions to a cultivated Renaissance audience which would
be difficult to avoid. Winter in Sicily would imply a pastoralism
already stained with an emotion more terrible than pathos.
Sicily was the island of Demeter/Ceres: it contained the flower-
filled sanctuary of Enna from which the god of the underworld
removed Kore, the Maiden, leaving its perfection in an eternal
state of violation. Sicily therefore bore the goddess's special
curse, corrosive and bitter. Golding's *Ovid* spells out its effects
most graphically:

But bitterly above the rest she banned Sicilie,
In which the mention of hir losse she plainely did espie.
And therefore there with cruell hand the earing ploughes
     she brake,

And man and beast that tilde the grounde to death in anger
 strake.
She marrde the seede, and eke forbade the fieldes to yeelde their
 frute.
The plenteousnesse of that same Ile of which there went such
 bruit
Through all the world, lay dead: the corne was killed in the
 blade:
Now too much drought, now too much wet did make it for
 to fade.
The starres and blasting windes did hurt, the hungry foules
 did eate
The corne in ground: the Tines and Briars did overgrow the
 Wheate.

(Ovid's Metamorphoses, V. 593–602)[42]

Sicily becomes the object of the corn-goddess's special hate, a
blighted land where fertility is wasted and the rule of natural,
seasonal law shattered. Shakespeare's *The Winter's Tale* is set, of
course, in Sicilia, and its elder heroine is named Hermione. We
have forgotten now that the name of 'Hermione' was
immemorially associated with Demeter, but that knowledge was
easily accessible in the Renaissance, as staple dictionary
information. Hesychius in his *Lexicon* recorded under
*Hermione: Hermione. Kai he Demeter kai he Kore en
Surakousais. Kai polis en Argei. Kai he thugater Menelaou* (Both
Demeter and the Kore according to the Syracusans. And a city
in Argos. And the daughter of Menelaus).[43] In addition, the
name Hermione, and the place Hermion (easily mistaken for
one another) are frequently associated with the goddess
Demeter in authors as universally known as Pausanias, so
voluminously cited in the Renaissance mythographies. A
sanctuary of Demeter stands 'Seawards, on the borders of
Hermionis' (II. xxxiv. 6–7). A statue of Hermione (daughter of
Helen and Menelaus) stands at a place the Delphians call
Omphalus, the Navel of the World (X. vi. 4). Demeter's most
frequent attribute celebrated in these shrines is her role as
Demeter Law-Giver, a role well-recognised by the
mythographers, who saw her as having brought humanity from
nomadic barbarism 'to a civil conversing...to live sociably, to
observe certain lawes and institutions' (*Countesse of Pembrokes
Yvychurch*, p.26a). This association of the goddess with civil law

is germane to Shakespeare's treatment of Hermione as the foundation of 'civil conversing', sociability and the rule of law in *The Winter's Tale*, and also of the political blight on Sicilia once that law of gods and men is broken. Historically, Sicily, home of Theocritus and birthplace of the pastoral dream, had been a centre of political corruption and tyranny exercised by the despot Dionysius II, and known in Shakespeare's time with a particular acuteness and intimacy through Plato's *Letters* recounting his own failed interventions in Sicilian politics, its embarrassing scorn of his teaching that 'Sicily, like other states, should be subject not to the tyranny of men but to the rule of law'.[44]

The Winter's Tale concerns a despot in Sicily; or rather, King Leontes *is* Sicily itself, as the king incorporates the whole body politic. The blighted land expresses its charnel passions in the distemper on his face, the black and inchoate words that break through and from him. 'What means Sicilia?' asks Polixenes, seeing Leontes' inexplicable distraction on his face (I. ii. 146). The whole nether world that lies beneath Sicily comes seething up in the surge of jealous hate that overwhelms Leontes and violates the garden-world of the rule of law. Civilisation itself is personified and arraigned in the form of the noble Hermione at her trial. Justice is condemned by injustice. It is as if we saw the statuesque benefactor of mankind, the goddess herself in her attribute as Demeter Law-Giver, brought before the tribunal of a corrupted human judgment. Grace, reason and nurture are ritually expelled from Sicilia. The stage which should represent the sanctuary of Demeter Hermionis is the exposing prison of mother and maiden. This play is Shakespeare's fullest exploration of the relationship between the Eleusinian myth and the shapes and meanings of human life. At the same time, it is the most human and personal. Its terrible anguish comes home to us through scene after scene of domestic realism, in which the playwright presents the breaking of the most sacred taboos of human life as they relate to women, children and the mother-culture:

> My second joy,
> And first-fruits of my body, from his presence
> I am barr'd, like one infectious. My third comfort
> (Starr'd most unluckily) is from my breast
> (The innocent milk in it most innocent mouth)
> Hal'd out to murder; myself on every post

Proclaim'd a strumpet, with immodest hatred
The child-bed privilege denied, which 'longs
To women of all fashion; lastly, hurried
Here, to this place, i' th' open air, before
I have got strength of limit. Now, my liege,
Tell me what blessings I have here alive,
That I should fear to die?
                    (*The Winter's Tale*, III. ii. 96–108)

Hermione's statement rings with tragic grandeur. Its rigorously controlled anger at the outrages it lists records a virtue which is won, word by word, from extreme human suffering. A sense of majesty, or even divinity, is felt within the speech, but this stems from the power to suffer as a human victim rather than from supernatural status. Shakespeare's Hermione does not gloss over the details of human cruelty from which pure comedy would naturally and decorously turn: visual details such as the breast-milk on the mouth of the suckling girl-baby forcibly weaned before it can hope to live without its mother; the mother's need to be with her boy-child; the exposure of her name to slander and her body in its post-natal weakness to the outdoor trial. Each image connotes rape. But, more humanely than Ceres/Demeter, Hermione who bears some of the goddess' themes, forbears to curse Sicily. More humanly than Pluto/Dis, Leontes' impiety dies at the moment of enlightenment. Sicilia, which curses itself, also atones for itself. Our tears come equally for Hermione and for Leontes. Evil inhabits him; each evil word it speaks through him is also an expression of his torment.

It is because of this deeply human quality of all the characters and their idioms that the mythic dimension extends itself through them to us with such energy and forcefulness. *Pericles* was a dream distanced as pageant, or as tapestry sewn with sequences of emblems, sometimes flawed, naïve and impersonal, its stylisations always declaring themselves through the frame of narrative. *The Winter's Tale* is a dream we belong in and would often like to awaken from: the nightmare of the rising up of the fathers in lethal ire against the mothers. In *A Midsummer Night's Dream* the lovers have mercifully forgotten when they awaken what it was they have dreamt. *The Winter's Tale* allows us to waken as it were with the statue into the wholesome-seeming world of daylight, time and community: 'Music, awake her; strike!/'Tis time...' (V. iii. 98), but does not erase the memory of the disturbances we have dreamed. The story that led the mythic Hermione, who is 'Both Demeter and the Kore according to the Syracusans' (see p. 153 above), from Enna to Eleusis was also charged with an almost human agony of loss, bereavement-pain and violation. It is this shared humanity which paradoxically unifies mythic and personal elements so indissolubly in *The Winter's Tale*. After he had made this synthesis, Shakespeare had no more to say on the subject of the myth that could not be encapsulated in the light bubble of the *Masque of Ceres* in *The Tempest*,[45] where Ceres' hymeneal blessing promises Miranda and Ferdinand *'Earth's increase, foison plenty,/Barns and garners never empty'* (IV. i. 110–1). The soul of the myth is fully played out on the human clay of *The Winter's Tale*, that perfectly cyclical play, leaving only a graceful resonance to follow. The final Act of *The Winter's Tale* may be felt as a religious as well as an artistic and emotional experience. The theatre in which the 'statue' of Hermione comes alive is the theatre of vision, bearing a sense of the sacredness of the drama, its power to project real illumination onto our field of vision, such as animated the world of the Greek plays. From wall to wall the theatre fills with a sense of the numinous, transmitted not only by the awed exclamations of the audience on stage but also by our own unfolding vision of the still figure transformed to motion. Yet even at the resolution of the play, we recollect the death of Mamillius and Antigonus, perceive the ageing of Hermione, the broken life of Leontes, and know that the characters move by the graveside. Time presses them on. Alcestis and Hermione must die again, in time, following Euridyce. Man's open wound is still perfectly visible by the torchlight of Eleusis.

Time delivers the cast-off baby, Perdita, and all the good luck thrown away with her, across the sea to the retrieval of the pastoral clown and shepherd. Here in the fourth Scene of the fourth Act of *The Winter's Tale*, Florizel identifies the grown girl with the fourth month of the year, 'Flora/Peering in April's front' (IV. iv. 2–3), dramatising a great metamorphosis, Ovid's *'Flora vocor quae Chloris eram'*. We call our old natures by a new name; the world shifts out of the shadow of winter and inclines towards the ripening sunlight. The myth of Proserpina

lightly touches the myth of Flora. This fact of experience can be
seen on stage by the audience's own eyes: a girl, garlanded.
Everywhere on the stage there is change, new life, fresh
characters, songs, disguises, jokes, a new generation. A wintry
gentleman is also present like a shadow cast from the old
Leontes into Bohemia, Polixenes tainted with the sins of the
fathers; but to balance him there is the magical, thieving, word-
mongering Autolycus, 'littered under Mercury' (IV. iii. 25), the
infinitely successful escapist and agent of change, the Hermes of
the play. The sense of lightening and quickening is universal. It
is Florizel who calls Perdita by the name of Flora, so that their
names reflect the identity of their natures. They stand at the
centre of the pastoral world like boy-and-girl twins. But behind
their mirroring natures in our memories (though blessedly
outside the scope of their experience) stands the shadow of
Perdita's elder brother, Mamillius, whom the whole power of
the tragi-comic structure cannot retrieve from the grave into
which his father's betrayal of his mother sent him. It is hard to
forget, as the Bohemian boy-'twin' is introduced, the
irreplaceable first boy-child, whose name emblematically
attaches him to the feminine,[46] and specifically to the maternal
function of nursing. It was the loss of Mamillius that 'killed'
Hermione: 'This news is mortal to the queen' (III. ii. 149). The
seven-year-old boy, so tenderly and humorously characterised in
the first half of the play, cannot survive unmothered.
Mamillius is constantly shown to us as being his father's
image, to the life. In denying this, Leontes denies his own
essential, life-giving relationship to the feminine, and the boy
dies, fixed in memory as a futureless child. Mamillius presents
an image of Leontes' own unfallen self, the innocent boyhood he
can never re-experience:

> Looking on the lines
> Of my boy's face, methoughts I did recoil
> Twenty-three years, and saw myself unbreech'd
> In my green velvet coat; my dagger muzzl'd
> Lest it should bite its master...
>
> (I. ii. 153–7)

This is actually a fabrication, to cover the fact that Leontes has
been sourly brooding on his son's possible illegitimacy. And yet

Leontes knows very well the boy is his own. The poetry
beautifully suggests the activation of memory so that the very
senses are alive with it: the rub of the velvet on childish fingers,
his eyes' pride in its familiar brilliant green colour. But the green
and pastoral boy is also armed with the miniature dagger,
symbol of the male potency and aggression, dangerous to
himself. Leontes has loved Mamillius with tenderness and
passion: 'this kernel,/ This squash, this gentleman' (159–60), but
by the end of Act 3 Leontes has metaphorically used the dagger
and the boy is dead. *The Winter's Tale* contains that grave; it
remains a tale of winter, Mamillius's tale. Even at the play's
most joyous and elastic moments, its events are rooted in his
grave.

Thus Perdita, in the lyrical flower-catalogue invariably cited
as the play's chief link to the Demeter/Ceres myth,[47] seems to
intuit a premature death to convert into elegiac music:

> O Proserpina,
> For the flowers now that, frighted, thou let'st fall
> From Dis' waggon! daffodils
> That come before the swallow dares, and take
> The winds of March with beauty; violets, dim,
> But sweeter than the lids of Juno's eyes
> Or Cytherea's breath; pale primroses
> That die unmarried, ere they can behold
> Bright Phoebus in his strength (a malady
> Most incident to maids); bold oxlips and
> The crown imperial; lilies of all kinds,
> The flower-de-luce being one. O, these I lack,
> To make you garlands of; and my sweet friend,
> To strew him o'er and o'er!
> *Flo.*   What, like a corpse?
> *Per.*   No, like a bank, for love to lie and play on:
> Not like a corpse; of if—not to be buried,
> But quick, and in mine arms.
>   (IV. iv. 116–32)

Perdita invokes Proserpina as if she were a sister or familiar
friend. Her pastoral elegy is full of the colour of those flowers
traditionally associated with Proserpina, 'Violets blew, or Lillies
white as Lime' (Golding's *Ovid*, V. 492) and the Golden Age
yellow of daffodils, together with a sense of their transience. She

lets us see the shaken expression on the face of Proserpina 'Frighted', as she looses her hold on the flowers which fall as testimonial to her rape and epitaph on her loss. The primroses are 'pale', like timid faces that cannot confront the sun-god. Before the masculine principle, the vulnerable flowers fail, speaking of Proserpina's long detention in the underworld. Other flowers display Perdita's own strength and perseverance: daffodils that easily take the March gales; the upstanding oxlips; the 'flower-de-luce' containing *lux*, light.

But spring is long past in the sheep-shearing scene. Perdita 'lacks' such flowers as she lists to 'strew' Florizel 'o'er and o'er'. His bantering query, however, might well evoke the abbreviated life of Mamillius, who, unlike Perdita, did not survive the hazards of the winter solstice to encounter those of spring and summer: 'What, like a corpse?' It is like stepping over a grave, swiftly. 'No, like a bank' Perdita replies, imagining a raised mound where the lovers may lie together. But the continuing presence of elegiac implications in her own imagery makes her grammar swerve to try to avoid them, playfully, then triumphantly, and yet for a reader painfully too: 'or if—not to be buried,/ But quick, and in my arms.' 'Quick' means, simply, 'alive'; and then it connotes haste, her passion's delighted urgency; and, finally, the 'quick' life of the unborn child moving in the body of the mother. Perdita's self-identification with Mother Earth cannot avoid the darker meaning of death. The 'bank' as a bed of love, strewn with flowers, is still a mound, and the mound resembles a grave. The recollection of winter is clear.

The play is called *The Winter's Tale*. Only Mamillius really knows that tale, and only his mother is privileged to hear it:

> *Hermione.*   tell's a tale.
> *Mam.*   Merry or sad shall't be?
> *Her.* As merry as you will.
> *Mam.* A sad tale' best for winter: I have one
> Of sprites and goblins.
> *Her.*   Let's have that, good sir.
> Come on, sit down: come on, and do your best
> To fright me with your sprites; you're powerful at it.
> *Mam.* There was a man,—
> *Her.*   Nay, come sit down: then on.

Mam. Dwelt by a churchyard. I will tell it softly;
Yond crickets shall not hear it.

(II. i. 23–31)

With gravity and application he begins to whisper his story into
his mother's ear. Her smiling indulgence tells of the
impossibility of her son's 'frighting' her with mere stories. To
the semblances in a story she will reply with the semblance of a
shiver. The tale serves as an occasion to unite mother and son,
whose high spirits have been exhausting to her. The Scene is full
of private laughter. She challenges him: 'Come on...come on'.
As Mamillius launches into his story, she promptly refuses to
listen until he is settled with her: 'Nay, come sit down; then on.'
The nursery scene is not so much idyllic as precisely observed.
We smile because of a sense that the public stage has for that
moment become the inner, private and domestic world of the
household, where in one sense not very much happens, but in
another sense everything happens. Art happens; a story is made
up; the bonds of love are tested minute-by-minute by rampant
childhood, tired adulthood, and the gentle bonds hold. The
inner and feminine world declares itself in snatches of simple,
apparently insignificant conversation. The talk seems to come
from the very basis of life itself: a dimension which is a universal
continuum, in the absence of which the universe would fall
apart. The Platonist image of Love as the force which, in
Spenser's *Hymne in Honour of Love*, links the universe together
'with Adamantine chaines' (89) and in Dante's *Paradiso* 'moves
the sun and the other stars' (XXXIII. 145) is located by
Shakespeare in nothing more elevated than the interior of a
human dwelling within which mother and child communicate a
pure, original language in words of one syllable, salted by
humour, face open to answering face. One of the Greek
meanings of Hermione's name is the equivalent of 'Grace', and
it is the language of Grace which we overhear in this intimate
scene between Hermione and Mamillius. Their tender and
humorous playing with words is the language belonging to a
serious game. But Hermione's gracious sense of humour is fatal
to her. Leontes becomes unable to follow the drift of her playful
wit. His language falls into the condition of nonsense: 'Go play,
boy, play; thy mother plays, and I/Play too' (I. ii. 187–8). The

fourfold repetition beats any original meaning out of the word: in the dialect of Leontes' fantasy, the serious games played between friends or within families, holding society together, distort to adulterous couplings played for pleasure only. In his fallen vocabulary, the idea of privacy is degraded to secrecy; liberty to libertinism; word-play to lying. Meanwhile, the private world of free and cheerful mutual speaking runs quietly on. Hermione expresses her love to her son, Mamillius offers his story to his mother. Looking into this privacy, we see clearly that this is Spenser's Love with magnetic chains, Dante's prime and continous mover of the universe upon its axis. The room in which mother and child are in touch with one another is the playroom on which all human action depends. Leontes therefore strikes—like Pluto on Persephone—at the root of civilisation itself, incurring 'a year/most dreadful and harsh for men; no seed' (*Homeric Hymn to Demeter*, 305–6) in the blight of his sixteen-year penance of childless loneliness. In discrediting and desecrating the creative feminine principle, Sicilia's crime is directed against the balanced arrangement of the cosmos itself. The room where mother and child play and speak resembles the unselfconscious garden-world of Enna, the theatre of inwardness. Its violation makes necessary the artistic fabrication of the play's equivalent of the temple at Eleusis in the final Act.

The abridgement of Mamillius' story casts a shadow forward over the entire remainder of the play. Nothing cancels it. Though Florizel becomes the adoptive male heir, there can be no complete substitution. The tragi-comic solution is both sweet and bitter. Even when Perdita returns to the court of her father in Act 5, she brings a vestige of her 'burial' with her, like spring shoots bearing traces of soil. A servant describes her to Leontes as 'the most peerless piece of earth, I think,/That e'er the sun shone bright on' (V. i. 93–4). Though the image of the sun evokes Apollo, oracular truth, spring awakening, the identification of Perdita with a 'piece of earth', however peerless, looks downwards to a source in dust that must return to dust. Illumination of human earth by sunlight can only be transitory; when the sun declines, the luminous clay cools and darkens. The mystery of Leontes' illumination by the delivered girl Perdita comes to us with the aroma of the grave still clinging around it. Paulina's remark about the age of Leontes' lost son when he is introduced to Florizel helps to emphasise the lasting pain of the wound the play evidences:

> *Paul.*   Had our prince
>   (Jewel of children) seen this hour, he had pair'd
>   Well with this lord: there was not full a month
>   Between their births.
> *Leon.*   Prithee, no more; cease; thou know'st
>   He dies to me again when talk'd of...
>
>   (V. i. 115–19)

Astrologically, Florizel and Mamillius are twinned: their signs are identified, like those of the childhood friends, Polixenes and Leontes, who were 'as twinn'd lambs that did frisk i' th' sun,/And bleat the one at th' other' (I. ii. 67–8). The tragi-comedy insists on the actuality of these separations and losses. Mamillius still dies recurrently in Leontes' mind in the fifth Act, as if cyclically: he goes over it again and again. The cyclical structure which is so comforting within the play is also seen to describe the circling of pain. At the culmination of the play, when the major mystery is revealed—the 'statue' of Hermione coming to life and moving to join her husband and daughter—this harrowing insistence on realism is not set aside. Leontes' joy at the return of Hermione is perceived as close to madness: it is *ekstasis* (V. iii. 72–3), affliction, shock. Its experience is close to that of grief, indistinguishable from its own opposite. The watchers of the mystery turn to stone (42); they seem to die while the apparently insentient and inanimate stone of the statue, warm and breathing, comes out of its veil. The dimensions cross, through the magic of the playwright's art. Mother and daughter are reunited, and with the fulfilment of the Eleusinian structure, the deaths of Mamillius and Antigonus are consigned to a completed past.

Shakespeare's classicism and his truthfulness to life are equally more authentically complex and dark than in *Pericles*. The tragi-comedy here is profoundly close to the atmosphere of Greek drama, and tragedy stemming from the rituals of the Dionysian orgiasts, whose solutions are based on a required blood-sacrifice, a sense of the terrible and incomprehensible workings of Fate, or (as in the parallel play, *Alcestis*, with its theme of the atoning

wife returned ceremoniously from the dead) an unnerving
knowledge of the smallnesses and defectiveness latent in human
nature.[48] Shakespeare's interpretation of the Ceres story in *The
Winter's Tale* insists on that area of experience which is filled
with the sensation of meaningless and inexplicable darkness, a
recognition intrinsic to the atmosphere of the original myth.
The play requires blood-sacrifice as a premise. Marinell/Adonis
weeps his blood into the earth of the pastoral Book of *The Faerie
Queene*. Antigonus and Mamillius are blood-sacrifices essential
to the completion of the 'happy' story of the pastoral *Winter's
Tale*. Demeter, like her fellow olympian mother-goddesses, was
never viewed as omnipotent. Hermione cannot staunch the
blood-flow of *The Winter's Tale*, and she resembles in this the
goddess herself, venerated for her struggle, search, power to love
and the consequent immortal power to suffer. Shakespeare's
feminine humanism shows most deeply here. The goddess is
venerated for her illimitable humanity, which it is possible for
mortals at their ripest to emulate. The Hermetic 'man the
miracle' and Pico's 'man the god' become in this late, strange
Shakespearean revival of humanism, woman the miracle,
woman the goddess, without jeopardising the validity of that
more Jacobean perception of the terrible 'absence, darkness,
death; things which are not' (Donne, *Nocturnall upon S. Lucies
Day*, 18) in the classicist vision. In *The Winter's Tale* our
ultimate sense of the high value of what can be recovered and
understood in human life comes into being because we are given
a scale of joy and pain which reaches far into the underworld of
perception of that which can never be rediscovered, palliated,
made sense of. Apollo's oracle is the core of the play, standing
for self-knowledge, reason, harmony, poetry, international law,
the divine sanity. Apollo is represented to us as real and
powerful. But in killing Mamillius and Antigonus, Shakespeare's play recognises the close intrinsic link between the
apparently opposite Apollonian and Dionysian religious cults
which was such a major feature of Greek religion, recognised by
Renaissance scholars and mythographers, but puzzling and
unsettling to Christian minds like Milton's which did their
utmost to sever the links between the rigour of Apollo and
Orpheus and the dissipation of the Bacchic. In Greek shrines,
Apollo's image tolerantly shares room with Dionysos. In Greek

religion, the procession of Bacchanals preludes the pilgrimage to
Eleusis.[49] Orpheus and Bacchus are mutually necessary. In
Shakespeare's *Winter's Tale* Antigonus is sacrificed. His fate is
remembered explicitly in the fifth Act: 'He was torn to pieces
by a bear' (V. ii. 64) explains one of the narrative Gentlemen
who mediate news of the recognition scene between Leontes and
his daughter. This is Dionysiac in its insistence. Antigonus has
been dismembered, mutilated and eaten, as a sacrifice to
whatever irrational powers inhabit the universe of the story.
The issue of Antigonus has been endlessly argued over as being
indecorous or problematic. But its macabre, absurd and terrible
detail is deeply proper to the classical frame of reference which
structures *The Winter's Tale*. As the Maenadic women tore the
sacrificial animal limb from limb and ate him raw—as they
feasted on poor Pentheus in Euripides' *Bacchae*—so 'mother
nature' in ursine form devours in Shakespeare's play that
enlightened and Hermetic messenger between worlds,
Antigonus. Linked at many points to the mythology of Eleusis,
the Dionysian cult represented a ritual killing, eating and then a
rebirth of the sacred child: carnage begets a divine birth.[50] Thus
the bizarre stage direction, amiably brief, '*Exit, pursued by a
bear*'. Antigonus has only time to set the sacred baby Perdita
down on the shore of Bohemia: 'Blossom, speed thee well!' (III.
iii. 46) when his statement that his 'heart bleeds' is ironically
followed up by storm, shipwreck and the bear's feast which is
narrated by the clown in a grisly manner. The audience laughs;
the tragic subject matter dissolves through lurid humour into a
comedy that will calm and compose into the gentle but always
threatened pastoral of Act 4. Antigonus *is* the transition from
tragedy to tragi-comedy. The bear's meal makes it possible for
the shepherd to speak the beautiful sentence upon which the
balance of the play is poised: 'Now bless thyself: thou met'st
with things dying, I with things new-born' (III. iii. 112–13). It is
as if Antigonus takes upon himself the curse (52) which must
expiate the sins of the fathers. His blood atones for his
generation, his tribe and his gender. One of the sanest and the
kindest dies, a coherent soul torn limb from limb by animal
nature. The event takes place upon the shoreline between
worlds, between genres, between grave and cradle, wild grief and
hysterical laughter. Beside the sea, which is at once destroyer and

creatrix, identity is for a moment lost where 'savage clamour' (56)—preluding Milton's use of exactly the same phrase in the elegy for Orpheus (*Paradise Lost*, VII. 36)—makes inaudible the harmonious and healing music of art.

In the final Act, the eyesight of Leontes and his court is washed clean; their natures are transfigured with ours as the hoarded secrets of time are unsealed. But the 'precious self' of the 'sacred lady', Hermione (V. iii. 79, 76) is wrinkled with time, Leontes can no longer hope for a condition approximate to that of 'boy eternal', and the final line speaks of the mutilation caused to the continuum of time 'since first/We were dissevered' (V. iii. 155). Our entrance into the Temple of Demeter Hermionis and the initiating vision of a holy art has been obtained at the price of the death of 'our prince/(Jewel of children)' and our knowledge of the Cain-like imputation with which the father-king's laws and institutions are branded, from generation to generation.

WOMAN AS MAGUS

The learned Egyptians, Hermes Trismegistus informs his pupil in the *Asclepius*, were magi who knew and practised the occult art of raising the statues of gods to life, fashioning them as 'statues living and conscious, filled with the breath of life, and doing many mighty works'. '*Statuas dicis, o Asclepi?*' parrots the more than usually stunned disciple as he tries to digest this new revelation. '*Statuas, o Asclepi*' (III. 24a) repeats the master witheringly, and comments unfavourably at the young person's incapacity to credit such simple utterances as if they should be hooted at, like an old tale. 'Yes, Asclepius. See how even you give way to doubt! I mean statues'. The Egyptian conjuring into life of statues was, as Riemer notes in his profound and enlightening *Antic Fables*, 'the single most notable and significant anecdote to have emerged from the Renaissance Platonists' fascination with Hermetic writings'; [51] he authoritatively links the raising of Hermione with this source. Her very name (Herm-ione) might have given this clue long ago, but so great has been the prejudice against the idea of Shakespeare as possessing learning ('small Latin and less Greek') that even Riemer has to apologise for attributing to Shakespeare a Hermetic knowledge which in fact the dramatist would have had to be blind, deaf and ignorant to avoid gleaning, given his place in the artistic circles of his period. Very little needs to be added to Riemer's chapter proving that Paulina, like Prospero, 'speaks as a Magus'[52] when she raises Hermione, for his arguments are documented and conclusive. But certain questions, not raised by Riemer, must follow in the light of the present study, from the fact that Shakespeare's art conjures up the unprecedented figure of the woman magus (Paul converts to Paulina), and connects her and her art with the female mythology of Eleusis. We need to enquire into the nature of this female magic that is claimed by Paulina as being so very legitimate, nothing to do with witchcraft: 'her actions shall be holy as/You hear my spell is lawful' (*The Winter's Tale*, V. iii. 95–6). What 'statues' do women have the power to raise to life, and how 'real' and 'natural' is their creative art? What kind of magic can we imagine as being, in Leontes' telling phrase, 'an art/Lawful as eating' (110–11)? With Leontes, in the statue scene, we want and need to know 'What fine chisel/Could ever yet cut breath?' (78–9). The play debates, and audiences and readers have endlessly discussed, the play's treatment of the ambiguous relationship between art and the life it imitates, which *The Winter's Tale* sets up through the reversed metaphor of life imitating art, '*Hermione standing like a statue*' (21). The discussion is infinite and insoluble, a serious game with words, if we consider it only in the terms of male art and male life, and conversation in these terms is of course both appropriate and delightful. But if we add the possibility of translating the question into the opposite gender, a source of self-complete meaning becomes available. In life there is one artistic process, and only one, which fulfils all the metaphorical requirements of the raising of the statue: birth itself, the whitest magic.

Perdita in Act 4 reflected upon the existence of an art which 'shares/ With great creating nature' (iv. 87–8), but neither she nor her mother set forth that art in a public way: that role is left to Paulina. We may think of Hermione-Perdita-Paulina as a triad, with Paulina as the connecting, intermediate agent, parallel to the Eleusinian triad of goddesses, Demeter-Persephone-Hecate, who are really aspects of the one deity. In the myth, the Hecate persona takes on the function of midwife, crucial to the fulfilment of the circle of loss and deliverance.[53] In the play, Paulina is a central and little-understood figure who follows Lychorida in *Pericles* in acting as a midwife figure who both delivers the child and mediates between male and female figures; but whereas Lychorida was not fully imagined and was dispensable in the earlier play, Paulina is needed as a vital character throughout *The Winter's Tale* in the world of Sicilia. The occult art she exercises in Act 5 is connected both with her role as Hecate and as Hermetic magus. She is therefore very unlike the 'master-illusionist' Prospero (Riemer, p.215) in her function as magus. Prospero operates the human actors upon his island as if he directed a masque, diverting them to rectitude, but conscious of age and tired both of himself and his craft ('the baseless fabric of this vision...this insubstantial pageant' [IV. i. 151, 155]). He may play with the astral influences and tap the *spiritus* in *materia* in his conjurings, but those influences pour through Paulina into the material world. Through her agency *spiritus* becomes visible, and the watchers are changed to *illuminati*. There is no need for her to renounce this magic at the play's end, for it has been seen to be a magic both awe-inspiringly holy and entirely natural. Paulina channels into the play the element of the holy which, despite Colin Still's ingenuity in ascribing it to *The Tempest* as 'Shakespeare's Mystery Play',[54] is not conjured into being by Prospero's lonely rod of power. Paulina is herself an aspect of the art she practises, as magus, as Hecate, but most of all as woman. The complexities of myth and learning which Shakespeare calls upon in this play net the simplicity of primal experience, a magic ordinary as eating, universal as birth and miraculous as both.

The name Paulina, so intimately associated with Grace in *The Winter's Tale*, inevitably alludes to that of St Paul. In *Pericles* the hero's journey may be traced to many of the places where the Apostle carried the saving gospel of Christ's Grace—Tarsus, Antioch, Ephesus, Mytilene. The Grace which Shakespeare celebrates in the Last Plays is both Christian and Pauline in origin, but it assimilates rather than denies the ancient Hellenic deities which were the objects of the great iconoclast's assault. In the *Acts* we are told of the social confusion which struck Ephesus when Paul delivered the Holy Ghost's power to 'speak with tongues' to the Ephesians upon whom he laid hands (19:6), performed exorcism (19:12), and caused the followers of the old matriarchal faith to burn their sacred books of 'curious arts' (19:19). Ephesus was Diana's city, an ancient and opulent shrine famous for its statue of the many-breasted goddess and for the atmosphere of magic and delusive craft which Shakespeare would exploit in his *Comedy of Errors*. In Ephesus Paul causes riot, and the mother-religion reasserts itself in the mob cry of 'Great is Diana of the Ephesians' (Acts 19:28, 34). Paul departs for Macedonia from this place of materialistic, sexually worrying self-delusion. The Last Plays of Shakespeare are committed to that unearnable Grace concerning which St Paul wrote to the Ephesians that 'unto every one of us is given grace according to the measure of the gift of Christ' (Ephesians 4:7). But in their humanistic syncretism these plays also seem to join with the artists of Ephesus in their great cry, *Megale he Artemis Ephesion*,[55] for in *Pericles*, in defiance of Paul, Shakespeare presents Diana and her city as a place of holy sanctuary in which the good may be maintained and revealed, and benevolent white magic worked (Cerimon is Ephesian). Shakespeare, like the iconographers,[56] reclaims the feminine as an essential component of Grace. He does so most fully in the person of Hermione, and through the agency of Paulina.

Clues to Paulina's significance are to be found in Act 2, when Leontes slanders her as a 'crone' (iii. 76), a 'gross hag' (107), and upbraids Antigonus with being 'woman-tired' (74), effeminately under Paulina's thumb and unable to control her ungoverned tongue (109):

Leon.   Will you not push her out? Give her the bastard,
          Though dotard! thou art woman-tir'd, unroosted
          By thy dame Partlet here. Take up the bastard,
          Take't up, I say; give 't to thy crone.
          (*The Winter's Tale*, II. iii. 73–6)

These repeated allusions to Paulina as 'witch', 'hag', 'crone' all confirm Leontes' personifications of Paulina as a Hecate-figure who, in speaking so voluminously on behalf of his wife and of all women, is associated with the malign and destructive powers he imputes to woman. Hecate, who had presided over the witches on stage in *Macbeth*, is conventionally symbolised by the figure of an old woman or crone. In *Macbeth* she is closely connected, subliminally, with Lady Macbeth's imagery of infanticide:

> I have given suck, and know
> How tender 'tis to love the babe that milks me:
> I would, while it was smiling in my face,
> Have pluck'd my nipple from his boneless gums,
> And dash'd the brains out, had I so sworn
> As you have done to this.
>
> (*Macbeth*, I. vii. 54–9)

This is a projection of man's fear of woman's power and his own unprotected vulnerability and dependence, as a form of black magic.[57] In order to understand the character of the white magic attributed to Paulina in the later play, it is elucidating to touch on Shakespeare's earlier formulation of the Hecatean black magic in *Macbeth*, which obscenely links the bearded hags on the heath stirring the lust for power in the seething cauldron of Macbeth's mind, in profound though unstated correspondence with Lady Macbeth's poisoning of the milk of human kindness in her husband. Here is the dark side of the female image, the moon beneath the horizon, originating in the remembered helplessness of babyhood dependent on the all-powerful, hunger-filling love of a mother who may offer or abstain from offering the means of life; who lifts the infant to soar through vertiginous heights and leans it back as if to drop in infinite space, impressing it with the fear of having its brains 'dashed out'. More specifically, *Macbeth* works through the male experience of his continuing bond with the feminine as a condition of dependency, threatening to his autonomy. Lady Macbeth is a personification of the 'witch' perceived in the mother. Yet she is always much more than this: elegiac pathos is associated with her blackest utterance. The lilting cadence of 'How tender 'tis', with its suggestion of a sigh, testifies to her remembrance of the perfection of the first love-bond. The 'boneless gums' of the baby are both a realistically observed detail and witness to a Golden Age before we grew our teeth, tore at our meat, and ground them at our losses; the 'smile' on the infant face again realistically calls up an image of the steady, unembarrassed gaze of the child studying the world in the microcosm of the mother's face. This recognition of the mystery and privacy of the maternal role is then violently challenged by the 'witch' aspect of the mother. She is willing to beat the brains out of the soft skull before its fontanelles close over. Symbolically, the speech is a threat and a challenge to Macbeth: he himself is the unweaned baby in his dependency. To prove himself a man he paradoxically severs himself from the feminine within his own nature, the sacred taboo of pity and trust.

In the Last Plays, the Hecate-figure as a dark homicide is still present (in the minor personages of Dionyza in *Pericles*, the Queen in *Cymbeline*, Sycorax in *The Tempest*), but she is a wraith of her former self. Her reign of terror is purged, as the honour of the feminine in each of her phases is affirmed. The plays' new classicism reaches back to the purer image which in Greece saw the goddess Hecate as an integral part of the cosmic adjustment of upper, middle and nether worlds, 'Lovely Hecate of the roads and crossroads' (*Orphic Hymn to Hecate*, 1), whose voice may not be the most comfortable or beguiling, but who is messenger and fellow-searcher with the goddess, and who finally joins and completes the reunited maiden and mother:

> an end to sorrow came for their hearts,
> as they took joys from each other and gave in return.
> Hecate of the shining headband came near them
> and many times lovingly touched the daughter of pure Demeter.
> From then on this lady became her attendant and follower.
> (*Homeric Hymn to Demeter*, 436–40)

In *The Winter's Tale* Paulina is Hermione's attendant; she is her shadow, her voice, her devoted follower. Only to the unseeing Leontes is Paulina a 'mankind witch' (II. iii. 68) though (because the possibility of comedy is never perfectly absent from this most moving of plays) we do see, or rather hear, what he means. Her raucous irruptions onto the stage with a view to shouting Leontes into a change of mind contain, of course, the ingredients of a stock comic situation, and are approached thus, with the hen-pecked Antigonus acknowledging his humiliated role by colluding in the joke against himself:

Leon.   A gross hag!
And, lozel, thou art worthy to be hang'd,
That wilt not stay her tongue.
Ant: Hang all the husbands
That cannot do that feat, you'll leave yourself
Hardly one subject.

(*The Winter's Tale*, II. iii. 107–11)

This comic function is in itself of primary importance in reconciling the tragic and comic elements of the plot, for Paulina with her noise on the stage incessantly harrying Leontes, with her counterpart Antigonus so cruelly eaten, draw together the play's generic tensions. They are messengers, crossing thresholds whether physically or metaphorically, enabling transition to occur, and in Paulina's case acting as priestess, fating power and stage-director. As 'shrew' she invites derision; as the haranguing voice of a conscience that will not be listened to, and whose spirit cannot be cowed, she claims our respect. Justice speaks through her, as personified in Hermione and linked indissolubly with Demeter. (Julian the Apostate, for instance, in his *Hymn to the Mother of the Gods*, himself an initiate, makes a point of associating the cult with the sign of Libra, the Scales of Justice).[58] She is the intermediate figure, the 'crone' who fords with Leontes the great gap of time between the generations and between Acts 3 and 4. As Hecate is often conflated with Death, Vengeance, the Erinyes,[59] so Paulina accompanies the penitent king into his future as a Fate. In the latter phase of action, she provides the initiate with the means of final enlightenment. Hag-ridden by her furious tongue, Leontes quails before her bitter eloquence as soon as he recognises his crime. Ironically, he takes the place of the absent Antigonus, whom he had mocked as emasculated, by welcoming the storm of her words as an expression of justice. In a Spenserian inversion of the patriarchal norm, Shakespeare's analysis of justice implies the pre-eminence and sanctity of female law, expressed in the mother-tongue, the language of Grace. Leontes' foul-mouthed blasphemies change, suddenly, to the quieter cadences of Grace, associated with the 'dead' Hermione ('Sir,/You speak a language that I understand not' [III. ii. 80–3]):

Paul.   A thousand knees
Ten thousand years together, naked, fasting,
Upon a barren mountain, and still winter
In storm perpetual, could not move the gods
To look that way thou wert.
Leon.   Go on, go on:
Thou canst not speak too much; I have deserv'd
All tongues to talk their bitt'rest.
                                        (III. ii. 210–16)

In Paulina's rejection at this bitter moment of the possibility of
atonement or Grace, the gods like statues avert their stone-cold
eyes from the suppliant, in unqualified indifference. As such, she
is the instrument of vengeance, Hecate as punitive Fate. Yet
Leontes' reply reveals a voluntary movement on his part
towards Grace: 'Go on, go on', and, as the scene closes, he
chooses Paulina as his guide: 'Come, and lead me/To these
sorrows' (242–3). This has a Sophoclean feeling, expressing the
repose of spirit achieved by classical tragedy, and Leontes seems
kin to the blind Oedipus led by Antigone on his journey to
Colonus: 'Lead me, my child. Take care of the blind old man'
(*Oedipus at Colonus*, line 21)[60] with the gods' promise of an
eventual sanctuary along the Sacred Road of suffering. Paulina
guides the wanderer through the land of the dead to a
destination in his sacred homeland of Sicily.

This destination is the 'chapel' (V. iii. 86) in which,
transformed to magus or priestess, Paulina practises her art of
raising the statue to life. A great synthesis is enacted of
Christian, Hermetic and Eleusinian elements. *The Winter's Tale*
is, in the end, sacred art, which takes the impossible on trust and
the ridiculous in earnest: *credo quia impossibile est*. Platonically,
from the world of the senses, in its most 'unreal' form as Art
(*Republic*, 598–9) the truest art being 'the most feigning'
(Sidney, *Apology*, pp. 123–4), she conjures the Real to manifest
itself and supplies to the incredulous audience the means of
believing in it. Dramatically, Paulina as magus retards the
process of revelation: the release of the spirit into the 'statue' is
conducted in a ceremonious sequence of phases, so that Leontes
has to be held back from touching and kissing Hermione until
the moment is perfect to do so. This suspense is real for the

audience too, from whom the secret of Hermione's survival has been faithfully kept:

> *Paul.*   Music, awake her; strike!   [Music]
> 'Tis time; descend; be stone no more; approach;
> Strike all that look upon with marvel. Come!
> I'll fill your grave up: stir, nay, come away:
> Bequeath to death your numbness; for from him
> Dear life redeems you. You perceive she stirs:
>   [*Hermione comes down*]
> Start not; her actions shall be holy as
> You hear my spell is lawful. [*To Leontes*] Do not shun her
> Until you see her die again; for then
> You kill her double...
>
> . . . .
>
> *Leon.*   O, she's warm!
> If this be magic, let it be an art
> Lawful as eating.
>
> (V. iii. 98–107, 109–11)

Paulina's utterances take the form of ordered commandments, drawing the vital life equally into Hermione and Leontes. The 'statue' seems to be reluctant to stir, as if Hermione's life really were in some tranced state midway between the living and the dead; Leontes is motionless as stone in his shock. The direction *Music* as the primary agent of revival implies that Paulina's magic is Orphic, as does the reference to a double death, which remembers Orpheus' tragic defect of faith and his double loss of Euridyce. The pauses between the phrases of her incantation direct attention to the power that is in words: for all concerned, both outer audience (ourselves) and inner (the participants) these are moments tinged with fear. The movement she directs is towards unity, both of husband and wife, and of youth, maturity and age. Hermione, who was 'tender/As infancy' is perceived by Leontes as 'wrinkled' with age (26–27, 28). The feminine Orphic and Hermetic magic insists on the reconciliation of human nature with natural reality—the fact that the process of time's circling does not return anyone to the self-same place, but perpetually moves us on to take one another's place. This is the sadness at the heart of the Eleusinian myth, but it is a reconciled sadness. Perdita/Persephone and

Hermione/Demeter become one with one another only in the autumn of the year, as the world is turning towards another winter. When Leontes welcomes Hermione into his arms, he takes his harvest to himself in a poetry that gestures towards the theme of nature's abundance and man's lawful harvesting of the crop, when he prays that such a magic may be 'Lawful as eating'. The active emotional participation of Polixenes and Camillo is also essential to us in understanding the communal nature of the vision ('She embraces him!' 'She hangs about his neck!' [111–12]). The 'Lawful eating' of a sacred meal is a crucial component of religious ritual: the Dionysian wine, the Eleusinian wheat, the Christian communion. At Eleusis the onlookers were also participants who saw the *phasmata*, the materialised person of Persephone: they took into themselves the blessedness generated by the humane deity. Polixenes and Camillo feel the reflected warmth of Leontes' beatitude, and radiate out to the furthest regions of the audience a joy that is not simply personal but general and communal.

The beginning of the story had shown a mother late in pregnancy, had involved the birth of a girl-baby and the death of that mother's only boy, Mamillius. The controlling symbolism concerns pregnancy, childbirth and nurture. The play ends with an act of white magic, through which a woman-magus celebrates the greatest good humanity can know, the power of genesis. The learned Egyptians, by questionable means, claimed power to raise the statues of their gods to life. Woman by a more natural magic gives life and value to the dormant universe of the unknown world by the creation of a child; the miracle-working 'art/Lawful as eating' is the white milk of nurture. Mamillius and Perdita in the course of the play are both lost to this nurture, Mamillius irrecoverably. Paulina's partially successful version of the generative white magic stretches as far as is humanly possible to the recovery of the lost feminine across 'this wide gap of time, since first/We were dissever'd' (154–5).

4

Milton

DEBORAH

Milton, notorious as one of the great misogynists of our literature, had one son. His name was John Milton. The boy died before he reached one year of age. Milton's first wife, Mary Powell, had blessed him only with girl-children, which his nephew, John Phillips, narrates thus in his memoir: 'His first Wife dy'd a while after his blindness seized him, leaving him three Daughters, that liv'd to bee Women'.[1] Blindness and daughters became related problems for Milton. His other nephew, Edward Phillips, told of how the poet 'supplied his want of Eye-sight by their Eyes and Tongue',[2] forcing the two younger daughters, Mary and Deborah, to read to him in a variety of languages, 'Viz. The *Hebrew* (and I think the *Syriac*), the *Greek*, the *Latin*, the *Italian*, *Spanish* and *French*'. Such a task might have seemed less intolerable had the daughters concerned been educated in these languages so as to understand what they were required to pronounce, but Milton—or 'Fate', as the sympathetic but judicious Phillips delicately puts it[3]—had refrained from passing on to Mary and Deborah any learning at all. To be fated to read in incomprehensible Syrian for hours on end might gall the most pliant of daughters, and Milton, being by nature irascible, was not likely to beget children of a mild disposition. Phillips tells of how they endured this confusion of tongues for a remarkably long period:

> yet the irksomeness of this imployment could not always be concealed, but broke out more and more into expressions of uneasiness; so that at length they were all (even the Eldest also) sent out to learn some Curious and Ingenious sorts of Manufacture, that

are proper for Women to learn, particularly Imbroideries in Gold or
Silver.

(Edward Phillips, pp. 77–8)

The exemption of the eldest from linguistic duties is a reference
to the fact that Anne was retarded and suffered from a speech
impediment. At his death Milton's will left everything to his
third wife and nothing to his daughters. They disputed the will
and spoke of him with hostility and bitterness—except
Deborah, whose later recorded comments were friendly.

Lovers of Milton have made frequent attempts to defend him
against the charge of unkindness to daughters, whether on the
grounds that the individuals concerned were termagants who
deserved no better, by questioning the authority of the accounts
of their sufferings, or by reinterpreting the tone of voice of
Milton's recorded remarks to or about them.[4] Thus his repeated
taunt '*One Tongue is enough for a Woman!*', referring to the
daughters' lack of enthusiasm for the Hebrew and Syrian
languages is read by apologists not as a slight but as a family
joke, intended to smooth ruffled tempers rather than to cause
aggravation. If we try to say the phrase in a light-hearted and
affectionate tone, prefaced perhaps by a forgiving 'After all ...',
it may be just possible to imagine such a remark as not unkindly
meant. But it is hard for a reader acquainted with Milton's
prose-works to conceive that the vein of savage sarcasm with
which Milton scathed the public world, and to which John
Aubrey testifies as a feature of his social behaviour ('Extreme
pleasant in his conversation, & at dinner, supper &c: but
Satyricall')[5] would have been restrained by the continence of
fatherhood. As their royalist mother, Mary Powell, had seemed
to challenge all his allegiances, humiliating and degrading him as
Dalila to his Samson, Eve to his Adam, so her daughters
sabotaged the patriarchal order of the autocratic republican's
home, from within. The Christian Homer's sacred duty was to
express the will of God on the printed page, though not granted
the eyes with which to do so, nor a free, just and appreciative
commonwealth in which to pursue this aim. Those frustrations
which he regarded as God-given he bore as a divine stigma,
lamenting but not cursing his blindness. Frustration in the
person of the human female was protected by no divine taboo.

His major characters feel free to censure and curse woman as an allowable scapegoat drawing to her the blame for an encompassing darkness of cosmic proportions, of eyes, of state, of spiritual home. Since Milton himself noted and sanctioned the practice of the expression of authorial views through the mouths of major characters in drama,[6] we in turn may be allowed to note that some of his own characters' most crucial speeches are charged with the personal gall of a long-standing Samson-and-Delilah complex. Samson's final opinion of Dalila is that she has proved herself a 'manifest serpent by her sting' (*Samson Agonistes*, 997), and Adam snarls out a view of his female offspring as:

> a rib
> Crooked by nature, bent, as now appears,
> More to the part sinister from me drawn;
> Well if thrown out, as supernumerary
> To my just number found.
> (*Paradise Lost*, X. 884–8)

'Sinister' means the left hand side, the side of human nature which is not dextrous, cannot be easily governed by the will and is therefore commonly feared as evil. The poet alludes to the ancient tradition of the female as associated with left-handedness, night, the moon, the unconscious, dark and curved line. Yet Adam's numerology is faulty: 'just' or 'even' number is not male but female. At the very moment that Milton allows his anti-feminine prejudice to spill over, his own double vision seems to criticise it. His Adam knows that the source of the 'sinister' is himself, the would-be even number with the dextrous brain and the straight-line will, and wishes to have been divorced from the woman-in-himself. The character therefore seeks to break down the wholeness of a divinely human nature; the under-meanings of the poetry comment satirically on the futility and sterility of such divorce. Nevertheless, the image of woman as scapegoat hangs over the major female characters of Milton's works. It is by no means the last word, nor is it a simple matter of crude misogyny: the present chapter will suggest a response almost totally contradictory to such a view. But it is an essential preliminary to recognise the animating rancour which Milton's works display towards womankind, in order to understand something of the poetry's extraordinary complexity.

Such outbursts should be understood not as a constitutional undervaluing of woman but as symptoms of thwarted idealism. In his earlier works he shows himself to be an idealist in relation to the feminine in a way that is recognisably in the tradition of Spenser and Shakespeare. *Arcades* and *Comus* were written under the patronage of Spenser's great patroness, the Countess of Derby, so that, as W.B. Hunter so beautifully shows, Milton looks through her eyes directly back to Spenser.[7] In her old age the great lady of the Elizabethan world briefly linked the last poet of the English Renaissance back to the flowering of its literature under Elizabeth Tudor. Milton was, and took pride in being, profoundly Spenserian. But Spenser was born in the very early 1550s and was dead (in 1599) before Milton was born (1608). Soon after Milton's birth, Shakespeare ceased writing. In Milton's life, therefore, we see an extension of the Elizabethan humanist dream, with a reverence for those values which Spenser also revered, but carried forwards into a new age of political and social upheaval and overt spiritual dissension, past the point where such a dream was really tenable. There is a sense in which both Spenser's and Shakespeare's celebration of the feminine is really conservative and backward-looking: Spenser's conservation of Elizabeth and her myth; Shakespeare's tragi-comic structures which circle back to mythic sources deep in the past. In the case of Milton, there is tension between this and its exact opposite. He is the new man, writing in a period of modern Hobbesian political realism, asserting a Protestant and individualist radicalism which declares a violently contemporary view of Christian rights and duties.[8] Milton is an embodied *Eikonoklastes*, speaking for the right of regicide, freedom of the press, male freedom of divorce. The *vita activa* and the *vita contemplativa* are in vehement argument in his works, along with humanism and Protestantism, idealism and cynicism, affinity with the male and with the female. The argumentative tendency of his work, its dialectical structure and the forceful claims of a heroic egoism all express the supremely personal character of Milton's poetry. It angrily resists the reader's search for singleness of voice and meaning. In *Of Education* Milton spoke of poetry as a kind of discourse that is 'simple, sensuous and passionate' (*CPW*, II, p. 403). The passion of his poetry defies its simplicity, for it is tense with conflict. What is vigorously affirmed may be at the same time passionately questioned, denied or even ridiculed.

We are warned against judging Milton by trivial remarks dropped in the heat of the moment, snatched up by the biographer and passed on to posterity as serious evidence of character. On the other hand, we can argue that it is precisely in such apparently inconsequent, habitual and unconsidered phrases that we declare our deepest bias. '*One Tongue is enough for a Woman!*' is a perfect instance. How do you say it? We inherit from Spenser and Shakespeare very little documentation of their personal views and lives outside the compass of the world of their art, but from Milton we have a mighty body of prose-writings by which we may readily judge tone-of-voice. More than this, a number of these voluminous works (the divorce tracts) deal directly with the subject of the feminine, and most of the others concern themselves by digression or by their own logic with woman's contribution to social, political and spiritual life. We should also note that Milton tended to write English prose with the rhythms of an intensely eccentric and personal speaking-voice, using the limits of his chosen decorum with the absolute freedom of his native tongue and idiolect, sometimes ranting out his polemic even where matter and manner require to be formal. Thus in the *History of Britain*, in which Milton often becomes incoherent with rage at the frantic boredom of cataloguing the acts of ancestors whose barbarous stupidity was only equalled by their viciousness, Milton must deal not only with the antics of English kings but also those of queens. The *History of Britain* is a tedious work. But when it comes to treating queens, its style acquires a vitriolic zest which enlivens the prevailing dulness. We hear of Queen Cartimandua that her subjects hated 'the uncomeliness of thir Subjection to the Monarchie of a Woeman, a peece of manhood not every day to be found among *Britains*' (*CPW*, V, p. 74). On Anglesea with the Druids a group of 'women like furies' were behaving themselves in the manner of 'a barbarous and lunatic rout'. When Milton comes to treat of that national heroine Boadicea, he presents her as a complete maniac, her reign indicative of a perverted state of society: 'the rankest note of Barbarism, as if in *Britain* Woemen were Men, and Men Woemen...right *Barbarians*...the wild hurrey of a distracted Woeman, with as mad a Crew at her heeles' (*CPW*, V. pp. 79–80). We can conjecture with some precision on what might have been this sage historian's response to Spenser's celebration of Britomart and the warrior-woman. As against the scarcely sane British, abdicating their manhood so as to serve their demonic or mentally retarded inferior, Boadicea, the Romans are shown as choice specimens of a male culture, under a 'public Father' (p. 85), ruling with reason, justice and order (except, of course, in the innumerable cases of the dissolute and despotic Roman emperors against whom Milton inveighs extensively elsewhere but prudently ignores here). Martial plainness, simplicity and rational discourse—'civilitie'—are the provenance of the male-centred culture and its language; volcanic irruptions of mass hysteria, disorder, ignorance and animality characterise female rule. The British women are like the Maenads who in *Lycidas* and *Paradise Lost* tear the Orphic poet and his rule limb from limb. Woman is the Dionysiac principle over against the Orphic and Apollonian principle of true patriarchy. In the cases where history obviously defies this prejudice outright, as in the case of the laudable Queen Elizabeth I invoked in *The Commonplace Book* (*CPW*, I, pp. 43–5), or where political pragmatism requires him to flatter a particular queen—Cristina in *The Second Defence* (*CPW*, IV, pp. 603–5)—Milton may grudgingly concede an exception to the rule of female inferiority. Alternatively, he may decide to deny history altogether. This pleasantly informal attitude to reality is demonstrated in his treatment of Queen Martia in the *History*. Milton's sources informed him that King Guitheline's wife, Martia, was responsible for instituting the laws used by King Alfred, laws whose legitimacy was for Milton one of the cardinal sanctions of the liberty of the English people.[9] Milton's desire not to believe this item of history led him to deny that it had happened. With the greatest candour in approaching the matter deductively rather than inductively, he explains that, being a woman, Martia could not really have thought the code up, 'for Laws are Masculin Births' (p. 32) for which woman's obstetric limitations disqualify her. Of the several variant spellings available to him,

Milton almost invariably selects 'Woeman' for its etymological piquancy: woe-to-man. It is not difficult to conclude upon the tone of voice in which Milton is likely to have remarked '*One Tongue is enough for a Woman!*', nor is much ingenuity required to imitate his habitual pronunciation of the word 'woman'.

On such grounds as these Milton seems richly to deserve the title of 'misogynist' conferred on him by tradition: this and its exact opposite. For the beauty and complexity of his poetry in part stems from an idealism about the feminine, reminiscent of Spenser's, which sounds against the voice of distrust. The fact that this represents a disappointed idealism makes it none the less tenacious and all the more poignant. The divorce tracts—*Doctrine and Discipline of Divorce Restored to the Good of Both Sexes* (1643), *Tetrachordon* (1644) and *Colasterion (1645)*—helps us to clarify the nature and grounds of this double vision, and yield insight into the acute personal pain which is felt throughout his works as a kind of inspirational affliction. Two incompatible images, of woman as *lux*, enlightening, lucid, associated with poetic creation, and of woman as *nox*, source of confusion, fear and mental darkness, are seen in the divorce pamphlets helplessly seeking to close with one another in reconciliation. These prose works evidence a gaping wound, the gap between momentous aspirations and expectations and the inevitable falling-short of the human reality these encounter. In the *Doctrine and Discipline* and *Tetrachordon* Milton quotes his sexual and emotional need in an emotive, self-exposing way, and allows the reader to perceive, between that need and its impossible fulfilment, the Abyss itself, the fall into a Godforsaken loneliness, both sexual, emotional and spiritual, which only the union with a cherished and highly valued woman could assuage. (*Colasterion* need not feature significantly in these reflections since it is written at speed and in a spirit of violent and crude contempt for his opposition in the debate: 'I mean not to dispute Philosophy with this Pork, who never read any'. [CPW, II, p. 737])

The divorce tracts plead for the divinely and legally sanctioned freedom of divorce on grounds other than adultery. They claim that marriage is a supremely noble and important institution; that the present law degrades it by reducing it to 'the prescrib'd satisfaction of an irrationall heat' (*Doctrine and Discipline*, *CPW*, II, p. 249), the compulsory coupling of two bodies yoked together even if 'their thoughts and spirits flie asunder as farre as heaven from hell' (p. 263). Milton's arguments are based on the pre-eminence of Charity in the Scriptures, emphasising God's love towards man, His will for man's happiness and His location of man's highest happiness in the gift to him of woman. The pamphlets therefore take a nobler view of woman than that of many of Milton's Protestant or Puritan contemporaries. They refuse to view her as a species of property, a sexual vehicle or a means of propagation, but insist on her dignity as the unique source of a divine and incomparable joy in the union of mind with mind, soul with soul. Milton does not believe, and never says, that man and woman are equal, but in his high valuing of marriage as a potentially paradisal estate, he manages to convey a sense that they are somehow more than equal:

> the fit union of their souls be such as may even incorporate them to love and amity; but that can never be where no correspondence is of the minde; nay instead of beeing one flesh, they will be rather two carkasses chain'd unnaturally together; or as it may happ'n, a living soule bound to a dead corps, a punishment too like that inflicted by the tyrant *Mezentius*; so little worthy to be receav'd as that remedy of lonelines which God meant us. Since wee know it is not the joyning of another body will remove lonelines, but the uniting of another compliable mind
>
> (*CPW*, II, pp. 326–7)

This 'correspondence...of the minde' is an idea close to the Shakespearean 'marriage of true minds', or to Spenser's image of the incorporation of Amoret and Scudamore in mutual trance (see pp. 100–2 above). Within the extract I quote above, the word 'loneliness' is repeated twice; it recurs like a refrain throughout the tract, accruing the suggestions of a condition of void, reprobation, the mind severed from the feminine being filled with emptiness, mocked by the travesty of the graphic 'two carkasses chain'd unnaturally together'. This 'perpetuall nullity of love and contentment, a solitude, and dead vacation' (p. 331) resembles Milton's depiction of the Satanic sufferings in *Paradise Lost*, where unfallen Eve seems to stand against the vacuity of hell itself, as the embodiment of our fullest knowledge of the bliss of heaven and the measure of Satan's loss of bliss in his fall into solitude, and soliloquy.

Milton's tracts speak with the voice of revolutionary Protestantism, which, for all its democratic impulses that worked to liberate women like the Quaker Margaret Fell and the antinomian Anne Hutchinson into assertions of equality,[10] also by a sharp irony worked to limit and confine their authority. Marriage became the last bastion of unquestioned male rule. Woman's possibilities were reduced and her figure withdrew into the shadow of her husband, who consecrated her life through its willingness to subject itself to incorporation in his. The *Doctrine and Discipline*, for all its insistence on the mind and spirit of the beloved companion, participates in this conservatism. Woman is recognised as helpmeet rather than equal partner; St Paul's recommendations to wives to maintain their servitude are quoted with sober relish. The burden of the argument is that if a woman should fail to co-operate in the divine plan for male welfare, she should legally and morally be set aside. Yet in *Tetrachordon* another note is sounded. St Paul's strictures on female obedience are glossed with a new emphasis, to the effect that 'Wives be subject...' does not signify or imply that man is 'to hold her as a servant':

> for it is no small glory to him, that a creature so like him, should be made subject to him. Not but that particular exceptions may have place, if she exceed her husband in prudence and dexterity, and he contentedly yeeld, for then a superior and more naturall law comes in, that the wiser should govern the lesse wise, whether male or female.

> (*CPW*, II, p. 589)

Just outside the door of this concession, an extremely draughty set of logical corollaries awaits, claiming right of entry. The polemicist shows a moment's alarm in a swirl of conditional clauses and a return to the major key of the male right to divorce on the grounds of his inalienable superiority as a general principle. But he does not close the door on female right to freedom from an evil or ungodly husband, for:

the wife also, as her subjection is terminated in the Lord, being her self the redeem'd of Christ, is not still bound to be the vassall of him, who is the bondslave of Satan: she being now neither the image nor the glory of such a person, nor made for him, nor left in bondage to him; but hath recours to the wing of charity, and protection of the Church; unless there be a hope on either side; yet such a hope must be meant, as may be a rationall hope, and not an endles servitude.

(*CPW*, II, p. 591)

The door is now fully opened upon the ultimate concession to woman's claim to freedom and dignity as a Christian soul: 'her self the redeem'd of Christ', licensed to make direct Protestant appeal to the highest law of all, to which earthly tribunals are universally subject. The concession may be grudgingly made, but it is fully and nobly done. Milton spoke of writing prose with his left hand, poetry with his right.[11] Here he employs the hand which justly elects Eve in the poetry of *Paradise Lost* to full participation in the image of God, expressing in her aspect 'Truth, wisdom, sanctitude severe and pure' (IV. 293), the classic Puritan virtues. The light reflected on the face of Milton's Eve, the beauty of her speaking-voice, the humility of her final posture, are images of woman seen not from the perspective of that Leontes-like, unself-knowing resentment with which Milton and his Adam are given to vilifying the feminine, but rather from the enlightenment which could recognise and assert the right to freedom of woman 'being her self the redeem'd of Christ'. Adam's tongue falls into rant against Eve as 'this fair defect of nature', but his tongue has fallen with his mind, out of a state of charity. No doubt the great misogynist took a more than covert pleasure in unburdening himself of these complaints, through the mouth of his spokesman, but he does not allow *Paradise Lost* to endorse the ugly voice of Adam that speaks, in a sense, against the voice of poetry itself, and the poem as a dream-vision, since Eve is above all a projection of the poet of *Paradise Lost*, this most personal of poems. Her early words in the poem, speaking of the dawn of her own life, carry with them a blessed lyricism: 'That day I oft remember, when from sleep/ I first awaked' (IV. 449–50); her last speech closes the circle of human articulations within the poem with the final word 'restore'. Milton's Eve lives in the tradition of Spenser's Florimell and Amoret, Shakespeare's Hermione and Perdita, because she has been born of the recognition and affirmation of the feminine within the poet's own nature. She 'restores' to the poet a lost sense of completeness, marrying the twinned halves of a single being: Psyche and Eros, Adam and Eve, poet and Muse.

According to Aubrey's account, England's epic poet had experienced some difficulty in defining himself as a man among men—'he was so faire y^t they called him the Lady of X^{ts} coll' (*Early Lives*, p.3). Hence, perhaps, his endless and touchy struggle to segregate and specialise the genders, to define himself as a 'Masculin Birth', denying his mother and consciously addressing himself *Ad Patrem*. Hence, too, perhaps, the irresistible current of desire which pulled him towards the feminine and led him to do her an unwilled justice. Throughout Milton's poetry we are conscious of his unease concerning the idea of female power, evoking in him a dread quite absent in Spenser, and outlived and repudiated in Shakespeare. Elizabeth I had been dead for over fifty years when Milton began to write *Paradise Lost*. His only adult experience of living under a queen had been the discouraging one of enduring Charles I's wife, the detested Catholic foreigner Henrietta Maria, considered both by Milton and many Protestant contemporaries as a single major cause of the civil wars.[12] After *Comus*, he seems always to have associated monarchy with degenerate female rule. But he named his third and apparently favourite daughter after one of the great warrior-women of the Old Testament, Deborah, the judge, poet, prophet and deliverer of Israel. The Song of Deborah is one of the most famous of Old Testament war-hymns, and possibly the most blood-thirsty. Naming a daughter after the mighty figure of Deborah the judge recognises that God the Father in the mystery of the Divine paradox has seen fit to subordinate the Chosen People to the leadership of a woman, as if what was so scandalous in Anglo-Saxon England ('as if... Woemen were Men, and Men Woemen'; see p. 180 above) might be considered gloriously correct in Israel. When God inverts the natural order, it becomes a sacred illumination. Deborah the inspired prophetess leads Israel to war. The querulous commander of the armies will only venture against

Canaan if Deborah will accompany him:

> And Barak said unto her, If thou wilt go with me, then I will go: but
> if thou wilt not go with me, then I will not go.
>
> (Judges 4:8)

Milton's Deborah acknowledges the gap between Milton's
favourite theories and God's incontrovertible practises.

THE MUSE AND THE MAENADS

In the four symmetrically placed Invocations of *Paradise Lost*,
the poet contemplates, describes and pleads with his Muse.
While the whole of the epic may be felt as an extraordinarily
personal, introspective and intimate work—despite the cosmic
grandeur of its focus—these four substantial pauses in the
narrative speak most obviously and simply with a personal voice.
Through them we learn a relationship between ourselves as
readers and the 'I' who tells the poem, the identity through
whose mind it has passed and who is, in these pauses, able to
look back reflectively on what has already been written and to
confront the poetry that is yet to be shaped and at present has
no existence. Through the Invocations we also gather
something of the relationship between the character of the
poem—its people and places—and that mediating 'I'. The
persona is not the 'I John Milton' of the *Defences* or the divorce
tracts, though he may allude to ·that personality and its
predicament, nor the theologian of *Christian Doctrine*, the
elegist of *Lycidas*, the agonist of *Samson*, but a signature
generated and circumscribed only by and for *Paradise Lost*. In
the Invocations, Milton explores his relation with the feminine
as the elusive counterpart of his own nature. He sings in the
Muse to the fourfold structure of his poem, both as the channel
of his inspiration and as an intrinsic part of the poem's subject
matter.

Hesiod tells us that there are nine Muses available for poets to
call upon, the daughters of Zeus and Mnemosyne, who bring
'Forgetfulness of evil, rest from pain' (*Theogony*, 55). If the nine
were not considered sufficient, it was open to a Christian

humanist poet to invent a new one or a new synthesis, as Milton partly does. In addition, the image of his Muse seems to change as *Paradise Lost* itself unfolds. An evolving Muse adapts herself to the needs of the story and its creator, pressed between the circling time-scheme of the story and the stress of day-to-day life. The poet presents himself throughout the four Invocations as involved in constant struggle and pain, allowing himself to give account of the specific pressures from which he suffers in the time-scheme outside the poem. Within the poem there is felt and articulated the acute difficulty of measuring up to the demands of the sacred story, along with the fear of falling into hubris, telling lies. Outside the poem, but bearing upon it, there is the problem of blindness—linking him with an elect group of blind seers including Homer and Tiresias—but presenting an overwhelming obstacle to setting the word on the page; there is his position in Restoration society as a stigmatised alien, fallen 'on evil tongues, and evil days'; awareness of increasing age and the possibility of being cheated of the poem's completion by his time running out. Because of this constant emphasis on pressure and difficulty in creating the epic at all, Hesiod's definition of the Muses as bringing 'Forgetfulness of evil, rest from pain' is peculiarly apt. A major function sought and found by Milton in his Muse is that of benign and cherishing protectiveness, a function which becomes more crucial as the poem develops. To argue, as some critics have done, that Milton's Muse Urania is an allegory for Christ the Son, the Creating Word,[13] so that the feminine suggestions are lost, is to miss a core of emotional and spiritual meaning in *Paradise Lost* around the narrative persona's sense of himself as in a medial position in relation to his material, a position of danger and isolation requiring human and humane consolation. It is to miss the essential mother-and-son archetype so central to the Orphic mythology and its magic, upon which Milton movingly calls.

As the immense enterprise of writing *Paradise Lost* unfolds, and the conception realises itself, the possibility which Milton had envisaged in *Lycidas* becomes a more acute anxiety:

> But the fair guerdon when we hope to find,
> And think to burst out into sudden blaze,

> Comes the blind Fury with th'abhorred shears,
> And slits the thin-spun life.
>
> (*Lycidas*, 73-6)

Busy, practical and armed with the instruments of her trade, Atropos casually and randomly attenuates an individual life. Against this dark, Hecatean death-figure in *Lycidas* stands the gentle Muse, Calliope, mother of Orpheus. Whereas the terror generated by Atropos stems from her impersonality, the sense we have of the Muse's power comes of her personal nearness to and involvement in human aspirations and losses. These are the qualities upon which both Spenser and Shakespeare called in their structural allusions to the classical mother-deities (see pp. 88ff., 120ff. above), and it is important to notice the range and depth of Milton's less overt commitment to this body of imagery and allusion. Calliope in *Lycidas* seems recognisably related to our own species, both through her sharing in its distresses and unfulfilled needs, and through the human quality of her motherhood:

> What could the muse herself that Orpheus bore,
> The muse herself for her enchanting son
> Whom universal nature did lament,
> When by the rout that made the hideous roar
> His gory visage down the stream was sent,
> Down the swift Hebrus to the Lesbian shore.
>
> (*Lycidas*, 58-63)

The elegist sings of the wholeness of a single life scissored prematurely; the powerful harmonies of individual poets and the corporate memory of the whole race mutilated into fragments. Through the Calliope/Orpheus icon, the effect has the poignancy of the forcible separation of mother and child. The image of the feminine as represented in the Muse implies infinite love without infinite power. The feminine is divine but not omnipotent, a source of security which is found finally vulnerable despite being the origin of Orpheus' lyrical enchantment of the natural world. The maternal archetype as the soul of tenderness lacks power to put its will into effective action. It is a fellow victim, not responsible for the evil in the universe, which it does not endorse and cannot allay. In *Lycidas* Milton significantly does not suggest the existence of a female magic equivalent to Spenser's *Venus genetrix*; he does not incorporate the Shakespearean adaptation of the classical corn-goddesses, representing both nurture and law. In weakening the feminine thus, Milton heightens the qualities of yearning and wistfulness in its image, which becomes an emblem of the best in human nature, together with the Christian conviction of the insufficiency of the merely human best. The flower of human nature is, like Eve, the 'fairest flower' of *Paradise Lost*, perfectly vulnerable. In *Lycidas* the flower-catalogue endorses this image of the perfect imperfection of nature, with the sudden tiny faces of the spring flowers bringing their moments of light and colour from the underworld itself, 'The glowing violet' (145) which has a whole line to itself, and 'The rathe primrose that forsaken dies' (142), echoing Perdita's Proserpina speech in *The Winter's Tale*. These ephemera of the natural world express the absolute goodwill of Mother Nature;[14] and, though they are spoken of with self-castigating scorn by the persona as leading us to 'false surmise', their affirmative lyricism prepares the poem for the imminent final Consolation.

Confronting the Orphic Muse in *Lycidas* as they confront the Sacred Muse in *Paradise Lost*, however, stands the threatening and sinister force of the Maenads, the Thracian women, followers of Dionysos, who are responsible for the dismemberment of Orpheus. As against Shakespeare's late, authentically classical synthesis of the Orphic and Dionysian, Milton's Protestant imagination reads the two cults always against one another, as eternal adversaries, the one rational, male-centred and enlightened, prefiguring Christianity; the other barbarous, animal, female and regressive. Milton draws back fastidiously from the wild rituals of the Dionysian cults, with their frenzied hunting and eating of the raw flesh of the sacrificial animal and their sexual and spiritual ecstasy, which Kerenyi sees as linked with women's 'overflowing vitality, their milk and physical energy...their greater visionary capacities'.[15] Shakespeare's Antigonus in *The Winter's Tale* had followed in the footsteps of Euripides' unfortunate Pentheus in taking the part of the god as ritual victim, to be killed, ingested and (meta-phorically) reborn, as did the sacrificial animal, or Orpheus

himself.[16] Milton's references to Orpheus always emphasise the
quiet of Orpheus;[17] we experience that quiet against the furious
noise he associates with the Dionysian in *Lycidas*, 'the hideous
roar' (61) that seems to mingle itself with the roar of the
destroying waters; in *Paradise Lost* 'barbarous dissonance' (VII.
32), 'savage clamour' (36); in *Comus* the cacophany of the
followers of that 'sorcerer' associated with dark female magic:

> Of Bacchus and of Circe born, great Comus,
> Deep skilled in all his mother's witcheries...
>   (*Comus*, 552–3)

These devotees of Hecate (535) fill the air with 'barbarous
dissonance' (550) prefiguring the uproar of the Dionysian
modern world in *Paradise Lost*, surrounding the Orphic artist in
his initiated élite of one. The Maenadic female principle
incarnated in the Restoration monarchy and associated with the
female element, water, in flood, is dreaded as the noise of death
to poetry, 'drowning' the meaning of words, the rhythms of
music.

However, in *Comus* Milton had dramatised the Orphic
resistance of one, rigorous, reformist and temperate, in the
person of the Lady, and we sense here a deeply Spenserian
impulse in the Masque's lyricism and its feminine centre, which
was never absolutely lost to the poet. The Lady's Song, '*Sweet
Echo, sweetest nymph that liv'st unseen*', is a Platonist adaptation
of the myth of Narcissus which Milton later associates with Eve
in *Paradise Lost*. The unseen voice sings in the night, and causes
in the barbarous breast of Comus a true sense of 'divine
enchanting ravishment' (245), an ecstasy carefully distinguished
from the sensual 'sweet madness' of his own Bacchic and sensual
music as bringing 'sober certainty of waking bliss' (261, 263).
The Lady's music enchants the enchanter himself. As a voice
liberated from the body, it works a natural magic according to
the sober laws of musical language. But it is important to note
that Milton associates this rigorously obedient music with an
experience of 'ravishment', rapture, taking leave of one's senses,
and that in this earlier phase of his development he found it easy
and natural to ally this Orphic power with the feminine. In
Paradise Lost, begun more than twenty years after *Comus*,

Milton has a subject which requires a state of mind beyond reason, sense or learned application of the rules of poetry. He returns massively to the resources of an earlier Platonism.[18]

Milton had a most cogent personal reason for allying himself with the Platonist adaptation of Orpheus: his blindness. Pico writes in the sixth of his *Orphic Conclusions*: '*Ideo amore ab Orpheo sine oculis dicitur, quia est supra intellectum*'.[19] He elsewhere remarks that there is a tradition in which those capable of the rapture of the vision of spiritual beauty 'were by the same cause blinded in their corporal eyes'.[20] This damage to his life, the stigma with which he had been taunted by his opponents in the civil wars, may thus be seen as a special sign of Orphic status rather than a handicap. Milton knows Love *sine oculis*, writing in this great tradition of Platonic Love-blindness, which admits him to a world from which the millions of the myopic normal are debarred, the vision *supra intellectum*, into which the poet can only enter if he is ravished, blind, open to the force of his psychic energies. In this state of mind in which perception is possible beyond the intellect, there is no guarantee that one has not deviated into the comparable but opposite world of the Maenads, as threatening forces within the psyche of the poet rather than simply in the external world. Thus the relationship between the poet and his Muse is uniquely passionate in *Paradise Lost*. His need to be sheltered and defended from the lawless, delusive forces latent in all human nature becomes more critical as the poem gathers substance and life: 'nor could the Muse defend/Her son' (VII. 37–8). He must fashion or find a Muse strong and definitive enough to lead her blind son, the modern Orpheus, through mysteries which the 'wild rout' (34) of egoism continually threatens to reduce to confusion. Both the Muse and the Maenads are forces within the mind itself. The tender but finally weak feminine archetype of mother-protector has to be recast into new and powerful form through the poem's energies in order to obtain what came so naturally to the Lady in *Comus*, assurance of music creative of 'sober certainty of waking bliss' in the eternal night of blindness. Milton must recall the feminine from his own divorce from her.

The figures of Eve and the poet are therefore in close secret harmony within the poem. The Orphic mystery-cult was deeply, and specifically linked with the Eleusinian mother-and-daughter cult. In both, spiritual illumination was held to come of cleansing the senses, the cultivation of the land, both of spirit and mind. In *Paradise Lost*, while the poet identifies himself with Orpheus resisting a kind of 'rape' by the darkness of a Maenadic world, he represents Eve as a Proserpina/Ceres figure who must deal with the rape on her spirit performed by the powers of darkness personified in Satan. The connection between Orphic poet and Demetrian heroine is powerfully felt. Through these two areas of struggle, in the 'mother of our race' for an Eleusinian illumination and the poet as son of his Muse for Light, each course reflects the other in a poem which is shaped as a great circling system of Platonic reflections. They run through the Platonic circle of Grace: *emanatio: raptio: remeatio*.[21] The soul departs from the One on its journey into creation, *emanatio* ('That day I oft remember when from sleep/I first awaked' [Eve, IV. 449–50]); it reaches its furthest limit and, ravished, turns for home, *raptio* ('Half yet remains unsung' [Milton, VI. 21]); it makes return to source, *remeatio* ('By me the promised seed shall all restore' [Eve, XII. 623]). Their circle is also a search, for light, vision, dream-inspiration and eyesalve for their blindness; it is equally a search for Love in the self-completing union with a counterpart of the other gender.

Milton's Muse is not conceived as a fully feminine figure until the second half of the poem. Before he has created Eve on the page in Book IV, placed her in Eden, heard her speak and gifted Adam with her love, he identifies his Muse in a sexually ambiguous or androgynous way. The first exordium calls to the first Creator of all being, the Holy Spirit, to enter into the mind of the creator of *Paradise Lost*, making the poem through him. It seeks for an inspiration as vast as the whole heavens, and a wish for wings, to fly to or above the summit of the mountains, where earth ends and heaven begins, to receive there Word from the Almighty. We are not presented, initially, with the Christian Homer (a new classicism) but with a Christian Moses, receiving straight from God the sacred poem of the Pentateuch. Mount Helicon, the mountain of the classical Muses, is disdained as too 'low' for such huge need of breath to 'soar' nearly above the range of the possible:

And chiefly thou O Spirit, that dost prefer

Before all temples the upright heart and pure,
Instruct me, for thou know'st; thou from the first
Wast present, and with mighty wings outspread
Dove-like sat'st brooding on the vast abyss
And madest it pregnant: what in me is dark
Illumine...

(*Paradise Lost*, I. 17–23)

This is the Holy Spirit, unmediated through images drawn from the fabrications of human mythologies. There is a sense of how improper to the vision of Creation would be the introduction of a classical Muse, stiff with the draperies of an outlived convention, her home a shrine in a small Hellenic locality: indecorous when there is a whole universe to be scanned, all time and all history, together with the terrible mysteries of what came before birth; how pain was born; how the forces upon whose tension the whole universe continues are to be contemplated. Eleusis would be insignificant here, Orphism a dream. Unlike Spenser, Milton always subordinates the fictions of classical mythology which play such a crucial part in his humanistic synthesis, to the Christian truth of the Scriptures. The poetry here convinces us that it sets itself a subject requiring something like the terms of quantum physics, or pure mathematics, to approach its mysteries. A gendered equation, then, perhaps we would not expect. Yet it is precisely in this power to render unexpected questions and previously unguessed solutions that Milton's grasp on our imagination lies, enabling us suddenly to enter secret (because unimaginable) areas of experience. Thus in the first Invocation he uses his biblical source in an extraordinary way, creating a radical image of the Muse he seeks, by bringing into the foreground its implied allusion to gender and fertility. Milton is aware of a need for power of language, able to speak what was 'In the beginning' (*Paradise Lost*, I.9), 'from the first' (19). To generate his own poem, he therefore goes back to Genesis for inspiration:

And the earth was without form, and void; and darkness was upon the face of the deep. And the spirit of God moved upon the face of the waters.

(Genesis 1:2)

Milton's adaptation of the Spirit of Genesis, conflated with the dove of the Gospel of St John, fuses both mother- and father-images without disturbing the theological obedience of his sacred poem, for the 'Spirit of God' that in the Authorised Version 'moved upon the face of the waters' was in patristic translations 'brooded' (*incubabat*).[22] The resulting androgynous image unites a sensation of infinite gentleness with terrifying power, a full-scale version of the 'dear might' of Christ in *Lycidas* (173). The mother-dove, emblem of patient vigil and nurture, is called up; the image is homely and reassuring. It is then stretched out in imagination to occupy the entire cosmos. The dimensions of the ordinary world are, with the magnification of this insight, 'outspread' (*Paradise Lost*, I. 20) with the 'mighty' bird. Its nest, in the familiar world, a network of twigs, becomes, in our outspread vision, a nothing. But again, its amplitude is emphasised: we are asked to see an extension of nothing, 'the vast abyss' (21). The suggestion of gender is then altered: 'And madest it pregnant' (22). Female incubation becomes male impregnation, but without losing the prior associations of disseminating warmth.

From the outset of the poem poetic relativity plays powerful and incompletely understood games upon our expectations. Here we contemplate an image of huge totality, in which there are no seams or edges between opposites. Great and small, male and female, time and eternity are perceived as One for as long as we look upon the image. The reader is called upon to think about thought itself here; to 'brood' upon the act of 'brooding', which unifies the disparate so that subject and object, reader and image come to have no opposition. In doing this, the reader co-operates in a divine function, that of Aristotle's God whose nature it is to 'think about thinking' and do nothing whatever—the Platonic and Neoplatonic Mind which eternally meditates the archetype.[23] But the symbol is not reassuring: the homely mother-dove, when raised to the power of infinity, challenges and awes. Milton's image suggests silence, rest, but also the gathering of an energy which, when brought so close to the egg-shell thinness of the mortal mind which invokes it, implies threat. We sense the terror of the holy journey Milton embarks on. 'What in me is dark/Illumine': inviting impregnation by that first principle of creativity, he offers his mind's darkness as the human counterpart of the original 'abyss'; he himself solicits the incubating warmth that lay across the entire universe, forcing it into a cosmos. There is a disturbing suggestion of the potentially destructive powers of the divine when it is brought against the vulnerability and limitations of human nature, a threatening potency in keeping with Milton's habitual thinking concerning the nature of creative power. Destruction and creation are intrinsic to one another, as he tells us in *The Doctrine and Discipline of Divorce* when he evidences:

> the first and last of all his [God's] visible works; when by his divorcing command the world first rose out of Chaos, nor can be renew'd again out of confusion but by the separating of unmeet consorts.

> (*CPW*, II. p.273)

Thus the primal creative act requires the breaking apart of the original darkness by a creativity which works by 'divorcing command'. This sense of the terror for human nature in proximity to God's creative power is reinforced by the Orphic symbolism implied by the dove-like Spirit's brooding: the Orphic egg which was shattered to give birth to the whirling energies of Light (*Orphic Hymn to Protogonos*, 1–9).

This conjunction of male and female in Milton's first image searching out his Muse gives a dynamic energy to the idea of the feminine by associating it with its twin male function in the act of generation. And it has an absolute bearing on the poem as it unfolds. For if the Muse is conceived as incorporating both male and female agencies, so too by extension the poet receiving inspiration declares an andyrogynous nature. His 'female' self is impregnated to conceive by the 'male' Spirit; his 'male' self is warmed into life by the 'female' mother-Spirit. And those three functions of fertility (conception, gestation, birth) are defined within the symbol as simultaneous. In terms of poetic creation, conception and expression in language are a single act, thought and words one single process, atemporal, just as the image of the Creation seems chronologically to reverse the natural processes. The Spirit is first seen brooding (as if conception has occurred), then impregnating (it is occurring). The bisexual poet receiving

inspiration from a bisexual deity is, throughout the poem, seen
to create a bisexual world. Milton the man and theologian had
sneered at this idea of man as an original hermaphrodite as a
Jewish fable and a piece of '*Plato's* wit, as if man at first had bin
created *Hermaphrodite*' (*Tetrachordon*, p. 589), but the poet of
Paradise Lost and the lover of Spenser seems to have found it
irresistible. Man and woman in Milton's Eden are only just
different: Eve tells over Adam's words in calling her 'Part of my
soul...My other half' (IV. 487, 488). This suggestion of a
belonging together that makes them incomplete apart is linked
with the explicitly hermaphroditic sexuality of Milton's
Heaven, in which angels are said by Book I to be either or both
sexes, 'so soft/And uncompounded is their essence pure,/Not
tied or manacled with joint or limb' (424–6). Raphael explains to
Adam in Book VIII, on the verge of the human Fall and its
dislocation of the sexes, that Spirits enjoy the act of love not as a
transient meeting of like with like, or even unlike with unlike,
but as a complete becoming of the beloved, 'air with air.../Total
they mix' (626–7). There are no surfaces in heaven to define one
happiness against another. Self dissolves into self, and in that
dissolution the two sexes become one another. This is the secret
of sexual and spiritual joy, which are not in Milton's epic
distinguished: the containment of self in the solitary
confinement of individual identity is a painful consequence of
the Fall. Even the planets in Milton's cosmos are seen as
gendered, sentient and animate. Raphael speculates with Adam
about the possible existence of other populated planets in the
galaxy, so that other suns and their attendant moons may be
seen

> Communicating male and female light,
> Which two great sexes animate the world,
> Stored in each orb perhaps with some that live.
>   (*Paradise Lost*, VIII. 150–2)

The world—that is, the cosmos—is *divided* into 'male and
female' only in order that they may seek return into one
another's being. We understand the androgynous fertility of the
Muse and the love-bond of Adam and Eve within the reflective

pattern of this impassioned cosmos, which displays in its great flow of mirror-resemblances the Platonic vision of 'the whole in the part and the part in the whole'—*emanatio: raptio: remeatio.*[24] The mutual attraction which Newton would assign to gravitational fields, Milton describes in Platonist and alchemical (as well as human) terms as sexual desire. Father Sun and Mother Earth, in Book VII and in frequent alchemical images which allude to the secret art of unifying contraries, are celebrated as desiring one another. Male solar light and female lunar light do not polarise experience into units of solitary opposition, but 'communicate' back and forth, desiring return to unity. 'Two great sexes' define Milton's universe as a dynamic duality[25] whose end is not diversity (though diversity is a beautiful and fascinating aspect of its process) but the urge of love into greater nearness. The gendered planets 'animate' the perfect motion of the cosmos. The verb contains the Latin *anima*, spirit: spirit thrills through into matter, and the two are really indissoluble. Insistence on this fundamental identity of spirit and matter, one of the poem's less orthodox pieces of Christian Platonist doctrine, formulated by Raphael at length in Book V in terms of organic imagery ('So from the root/Springs lighter the green stalk' [479ff]), allows Milton to give to sexual desire a unique spiritual value, to things of the spirit a palpable, lively and joyous reality. The planets of his cosmology are not heaved round in their grooves by disembodied Aristotelian Intelligences, neither are they worked according to the impersonal laws of modern physics: Milton goes back to the High Renaissance of English Spenserian art for his vision of a universe whose planets all yearn inwards through fusion with one another towards the One from whom they originate. Nothing but hell is visualised as dead matter in *Paradise Lost* (and even hell is *living* death [II. 624]). The cosmos is personal as we are personal, we are thus cosmic in our nature and actions; and even God, so often irate, can give a playful human smile in complicity with Adam's boldly expressed desire for a mate (VIII. 368). The Platonic doctrine of emanation is thus figured throughout the poem as a vision of matter warm with love-longing; until the Fall's adulthood cools the planet, distorts the planetary system and chills man into impercipience of the remaining harmony.

The poetic energies of *Paradise Lost* are poured out in expression amounting to mimesis of this huge concept of a universe whose each particular relates to the others as a colossal flow and discharge of loving energy, the cosmos itself conceived in the image of the hermaphrodite-Muse of the first Invocation. This Muse is therefore doubly vital. It is the seed from which the epic action springs. The source of the concept of the androgynous creator and androgynous world is unmistakably Hermetic; it is important to understand this source in some detail, to see the force of the feminine in shaping the structure of *Paradise Lost*.[26] In the *Pimander* the Renaissance had found the idea of an androgynous Creator in combination with theories of emanationism, *ekstasis*, the divinity within man, and the love-lorn universe. Hermes tells of the primal Creation in terms of:

> the breath-like Word which moved upon the face of the water.
> And the first Mind,—that Mind which is Life and Light,—being bisexual, gave birth to another Mind, a Maker of things
> *(Pimander*, 8–9, in *Hermetica*, p. 119)

When God makes Man, in his own image, Man breaks through the spheres of the universe, to view its core, Nature:

> and showed to downward-tending Nature the beautiful form of God. And Nature, seeing the beauty of the form of God, smiled with insatiate love of Man, showing the reflection of that most beautiful form in the water, and its shadow on the earth...And Nature, when she had got him with whom she was in love, wrapped him in her clasp, and they were mingled in one; for they were in love with one another.
> And that is why man, unlike all other living creatures upon earth, is twofold...He is bisexual, as his Father is bisexual, and sleepless, as his Father is sleepless; yet he is mastered by carnal desire and by oblivion.
> *(Pimander*, 14–15, in *Hermetica*, pp. 121–3)

The beauty of the Hermetic cosmic structure, like that of the Miltonic, is in the fact that it is not machine but process, in a state of steadfast volatility; each part surging towards another in an excitement which is interpreted by the magus as Love, not turbulence. The personified universe falls in love with itself, aspect by aspect, because each part mirrors the Good and the Beautiful, which is the deity. No stain is imputed to nature for 'wrapping' man in herself, 'mingling in one' with him, though this clogging of the soul with matter has unfortunate side-effects for men, 'stuffing them up with the gross mass of matter' (*Hermetica*, VII. 3, p. 173). The universe cannot help adoring the image of the Good, and even though that may be a narcissistic self-image, the motive is virtuous. Bisexual man, however, was untied from himself, at a due period, so that procreation could take place (I.18), which explains why we find ourselves in our present state of singularity. Later Hermes goes on to speak of God's placing a sort of 'basin' of Mind in our world, in which we could dip ourselves to obtain *gnosis* (IV. 4); his kindly God takes care of his universe by sending 'radiations' of divine forces, including birth and the arts, and 'good daemons' who look after us (X. 22b–23). Each of us has in himself a womb, in which one may be reborn as a baby, or as a child before its own conception, a pre-existent being who is yet 'the All' (XIII. 11a–11b). This sexually charged, acutely imaginative and ecstatically active universe of the Hermetic philosophy is directly comparable with the dynamic universe of *Paradise Lost*, where all is force and motion, places are described as if they are persons, and the planetary system is animated by 'two great sexes'. In this Milton is profoundly Spenserian (see pp. 89ff. above), but he outdoes Spenser in the aptness of his poetic style to the Hermetic conception. Spenser's immaculate sealed units of stanza and canto give way to the dynamic flow of Milton's immense verse-paragraphs, with the sensation they convey of the infinite harnessed in finite space, which spills again towards infinity, naming its own paradox as it goes, 'numbers without number' (*Paradise Lost*, III. 346), an eternally generative grammar of creation.

There are clear implications when we come to evaluate the female principle in *Paradise Lost* in the light of the Hermetic model. Combining with the intensity of Milton's feeling of the power and beauty of sexual love, it seems to have helped make possible for the poet a generous avoidance of the kind of misogyny which characterises his fallen Adam, and the vengeful feelings which reduce the female antagonist to the status of a thing in *Samson Agonistes*, where the Chorus seems unable to assign Dalila to its own species at all: 'Female of sex *it* seems' (711; my italics). The Hermetic text has not only a passionate quality in keeping with the spirit of *Paradise Lost* but also a concern voiced in each of the four Invocations as to how that God-reflecting passion can, in the nature of things, be expressed in language. This query makes the character of the Muse and her capacities vital to the poem. *Paradise Lost* repeatedly questions its own power to receive correctly or enunciate intelligibly its divine subject. Even the angels cannot sustain the contemplation of the full light of God in Book III:

> Dark with excessive bright thy skirts appear,
> Yet dazzle heaven, that brightest seraphim
> Approach not, but with both wings veil their eyes.
> (*Paradise Lost*, III. 380–2)

When reality cannot be seen as itself, but light too intense is apprehended as its own cauterising opposite, joy opposes itself as a kind of pain, and the whole being of the angels is exerted in the shading of the vulnerable retina 'with both wings'. The Hermetic text presents a rueful but also sanguine awareness of this paradoxically visionary condition:

> But in this life we are still too weak to see that sight; we have not strength to open our mental eyes, and to behold the beauty of the Good, that incorruptible beauty which no tongue can tell. Then only will you see it, when you cannot speak of it; for the knowledge of it is deep silence, and suppression of all the senses.
> (*The Key*, 5–6, in *Hermetica*, p. 191)

This is the silence that *Paradise Lost* must call, or dream, into speech—a contradiction in terms, since it is 'Beatitude past utterance' (III.62). In the Invocation to Book III the doubt is hazarded as to whether the poet 'May...express unblamed' the Light which is God's first-born offspring, or emanation (3). The hubris of the attempt, encouraged by the Hermetic cry to 'make yourself equal to God...Leap clear...rise above all time' (XI. 20b), the humanistic dare to 'be reborn into the highest ranks, those of the divine',[27] must constantly fly for refuge to the validating shelter of the 'mighty wings outspread/Dove-like' of the maternal-paternal Muse. The Muse thus gives birth to the maternal-paternal poet, who in turn, regenerated moment-by-moment by cyclical return to source, can give form to the story in which he participates.

In each Invocation Milton uneasily, or with the lyricism of renewing hope, reviews the story as a pilgrimage in which he has personally visited the places and confronted the figures and actions, and looks ahead to what must occur in the poem's future. In Book III he emerges from hell into the upper world, as if the companion of Satan's odyssey, shaking off the contamination of the journey in prayer. Where the characters go, he must go; and what they do, he must mime. This partly explains a growing sense of his closeness to and identification with Eve after Book IV: he *has* to identify with every person and event, and, in the poem as in the Bible story, Eve has to be the focus of the crucial action of falling. Fallen poet and falling woman are kin, as Adam and Eve are kin within their shared state of innocence. Repellently, he must accompany Satan, and meet the person of Sin, also near kin to fallen man. Thus he thinks of his Muse in Book III (in an image which is genderless, but has been thought of as associated with Christ)[28] as the creating Light, the 'first-born' from whom he may obtain purifying rebirth in the Invocation:

> Thee I revisit now with bolder wing,
> Escaped the Stygian pool, though long detained
> In that obscure sojourn, while in my flight
> Through utter and through middle darkness borne
> With other notes than to the Orphean lyre
> I sung of Chaos and eternal Night,
> Taught by the heavenly Muse to venture down
> The dark descent, and up to reascend,
> Though hard and rare: thee I revisit safe...
> (*Paradise Lost*, III. 13–21)

Each Invocation affords space and time for a conscious rebirth of the poet to continuing action within the body of the poem. The Invocations are sanctuaries, areas of sacred refuge in which the speaker argues himself towards a ritual peace into which Light flows. Here he looks back not so much on Satan's fall as on his own downward flight, his own visit to the tar-black

waters of the Styx, his own underworld in which there was no
Euridyce to redeem and where the song seemed made out of the
black, polluting materials it had to describe: an explicitly non-
Orphic song (17).

In that interval between the first and second Invocations
(Books I and III) Milton has, impersonating Satan, met with the
first female character to speak in the poem, Sin; in likewise
impersonating her he has, in Platonist terms, also 'been' her.[29]
Sin, descended from Homer's woman-monster, Scylla, and
Spenser's Errour, is a projection of man's most primitive and
fundamental fears of and recoil from the female. In her
incestuous relationship with her father, Satan, and her son,
Death, she presents a betrayal of nature; a reversal of natural
processes, so that she takes back her own young into herself and
as Satan's concubine goes back into her own family. Life
reverses; the creative womb takes back what it has given; the
positive future is undone as a possibility. The relation of love
within a family is reversed, so that Satan, Sin and Death are
bonded by mutual enmity. Like Antiochus and his daughter at
the beginning of *Pericles* (see pp. 132–3 above), Sin and Satan
acquaint us with the dark meaning into which life and language
easily degenerate. The self-loving universe, radiating mirror-
reflections of beauty, becomes in his nightmarish version a
vicious twisting inwards of like to like, joined at the root of sex.
Archetypally she is the Dark or Terrible Mother humanity
fears,[30] because like Mother Earth she threatens to crush life
back into the passage from which it gained admittance. Womb
becomes grave, and, just as man had no power over his forcible
extrusion into being, so he has no ability to control his exit and
re-encapsulation in the original earth. She is a fear of matter
itself, in Hermetic terms men's physical incarnation which
'stuffs them up with the gross mass of matter' (see p. 199 above).
The poet's return to this unbegetting womb may be seen as a
metaphoric rendering of the Platonist's horror of return to the
cave of the senses, the furthest possible place, within the bowels
of matter itself, from the sunlight of Reality. Sin and Death are
perceived by the poet as themselves unreal: Sin only '*seemed* a
woman to the waist' (II. 650; my italics); Death is a shapeless
shape (666–7) and wears only the 'seeming' of a head (672). Sin's
rapacious sexual energies are expressed in her unctuous manner

of speaking, in which the coiling, sibillant sentences declare her affinity with the serpent and the underworld, 'volup-tuous.../Thy daughter and thy darling without end' (II. 869–70). This reptilian voice, and the reduction of Sin to the womb she contains, offer a passage down which Satan, poet and reader are endlessly invited to slide: to abort life, to go back into the dark, to be eaten and erased. The constant chant of the word 'womb' as she tells Satan of her history (747–814) leads the reader back again and again to the claustrophobic horror of birth, and a sense of traumatised pain hangs over the whole episode. The image of her violation by her offspring is important. They:

> never ceasing barked
> With wide Cerberian mouths full loud, and rung
> A hideous peal: yet, when they list, would creep,
> If aught disturbed their noise, into her womb,
> And kennel there, yet there still barked and howled,
> Within unseen.
>
> (*Paradise Lost*, II. 654–9)

Here, the object of horror, Sin characterised as female, is exposed to an obscene and complicating state of pain. The pain is partly created—as for Milton in the later Invocation, in the bedlam of a Maenadic 'savage clamour' (VII. 36)—by noise. The muffled din of the hell-hounds in full cry, on the scent, but enclosed in a parody of the *hortus conclusus*, in and out of which all creatures can scramble who are the children of sin, is an image of possession: the violation of private inner space by occupants ravening round the soft interior. Sin's womb becomes a world, an equation frequently made by the alchemists,[31] just as Hell itself is a world and had a womb, referred to in a disturbing travesty of the bisexual Creator-spirit as '*his* womb' (I. 673; my italics)[32] and set against the privacy of men's 'mother earth' (687), rifled by her gold-digging children. If Sin's womb is a world, plagued by intrusive noise it cannot void because it is self-generated, the implied relationship between this world of false creation and the creating mind of the poet who knows her story becomes alarmingly suggestive. This is the dark side of creativity, in which the magic lunar principle takes on a

nightmare Hecatean power, which the epic simile, as so often,
elucidates:

> Nor uglier follow the Night-hag, when called
> In secret, riding through the air she comes
> Lured with the smell of infant blood, to dance
> With Lapland witches, while the labouring moon
> Eclipses at their charms.
>
> (II. 662–6)

As Cornelius Agrippa tells us in his *Occult Philosophy*, sorceries
are most poisonous at the decrease or eclipse of the moon.[33]
Here the Lapland witches have power to cause the moon's
eclipse. Their orgiastic dance accompanies rites associated with
the products of infanticide: their secret power, predatory and
carnivorous, attacks life at its vulnerable outset. The 'Night-
hag' and her crew undo all that is civilised and natural, breaking
down the principle of growth. Thematically within the poem,
Milton links their arts with the mutilating rites performed by
the Maenadic women over the body of Orpheus. The
composing poet feels himself open as a child to forces he cannot
control. The 'infant blood' is *in-fans*, incapable of utterance.

Perhaps this therapeutic projection of his own deepest fears of
woman on to the person of Sin, at this early place in the epic,
made it possible for Milton to avoid burdening 'our general
mother' Eve with them (for he does very largely avoid this). In
projecting them onto the allegorical and Spenserian personification of Sin, he can also criticise and focus these feelings, so as
to turn his misogyny against humanity in general rather than
woman in particular. Sin is a female, but the female is not sinful.
Sin is inside all those who visit her in their odyssey, and they are
within her. We all breed her, as Satan originated her from his
head. Satan's birth-pangs are described as a sort of migrainous
crisis:

> All on a sudden miserable pain
> Surprised thee, dim thine eyes, and dizzy swum
> In darkness...
> ....
>   a goddess armed
>   Out of thy head I sprung...
>
> (II. 752–4, 757–8)

The point of the bisexual scheme upon which Milton structures *Paradise Lost* becomes clear at this point, where Sin like a defective Athena comes clear of Satan's head, in parthogenesis. A mind is equated with a world, a world with a womb. In attributing the female creative function to the closed structures of his cosmos, Milton can implicitly use the feminine as a measure of all things. In Book III the reflective narrative voice speaks of his own escape from 'the Stygian pool', as if he had in his own person nearly drowned in those dark, underground waters. The terrible music of his flight out of the Hades of his poem has been Satan's song 'through utter and through middle darkness borne' (16), 'utter' meaning 'outer' but also 'absolute' and 'speaking out, expressing'. In the 'dark descent' and reascent through the womb of his own mind, the poet's song has almost voided from the God-centred universe altogether. He has been Satan, remembered loving Sin (she is born with us, and of us) and made a new conspiracy with her. The tainting quality of the dark story is poignantly evident in Milton's relief at revisiting the less threatening but still anguished darkness of his blind eyes. The Invocation becomes more precisely personal as he shakes off the horror of the visit to hell:

> thee I revisit safe,
> And feel thy sovereign vital lamp; but thou
> Revisit'st not these eyes, that roll ·in vain
> To find thy piercing ray, and find no dawn;
> So thick a drop serene hath quenched their orbs,
> Or dim suffusion veiled. Yet not the more
> Cease I to wander where the Muses haunt
> Clear spring, or shady grove, or sunny hill,
> Smit with the love of sacred song; but chief
> Thee Sion and the flowery brooks beneath
> That wash thy hallowed feet, and warbling flow,
> Nightly I visit...
>
> (III. 21–32)

Warm light on an upturned face that has long been obscured in the chill of darkness is tangibly felt as a grateful release; but it is qualified by the image of sightless eyes that can never be warmed into vision. These eyes 'roll in vain' like planets that circle the life-giving sun. Alchemical images throughout *Paradise Lost* show the sun as the vital male principle that calls out its warm, living likeness in the otherwise cold and null matter of the cosmos through:

> his magnetic beam, that gently warms
> The universe, and to each inward part
> With gentle penetration, though unseen,
> Shoots invisible virtue even to the deep...
>   (III. 583–6)

The reiterated lull of 'gently...gentle' creates a strangely peaceful excitement. The soft motion of the creative principle which is like that of the Dove-Spirit in Book I, and like Adam's physical love of Eve so gently conjured in Book IV, is God's love sensuously pictured as the opposite of coercion. It causes the relaxation of what it touches, like the genial, warmth-giving God of the Cambridge Platonists with whom Milton has so much in common.[34] To the male principle is thus attributed the gentleness of a traditionally female nurturing, within the bisexual universe. Later, in Book VII (the lyrical Book of Creation), the light which will be expressed in the sun, and which pre-dates 'him', is personified as 'she' (248, 245). Where gender melts or shines into gender, unconfined by strictly drawn outlines, the sunlight so longed for by the blind poet achieves a totality of effect as having a power equal to all the powers of both the sexes, quintessentially represented. The extreme poignancy of the poet's blindness is also understood as a failure of 'gentle penetration'. The sunlight reflects on his skin as a superficial sensation only; it cannot enter the mind's womb through the eyes. The 'piercing ray' that can penetrate the nature of any common plant or stone, is sealed out by human blindness. He represents his interior as veiled, a window or door closed: 'wisdom at one entrance quite shut out' (III. 50). In this sense the poet stands as female to the sun's male; his channel of vision a birth-canal through which no generative imagery can enter to form new conceptions. The grief realised in the image he gives us of eyes 'rolling' to catch the light is produced by its sense of endless strain, along with exclusion from 'the cheerful ways of men' (46). The closed self that cannot be entered by light is trapped in a continual inner representation of the Fall, in a way that his cheerful fellows are not.

The more this personal loneliness is admitted, the further the poet of *Paradise Lost* moves towards the feminine, both as a source of consolation, and as an exact affinity. Even in his presentation of Sin, Milton showed the female as carrying, or enclosing, a burden of pain and alienation. Later the poetry will reach to enclose the stigmatised person of Eve in its self-identifying concern and protection. The female is stigmatised in a manner that is strangely close to the poet's own—stigmatised by and through her power to give birth, as the poet is. As he returns to the stability of earth in Book III, the double negative 'Yet not the more' draws him towards the previously abdicated territory of the classical Muses, the mind's own territory which it can conjure up from remembrances. The Muses do not exist, the poem chants; the classical deities are acknowledged fictions. Yet these unrealities call to be conjured up by Milton for the pressing needs of the moment of writing. He is willing in this Invocation to shade them into inspirations of 'sacred' song, despite recognition that the inspiration of Sion is more holy, the Hebrew Word more magical. The outpouring of divine light shining 'inwardly' which the blind poet can hope for, and which steadfastly eludes the open-eyed who can tell night from day, is a kind of terrible penalty even when it succours. The further the poet comes down to earth, to his mortal predicament, the more freely he allows himself to want and seek reassurance from the feminine principle. In shadow, he lives in a nocturnal world, and the night-world is always associated with the female. The shadow may be apprehended as the negative manifestation of Divinity, as in Pseudo-Dionysius' *Celestial Hierarchies*;[35] the mystic's apprehension of God as absence of nameable or visible attributes.[36] But this place of Orphic *nox*, or cabalistic *Ensoph* (the Nothing which is the highest Name of God) may be divine but is not naturally human. In that blind shadow, nothing human grows. The Invocation which equates the rapture of physical blindness with the power of more-than-human vision also records a wistfulness for the security of the merely human, and a sense of existential terror in the dark that precedes the power to sing and is never really dispersed by the achieved song. The mediatorial Muses gracefully enter his night, as clement figures bringing spellbinding relief from pain. In the night-world, only the most solitary, rare birds sing:

> Then feed on thoughts, that voluntary move
> Harmonious numbers; as the wakeful bird
> Sings darkling, and in shadiest covert hid
> Tunes her nocturnal note. Thus with the year
> Seasons return, but not to me returns
> Day...
>
> (III. 37–42)

We cannot think of the nightingale without recalling Philomela, Tereus' rape and the cutting-out of her tongue. Milton explicitly associates himself here with the archetype of the violated girl, whose person enters the natural scene as a requiem to her own lost humanity: an incarnate voice, beauty born from savage pain. Philomela and the poet represent an Orphic survival of barbaric mutilation. Considered as a divine transformation, theirs are cases of success, rebirth, recreation—in human terms, tragic impairment. Milton's repeated insistence on the 'unpremeditated' character of the poem, intuitive as birdsong, perfectly shaped out as dream, is first stated here in association with the feminine as exile from the fruitful sunlight, entered by force, generating a lonely music, unwilled as birth itself.

Between the Invocations to Book III and VII the reader has been introduced to Eve, 'our first mother', to the erotic love between Adam and herself, to a history of her life, told in her own words (IV. 440–91), and to her false dream, insinuated into her sleeping mind at night by Satan (V. 28–94). Suggestions of Eve's sexual openness are balanced by suggestions of Satan's sexual rapacity. Before contemplating this motif it is important to register just how high a place on the ladder of being Milton's Eve originally occupies. Before cleaving the idea of humanity down the centre into gendered, specific and unequal identities, the poet first insists (and goes out of his way to insist) on the unanimity and unity of human nature in virtue and divine quality. I have written elsewhere of the Edenic kingship as involving the solidarity of a jointly manifested 'naked majesty'.[37] Adam is not the totalitarian 'lord of all': Adam and Eve reign as 'lords of all'. The first visual presentation in Book IV suggests that grandeur of the humanist and Platonist 'noble shape' of Donatello or Michelangelo, sensuously and sculpturally beautiful, each 'erect and tall' with the rigour of the Puritan truthful soul:

> Two of far nobler shape erect and tall,
> Godlike erect, with native honour clad
> In naked majesty seemed lords of all,
> And worthy seemed, for in their looks divine
> The image of their glorious maker shone,
> Truth, wisdom, sanctitude severe and pure...
>   (IV. 288–93)

This stability of both genders within the framework of human perfection is carefully established *before* specialisation of gender is announced, in terms of which Eve is said to be made for 'softness' and 'grace' (itself a very double word, which can magnify into Grace) and Adam for 'contemplation' and 'valour'. There is passionate emphasis by the narrative voice on the erotic bond between these two distinguished genders, drawing Eve to 'lean' upon and towards 'our first father' (494), Adam to bend to her as his 'Sole partner and sole part' (411), implying not only her uniqueness but also that she is his 'soul-partner', even 'solar part', the part of Eden which reunifies the many into the One for him.

I read Eros in Book IV of *Paradise Lost* as the Platonistic and Hermetic agency of a secret magic of reconciliation in a Creation which has already been split in the very course of its making. This partly explains the sense of heightened personal feeling in Milton's description of Adam's and Eve's sexual longing for union—not merely the natural excitement a poet, being only human, is bound to feel at the chance to write erotic poetry, but a quality of philosophic or religious passion within the lines, which communicates the mystery and sanctity of sexual love in a state of innocence, so that we draw back from what is not quite exposed to us, as not liking to trespass upon holy ground. The poetry's power to conjure in a reader such awe has its travesty in its total revelation of the staring, greedy eyes of Satan in his intrusive, voyeuristic solitude, preying on the self-complete bliss in which he cannot participate, his frustrated desire and his ability to love these two beings 'imparadised' in one another (363). His sexual frustration makes what to us appears wistfully beautiful seem to him 'Sight hateful, sight tormenting!' (505), since one of the major sufferings in hell is eternally aroused, eternally unfulfilled sexual need (510–11). In the initial set-piece description of Eden (through Satan's eyes), the impression is given of its feminine nature, like a womb full of seeds (131–65). Disgorged from the womb of hell, Satan's rapist penetration of the universe resembles the journey of semen carrying a potentiality for contaminated growth. Eden is a *hortus conclusus*, like Spenser's Garden of Adonis, 'a spring shut up, a fountain sealed', which Satan's illicit entrance does not unseal (for he forces no gate, only leaps the wall). The Garden is an externalisation of the fruitful person of Eve, and an allegory, as in the patristic tradition,[38] of the psyche itself. It is linked, as she is, to the astral influences of the whole cosmos, which pour down to the sleeping world by night, renewing with lunar silver light what the sun will warm by day (670–3). Eve is to the Garden as Creation is to the All. A sense is projected of her containment of the seeds of everything that is to be, a sense too of her mysterious closeness to the source and end of all legitimate desire. Adam's sexual bliss does not just represent but actually is his re-entry into the ecstasy of union with his Creator. Book IV's attention to questions of cosmography as well as to Eros reinforces this mysterious meaning of sexuality. Like Bruno's in *De gli eroici furori* and *De l'infinito, universo e mondi*, Milton's vision of the enraptured body and soul in love is a vision of the accessibility of the cosmos and the Creator to the longing soul. Bruno's aggressive misogyny more than matches Milton's, and he is able to contradict it as joyously by calling sexual love 'that sweetest apple which the garden of our earthly paradise can produce'.[39] Sexual knowledge is intuitive, the only kind by which we can 'know' God, beyond reason. Bruno's elevated view of matter is also like Milton's: matter and spirit are opposites in the same kind.[40] An archangel can share man's meal with enjoyment; man has a language in common with the highest celestial orders; even in the fallen world his poem can mime their knowledge; men and angels want and need to make love, and the human methods are different not in kind but in degree. Making love is an act of *gnosis*, ecstatic initiation.

It is a fact often noted that, though Milton's Eve is declared to be naked, she is also seen clothed (with her hair); that though she is supposed to be freely erotic, she practises the art of 'sweet reluctant amorous delay' (IV. 311), which is held by readers to be as suspect as the sin-bred 'honour dishonourable' (314) of prudery against which Milton inveighs with scandalised indignation.[41] But it is crucial to see that these details emphasise the mystery of Eve's nature:

> half her swelling breast
> Naked met his under the flowing gold
> Of her loose tresses hid...
> (IV. 495–7)

What is 'naked' cannot logically be 'hid'. The poetry mimes Adam's perception of her nature, as if through a veil, hinted through only partial contact. She is hidden by herself. The divine experience sought in her is only to be found by guess-work, intuition, remembrance and by the final invisible (therefore 'hidden') inwardness of physical love-making. Her hair is God's colour, the gold of the sun. As 'flowing gold' it suggests alchemical virtue, the secret 'potable gold' made by the alchemist in his crucible. For Adam (mimed by the narrator and followed by the reader) it is as if all the beauty in the universe collects in the crucible of Eve's nature, and like Solomon's secret gold it evades definition, is seen purely by virtue of its hiddenness. In sexual union, the Hermetic *Asclepius* told the Renaissance, we are able momentarily not just to know but actually to become our own opposite:

> For if you note that supreme moment when, through interaction without pause, we come at last to this, that either sex infuses itself into the other, the one giving forth its issue, and the other eagerly taking hold on it and laying it up within, you will find that at that moment, through the intermingling of the two natures, the female acquires masculine vigour, and the male is relaxed in feminine languour.
>
> (*Asclepius*, III, 21, in *Hermetica*, p. 355)

Hermes explains that the act of sex must be secret because of this mutual exchange of gender; vulgar persons must inevitably mock this deepest mystery of all, which leaves the male unprotected by his customary status. Sexual love is thus seen in Hermetic terms as a mysterious return to our primal androgyny.

The spiritual centre of Book IV is the Hymn to Love, 'Hail wedded love, mysterious law', which covers the climactic moment in the inmost Bower of Eden, where Adam and Eve consummate their love and make secret exchange of knowledge. In fact we see nothing at all of this. Covering the consummation scene, Milton lets loose a tirade against the modern perversion of love (whether Roman Catholic, courtly or commercial), and returns to Adam and Eve only when they have enjoyed the mystery of sexual intercourse, to speak to them in the very personal voice which we have learned to recognise from the Invocations:

> Sleep on
> Blest pair; and O yet happiest if ye seek
> No happier state, and know to know no more.
> (*Paradise Lost*, IV 773–5)

We have a sense of intense emotion withheld, mysterious rites not pried into. There is the tenderness of the poem's father over the poem's momentarily sleeping and transiently safe children; conversely, regret on the part of one of the children of the Fall at the extent of the loss to the human inheritance, in the form of knowledge as pure joy:

> which lest we should think faulty, God himself conceals us not his own recreations before the world was built; *I was*, saith the eternall wisdome, *dayly his delight, playing always before him*. And to him indeed wisdom is as a high towr of pleasure, but to us a steep hill, and we toyling ever about the bottom... [Solomon] in the Song of Songs, which is generally beleev'd, even in the jolliest expressions to figure the spousals of the Church with Christ, sings of a thousand raptures between those two lovely ones farre on the hither side of carnall enjoyment.
>
> (*Tetrachordon*, pp. 596–7)

Eve in the Bower is the protected centre of Eden, circle within circle. She is a version of *Tetrachordon*'s 'eternall wisdome' (related then to the figure of Wisdom, sister to Milton's Muse in the Invocation to Book VII, 9–11). She is 'part' of Adam, whom he enters. He enters, therefore, himself and exists there in his most complete form. In a sense nothing can be said about this by the poet, nothing known, except from within. In *Pimander* Nature embraced Man in herself as part of the Divine Creation; Pimander advised Trismegistus to 'go toward himself' through knowing himself; that is, his true reflection in Nature. He tells of the gnostic trance, in which the soul leaves the body behind asleep, while it soars in enraptured love.[42] It is possible to see in Adam and Eve's mutual sleep this gnostic trance, cyphered in the fourfold incantation of the final line of the lullaby: 'No happier state, and know to know no more', which becomes 'know' four times, and simultaneously the elegiac call against the passing of a history which has long been irrevocable: 'no, no, no, no'.

If this *gnosis* is thought of as central to the lyrical presentation of Eros in Milton's Paradise, the Hermetic theme of the highest knowledge as being *nox, nihil, Ensoph*—the nothing—human love is seen as reaching to the threshold of the Divine, the 'unutterable' which words cannot encounter, a silence beyond speech. Its theology may be seen as being optimistically at variance with the surface polemic and as being gathered at the end into a powerful affirmation of the *felix culpa* theme. Considered in the light of such a motif, the total meaning of Book IV may be revised. The balance moves towards the feminine as a mysterious—or the mysterious—revelation of the divine. Eve's account of her 'birth', her quest for her image, her flight from and seizure by Adam (IV. 440–91) has traditionally been seen as evidence of her dangerously fallible nature, its tendency to vanity (through the implied emblem of Narcissus) and, by some, a sign of her already fallen disposition, incriminating to her maker, who should have known better.[43] But this is to simplify the Narcissus allusion in a way which Renaissance mythography would have thought crass. Eve's search in water for a reflection of her true self is a genuine parable of man's quest for identity, adapting the Narcissus story (in a Neoplatonist interpretation) to the Hermetic creation myth, whereby (in the *Pimander*) newly created Man fell in love with his own divine 'reflection. . .in the water, and its shadow on the earth' (see p. 198 above). Eve remembers that the 'liquid plain' of the still lake 'to me seemed another sky' (IV. 455, 459), and her perception is not inauthentic. In being heaven-reflecting, the lake is a true image of reality, leading to a truer image. Renaissance Platonism did not impute a blameworthy or sterile vanity or 'narcissism' to Narcissus but rather saw his myth as incorporating the potentially fatal difficulties of the dualistic scheme according to which soul and matter were married in indissoluble embrace. Ficino, translator of the *Hermetica* as well as of Plato, allegorised 'The young Narcissus' in his *Commentary on Plato's 'Symposium'* as 'the soul of rash and inexperienced man' who:

> does not look at his own face, does not notice his own proper substance and qualities, but pursues his shadow in water and tries to embrace it...and turns his back on his own beauty.
>
> (Ficino)[44]

In Ficino's Platonist adaptation, the Narcissus myth acquires philosophical dignity and a nobler meaning. In the *Commentary* he has explained that 'the sun's light in water' is at four removes from the real sunlight. It is a shadow of light in air, which itself shadows radiance in fire, itself a shadow of the sun's light. Eve is born, it seems, into some such area of quadruple shadow, having to find her way by stages to a knowledge of the real. But to admit this is only to agree that she is human-born, like us (Adam is not), and that she is 'young' like Ficino's Narcissus. She speaks of her 'inexperienced thought', and the story she has to tell (together with the gentle mood of the poem as it reflects on these experiences) is really a parable of how, through the senses, one may reach beyond the delusive world of sense-impressions, rather than an initial subversion of Eve's dignity on the part of Milton, or a defamation of character.[45]

An association of the cupped lake with a genuine kind of knowledge is offered by the Hermetic text *A Secret Discourse of Hermes to Tat*, in which the Deity is quaintly said to have let down a basin into the cosmos, inviting humanity to dip itself therein and get 'a share of *gnosis*...and so become complete men' (*Hermetica*, p. 151). Eve, like the gnostic seeker, looks for a union of identity with the universe in which she finds herself a separate unit of being. The voice which calls her away from her own surface-reflection leads her to a fuller enjoyment of her self, a reality of which she is the image:

I will bring thee where no shadow stays
Thy coming, and thy soft embraces, he
Whose image thou art, him thou shall enjoy
Inseparably thine, to him shalt bear
Multitudes like thyself, and thence be called
Mother of human race...

(Paradise Lost, IV. 470-5)

The voice of God does not forbid Eve to enjoy her self, though it points out the drawback of loving one's own image: 'With thee it came and goes' (469). Rather, the voice encourages a more sustained and comprehensive Narcissism, in the higher, gnostic and Platonist sense. Having seen the image of herself, like Pimander, and like Bruno's Actaeon in *Gli eroici furori*, she may move more deeply towards the reality. Bruno's Actaeon sees the most beautiful possible reflection 'Here, amongst the waters, that is in the mirrors of similitude...the brightness of divine goodness and splendour'.[46] Eve is persuaded to move more closely into the divine reality of herself, 'where no shadow stays/Thy coming'. The tone is one of gentle elucidation, faintly amused, as of the Ancient of Days to his youngest child, and our sense of Eve's youth is strong. She is from the very beginning far more like us than Adam can be, having the metaphorical equivalent of an infancy (the baby playing with its image in a mirror experiences the conspiracy of genuine friendship). Through this intimacy we witness Milton's poem expressing the Hermetic urge to synthesise reflection with reality; for the disjunction into hierarchy to reunite, so that higher moves to lower (Adam chases Eve) and lower can naturally rise to higher (Eve is not kept in an abject state of childish ignorance; her *gnosis* expands).

This movement of the two into one, miming the democratic tendency Christopher Hill sees in Hermeticism,[47] also reflects the passionate emphasis on Christ's mediatorial function throughout Milton's works. The second person of the Trinity longs to come down to be with, and to be, mankind, paralleling the desire of the male to take to himself his supposed inferior, to be in the female, and to be her. Eve remembers Adam chasing her, calling 'Return, fair Eve'. For the Platonist these words must be charged with philosophical implications. She emanates (*emanatio*), is called upon to turn, her perception clarified (*raptio*), to bring her expanded and animated nature back into its source (*remeatio*). Syntax constantly identifies subject and object, as in 'Whose image thou art, him thou shalt enjoy' (472): *him thou*. Here she is active to his passive, and shortly afterwards passive to his active, as he pursues her, as Apollo did Daphne, but a Daphne whom no dehumanising tree-magic will root down, to prevent the breeding of new images of her own divinely beautiful self as 'Mother of human race'. In describing the final phase of her initiation, Eve recounts a rapture which is imaged in the male's seizing of the female. The poetry seems to emphasise the roughness of this seizure:

> Part of my soul I seek thee, and thee claim
> My other half: with that thy gentle hand
> Seized mine, I yielded, and from that time see
> How beauty is excelled by manly grace
> And wisdom, which alone is truly fair.
>
> (IV. 487–91)

Adam identifies himself as the basis of an original creative androgyny, conferring his soul on her and claiming hers in return. The 'seizing' of Eve's hand leads to her 'seeing' a higher truth than she had know before. She is rapt, or enraptured. The poetry insists on the element of violence in the simultaneously gentle release of the soul from lower to higher knowledge. As blind eyes are fiercely burned by the light of truth, like Bruno's *illuminati*, as the poet is '*Smit* with the love of sacred song' (III. 29), so the lover is 'Seized' with joyful awareness of the beauty of Wisdom, and the mystic is seized by the nature of God.

Alongside the magical knowledge which centres around Eve and the female, Milton recognises the subversive power of the daemonic magic. The world of *Paradise Lost* is populated by daemonic spirits, both good and evil. The words of the poem, like the sacred Hebrew mother-tongue of the Bible, seek to stay the destructive force of the evil daemons. In Book IV Satan is ranged against Gabriel, Uzziel, Ithuriel and Zephon. The Book of Love contains the threat of war. Eve's divinely open nature offers access to its enemy, who can enter through the dream which Satan, 'squat like a toad' pours into her sleep in Book IV and she recounts in Book V.[48] The closeness of this flood of potentially contaminating dream-poetry, which travesties the 'ravishment' (V. 46) experienced with Adam, to the poet's experience of the danger latent in *ekstasis*, is very clear, and clearly recognised in the Invocations to Books VII and IX. These Invocations reflect the state of mind in which the meditating poet finds himself, awakening from the love-trance of composition and ritually searching out his way back. They also reflect his judgment on the reality of the poem, on the problem of whether it is authentic light or shadowed imagery at several removes from its true source. Images of presumptuous flight predominate, such as Eve's bad dream entertained (V. 78–93): Milton has 'presumed' (VII. 13) as a guest-observer in Heaven; he has 'soared' above Mount Olympus; the flying steed of sacred poetry reminds him disconcertingly of Bellerophon's 'unreined' (17), and he has a sense of possible loss of control, returning headlong, as if:

> Dismounted, on the Aleian field I fall
> Erroneous there to wander and forlorn.
> (VII. 19–20)

In Eve's prophetic dream, she:

> flew, and underneath beheld
> The earth outstretched immense, a prospect wide
> And various: wondering at my flight and change
> To this high exaltation; suddenly
> My guide was gone, and I, me thought, sunk down,
> And fell asleep...
> (V. 87–92)

The dream-poet and the human dreamer both nurse the same horror of offending, as it were, in their sleep—the intuitive life breaking its constraints so that they 'sink down' onto a pathless world of exile. The tone and mood of the Invocation to Book VII, with its brooding introspection as to the possibly 'erroneous' character of the poet's choices, with the consequence of a fresh loss of Eden through the poem's presumption, is close to the treatment of Eve in the concluding moments of solitary innocence in Book IX. While the poet may awaken to find himself on the Aleian, or alien, field, cursed, an exile from God, whose image he has distorted in the making,

Eve is imagined in Book IX as causing Heaven to become 'alienated' (9), keeping 'distance and distaste'. *Paradise Lost* recognises that it may ultimately be judged as a grandiose mistake. It addresses Eve with an elegiac sense of affinity: 'O much deceived, much failing, hapless Eve' (IX. 404). Poet and woman are subjected to temptations which speak to them in a kind of dream language, so that each is credulous (the converse of the real faith each truly has) and rather deceived than fraudulent. Each is seen as profoundly unsafe, as if by nature forced to inhabit a borderline of intuition, keeping a nearly impossible balance, surrounded by staggeringly disproportionate forces of emnity.

The Invocation to Book VII echoes the word 'safe' (15, 24) and the word 'evil' (25, 26) in close association. Likewise, as Satan approaches Eve in Book IX, we perceive her vulnerability to the preying eyes and evil presence that stalks her:

> Standing on earth, not rapt above the pole
> More safe I sing with mortal voice, unchanged
> To hoarse or mute, though fallen on evil days,
> On evil days though fallen, and evil tongues;
> In darkness, and with dangers compassed round,
> And solitude...
>   (VII, Invocation, 23–8)

> Such ambush hid among sweet flowers and shades
> Waited with hellish rancour imminent
> To intercept thy way, or send thee back
> Despoiled of innocence, of faith, of bliss.
> ....
>   fairest unsupported flower,
> From her best prop so far, and storm so nigh.
> Nearer he drew...
>   (IX. 408–11, 432–4)

It is curious that although Milton speaks of himself as 'more safe' having returned to his middle position on solid earth, we feel his position as being in fact less safe than when he was (as if obliviously and in dream) 'rapt above the pole'. The raptured trance that leaves the individual's present miseries behind, being dispersed, there is a reduction to self-consciousness, to the toll of words which obsess the mind in the world of shadows and dark speech, outside Eden: *fallen/evil days/evil days/fallen/ evil tongues/darkness*. The blind self crushed in the tiny space at the centre of the chiasmus hangs on an unatoning cross of words. The passage represents for us, unforgettably, Milton's republic of one man, surrounded by Restoration England with its eyes upon him, hunted and spoken against. He has incanted with the powerful Word, and called up visions. But in Book VII we seem to hear the hissing of 'evil tongues' around the life-sized poet who has fallen into the proximity of an 'ambush' not very distinct from that of Eve, whom darkness, evil speech and an evil day approach in Satan's form. In each case we have a sense of the singling out and segregation of an individual from his or her secure source; a trap laid and to be sprung—in Eve's case a 'rape' being meditated and very close to being committed. At the moment preluding defloration, or recording it, we feel most intensely the uniqueness and divinity of what is being tampered with.

Responding to this acute awareness of 'descent', Milton's Invocation to Book VII calls up a host of feminine figures and personifications to fence him round. But these figures have the gossamer faintness of Diana's nymphs in Spenser's *Faerie Queene*, seeking to protect her truth from being seen into (see p. 81 above). As Milton's epic draws towards portrayal of, and implication in, the human Fall, his vision threatens to lose the power of ascent in *gnosis*, and the Muse is increasingly isolated in the unassimilated feminine. Searching to name the benign presence who inspires his dreams, he signals his uncertainty by a conditional:

> Descend from heaven Urania, by that name
> If rightly thou art called...
> . . . .
> The meaning, not the name I call: for thou
> Nor of the Muses nine, nor on the top
> Of old Olympus dwell'st, but heavenly born,
> Before the hills appeared, or fountain flowed,
> Thou with eternal Wisdom didst converse,
> Wisdom thy sister...

(VII. 1–2, 5–10)

Having isolated the Muse and tentatively named her, a problem of sisters fans out and elaborates itself through twelve lines. Her eight classical sisters are roused only to be cancelled out, but somehow their images remain like shadows on the retina; a replacement sister is produced, sacred Wisdom, guaranteeing twofold protection and leading back to a time before Genesis, in the beginning ('Before the hills appeared'). The strange difficulty of naming the Muse is elaborated in line 28, where Milton defies his exposed position in the modern world:

> yet not alone, while thou
> Visit'st my slumbers nightly, or when morn
> Purples the east...
>
> (VII. 28–30)

We should compare this with Book IX, where we are told that Milton's Muse:

> deigns
> Her nightly visitation unimplored,
> And dictates to me slumbering, or inspires
> Easy my unpremeditated verse...
>
> (IX. 21–4)

Both occasions insist that *Paradise Lost* is at least in part a dream-poem, completely outside conscious control. The Puritan doctrine of inspiration merges naturally and easily with the classical *ekstasis*, but if the idea of the soul's enlightenment through Grace is Christian, its imagery implies the classical and feminine. The poet is the passive receiver of *her* 'nightly' dictation; with the threshold of dawn, waking words come in a natural flow. Both Invocations insist on the poet's lack of willed contribution. But between Books VII and IX some shift of mood has taken place—a burden eased. The female figures which divided into various groups in Book VII—the true Muse and her sister Wisdom; the gracious but regrettably fictitious classical Muses; the ferocious Amazons (fought by Bellerophon) and the parallel Maenads—have faded and simplified. Only one single, infallible figure remains, to convey authority for the 'tragic' (6) material remaining. He does not try to name her. But we may recollect the pleasing Platonistic conceit which had it that, if the universe is structured as a musical scale, then Urania is the topmost Muse on the scale of which Proserpina is the lowest: the breath of heaven, the breath of earth.[49] What intervenes to recreate Milton's Orphic confidence is, precisely, that the poet comes down to earth, mother-and-daughter earth—in the great hexæmeral Genesis hymn of Book VII, the most 'feminine' of all the Books in *Paradise Lost*. Here Milton sings the Creation of the world, and thus returns in spirit to the vitality of the beginning, circling back to the dove-like androgynous Creator-Spirit of Book I and looking forward to the dream of Eve, through whose womb the Word of God will enter the future: 'By me the promised seed shall all restore' (XII. 623). Through the bliss of shaping the visionary world of the mother-planet in Book VII, the poet redeems himself from the scattering, punishing experience of descent. Here he recreates the earth's unity with the heavens, mother with father, Pimander with Genesis, self with poem, poem with cosmos.

MOTHER EARTH

No baby, it is said, could have been introduced and sustained in the grandiose epic atmosphere of *Paradise Lost*: I doubt if that is so. Milton used to say in the mornings as he urgently awaited the arrival of his amanuensis to relieve him of the heavy burden of poetry that had accumulated overnight, that he '*wanted to bee milked*',[50] a bovine analogy not absolutely disparaging to the dignity of poetry considered as the food of life itself. The central theme of *Paradise Lost* is generated: the birth of our world and its creatures, the rebirth of the soul after loss of contact with the Creator, the birth of Christ the Light, Logos and child, 'our great Expectation.../The Seed of Woman' (XII. 378-9). To record this theme coherently, a mother-principle must be present. But Milton, who wrote so gratefully and graciously *Ad Patrem*, had never brought himself to write *Ad Matrem* and had clearly spent considerable time trying to persuade himself that he was, like law, a 'Masculin Birth' exclusively. It was not until he reached the sober stillness of emotion in *Paradise Regained*, with its absence of a sexual love component, that he was able to mute his antagonism sufficiently to write other than obliquely about a mother-child relationship. But what cannot be expressed forthrightly may find an all the more truthful and just expression through displacement into symbol. In Book VII of *Paradise Lost* we are guests at the birthday of Creation (256). It is the most magical Book of all. In his seventh Book, six plus one days of Creation are recorded, mystically figuring the mathematical beauty of the cosmos; the Word's creation of our world is spelt out to us in words which seem lyrically knowable representations of the first Word; talismanic-seeming images of the composition of the universe are poured out to us in a poetry whose bounty and fluency dramatises the infinite cosmos of Milton's vision. The material universe of Book VII is young, at its quick inception. It is only just parting company with its Original. The light, warmth and vigour of the loving Father are visible in His children, which burst from the egg of potentiality in astonishing outbreaks of self-declaration. Book VII is truly Orphic in the animation of its song, its incantation of the sacred matter vitalised by the Creator-Spirit. It sings life and motion into all creation. Stone is warm with sentient life, trees dance, the planets are stirred by emotion. The poet's vision includes an experience of mother-and-child, the mystery of the child's first opening of fresh eyes upon the universe. Out of his *nox*, the unnamable darkness of his apparently uncreative condition, the magus-poet is able to conjure the Creator's great and vital artwork, easily and freely, in serial acts of naming. These are sacred acts, remembering the cabbalistic belief that in naming the Divine we rapturously know it.

Bruno had spoken in *Lo Spaccio* of the rich colour-scheme of the universe, colour flowing all the way along the channel of Nature: 'the Sun in the Crocus, in the narcissus, in the heliotrope, in the rooster, in the lion', which may be discerned by mortal eyes which, through sensuously responding to the fluent pattern of the natural world, achieve immediate contact with the Divine.[51] He speaks of 'the womb of nature' from which all this golden meaning is generated.[52] Milton's song in Book VII yields a like vision of individualities all flowing together, not pre-formed but in their million 'sudden' (317) acts of emergence. What is inside springs out, 'forth...forth...up' (320-1); the latent becomes actual. Each life is motion, not stasis. Nothing is completed.

Genesis is not felt to be in the past, for what was created 'in the beginning' is recreated 'now' (463) in the moment of being described and in all subsequent acts of reading. We have a sensation of the likeness of our own (allegedly fallen) planet to the unfallen, teeming earth of Milton's hexaëmeron, whose heroic pastoral urges us to believe that the cosmos still and eternally reflects the glory of God's creativity. Though it is the case that Milton's God sets down no human infant in that first world, he draws from it infancy itself, so that the seas covering the mother-world 'With fry innumerable swarm' (400), and the birds:

> Their brood as numerous hatch, from the egg that soon
> Bursting with kindly rupture forth disclosed
> Their callow young...
>
> (VII. 418–20)

'Kindly rupture' characterises Milton's treatment of the Fall as fortunate (heretically inclining though that idea may be)—the Fall as a birth. In Book VII the poet 'descends' from heaven to earth on the verge of its own lapse, and finds there a multiplication of the One, a rupture in the sealed wall of the Divine Nature from which break pours being, both great and small. 'Kind' or species liberate their natures; the break is 'kindly' that yields the first view of the potency of God revealed in a blind and naked baby bird when first light enters its opened shell. So too, in a more complicated way, man's expulsion from the garden of his origins will reflect a pain instinct with joy and purpose—a fuller realisation of Divine Possibility. The 'callow young' are safe in their mobile world; for, it is important to see, the nest is not their home. They do not have to depend on an external shelter when 'feathered soon and fledge/They summed their pens...soaring' (420–1). Swift time 'soon' passing matures their power to exist independently. Their home is themselves; the appearance of supreme vulnerability (as 'callow young') 'soon' passes. Just so Eve awakens from her inspired trance at the end of the poem, with superb assurance that proves her 'fledged':

> but now lead on;
> In me is no delay; with thee to go

> Is to stay here; without thee here to stay,
> Is to go hence unwilling; thou to me
> Art all things under heaven, all places thou,
> Who for my wilful crime art banished hence.
>   (XII. 614–19)

Her speech is in the active mood, brisk and definite. It is a putting forth of the heroic will, with absolute conviction. Eve defines herself by internals, as a Puritan. Love asserts itself as a right and a faith, with its own characteristic language. This final speech of the epic is a love-poem, a commitment under the higher covenant with her Creator (Adam is all things and all places, but only 'under heaven'). The infolding of subject and object (*In me/with thee, thou to me*) in a rhythm of balance and certainty, informed by intense joy, leaves us with no cause to pity her. For Eve, the disclosure from Paradise takes the form of a 'kindly rupture', hatched into the future with the certainty of fruitfulness. It constitutes, therefore, at the end of the poem, a return to Genesis, the Word of God having breathed knowledge and an appropriate language into her mind through dream. Book XII returns to Book VII, which again returns to Book I, regenerating, so that at beginning, middle and end we sense the presence of the 'mighty wings outspread' of the Dove-Spirit. The chiastic structures within Eve's speech mime her sure return to the original androgynous condition of creativity, *stay here/here to stay*; so do its internal rhymes, *In me/with thee*; so do its tense attraction of the subject to object, *thou to me*. Adam has been subjected to two full Books of the most punishing education of his ego by Michael. His reason has been overhauled and taught the wholesome but unlovely virtue of Temperance. This is one form of knowledge, but it is not *gnosis*. Eve is granted the greater poetic miracle, to know by insight and to be reborn through that illumination. Through this timeless knowledge, she will become a home for new entities, taking on her role as 'mother of mankind'.

The maternal role in which Milton praises Eve and nature is seen as a metaphor for man's highest latent capacities. As created beings, we also long to create. This divine urge is imaged in Book VII as the pouring out of God's power into and through the great system of genders. On the first day of the

Creation, God's command is 'Let there be light' (243). Since
Christ has previously been identified with light, as first-born
Creator (III. 1-6), we might expect a masculine association. But
the Latin is feminine, *lux*. She is 'first of things', a daughter of
God, like Wisdom in Book VII, and because she predates the
sun, 'she in a cloudy tabernacle/Sojourned the while' (248-9).
When *Sol* is fashioned, 'she' will inform 'him'. 'He' will then
shine upon earth, which is female; 'she' will divulge the male and
female offspring of 'her' womb. The wholeness of the universe is
therefore urged not by a system of Aristotelian categorically
separated units but by the mystical action of 'her' in 'him' in
'her' and so on through the entire scale of being.[53] This arousal
of our sense of a powerful flow of genders helps to give Book
VII such a freely imaginative character. We participate in the
Creation through arousal at reading of its sympathetic pattern.
Milton's circling song of praise for God's art also echoes the
Creation, containing as it does the angels' song of praise, which
fluently rounds each day of Creation, 'circumfluous' as the
waters that lap around the created earth (270). The very
grammar declares this: 'Creator him they sung'. The active art
of the angels names 'him', and through this naming it
participates in the Creation. The power to sing is realised as
creative in a more than fanciful way. Like Orphic incantation,
and without the need of a classical Muse to 'defend/Her son',
Milton through singing Genesis, enacts it. Through conjuring
up light, he sees into each particle of Creation, and each process:

> The earth was formed, but in the womb as yet
> Of waters, embryon immature involved,
> Appeared not: over all the face of earth
> Main ocean flowed, not idle, but with warm
> Prolific humour softening all her globe,
> Fermented the great mother to conceive,
> Satiate with genial moisture...
>
>   (VII. 276-82)

The description of earth's gestation and delivery of her children
resembles a scientifically exact but emotionally highly wrought
description of human fertilisation and childbirth. Earth
throughout this paragraph is described in terms appropriate to a

woman's body: 'she' has a 'face' (316) and a 'bosom' (319), and
the hills, tufted woodlands, valleys and fountains (326–8) are
reminiscent of the traditional topography of the female body
used by Shakespeare in *Venus and Adonis* to more salacious
effect, and by Spenser in the Garden of Adonis (see pp. 87–8
above). Milton's allusion to the tradition is deeply sensuous. It is
personal in a particular sense, like those very personal 'scientific'
experiments in the alchemist's crucible, where Sol and Luna
combine in the person of a love-locked hermaphrodite
suspended in fluid, with such very human faces.[54]

Alchemical allusion is explicit and important in Milton's
account of the Creation, especially in relation to the theme of
Mother Earth. In alchemy the primal Mother, *Mater Natura*, is
an indispensable focus of the alchemical work, its essential
beginning and a final return: '*Terra enim est mater Elemen-
torum; de terra procedunt et ad terram revertuntur*', 'mightiest
nature of the natures...who comest with the light and art
born with the light, who hast given birth to the misty darkness, who art the mother of all beings!'[55] Paracelsus' beautiful
passages concerning Creation, and the creativity of woman,
do justice to the female principle:

> There are three different kinds of matrix: the first is the water on
> which the spirit of God was borne, and this was the maternal womb
> in which heaven and earth were created. Then heaven and earth each
> in turn became a matrix, in which Adam, the first man, was formed
> by the hand of God. Then woman was created out of man; she
> became the maternal womb of all men, and will remain so to the end
> of the world. Now, what did that first matrix contain within itself?
> Being the kingdom of God, it encompassed the spirit of God. The
> world encloses the eternal, by which it is at the same time
> surrounded. Woman is enclosed in her skin as in a house, and
> everything that is within it forms, as it were, a single womb.
>
> (Paracelsus, pp. 97–8)

He goes on to say that woman is 'the maternal womb of man'
(p. 100), the world into which he is born being another womb,
so that man is always *in utero*. Woman is superior to man as the
strong fruit-tree is to its vulnerable pears (p. 100); she is the tree
of life itself. Just as much as man, she is 'beloved by God' (p. 99).
This kind of alchemical link between the waters of the

firmament in Genesis, the receptacle formed by heaven and earth, and the creative womb of woman has an obvious relevance to Milton's account of the 'womb.../Of waters' in Book VII. The 'fermentation' process in which the softening liquors seep into the surface of the unseen world, preparing it for birth, is seen as a transmutation at once scientifically controlled and personally joyous. The inanimate universe at its origins is as open to pleasure as human nature is. 'Satiate' means full but also satisfied; 'genial moisture' is conducive to generation but also loving and friendly. God's great work, beginning with the operation of the Dove-Spirit upon the *prima materia* of the Abyss (235–42) is represented as an alchemical work. Light pours into the sun, flooding it with golden 'liquid light' (362), and fountains out again to warm, order and nurture the other stars (364–5). In this way, the universe is recognisably human before humanity enters it. With each new birth a reader may be enabled to be born again into a fresh sense of the beauty of the creation, asserted as sudden statements of individual being, each divine, rising into full freedom:

> The earth obeyed, and straight
> Opening her fertile womb teemed at a birth
> Innumerable living creatures ...
> . . . .
> The tawny lion, pawing to get free
> His hinder parts, then springs as broke from bonds,
> And rampant shakes his brinded mane...
>   (VII. 453–5, 464–6)

When man the miracle is born, last of all, he hardly appears more miraculous than the animal species breaking urgently out of their mother's body, and 'teeming' into the reader's mind. Birth is presented as a release into an astonishing variety of intuitive life: the animals know what they are to be, how to behave, and long to do it. The poetry's magic effects dazzling conjuring tricks. Verbs reinvent themselves from the Anglo-Saxon, tense as coiled springs: *upsprung* (462), or heavy with the load of being, *upheaved* (471). Birth delivers masterpieces of artistic illusionism: 'The grassy clods now calved' (463)—we see the turf at the moment of breaking open, its contents scrambling out. The tiger erupts from what seems at first a molehill; the stag's antlers branch up in the semblance of a tree, before that graceful and kingly creature is truly seen (469–70); flocks are born 'As plants', and as they emerge we hear them bleat. Glorious humour closes the gap between Genesis and the fallen reader. By its alchemical transformations of familiar objects which our senses falsely think they know, the poetry of Book VII divulges original truths. By displacing his treatment of the feminine from the human to the physical universe in relation to its children, Milton evades the poetic restrictions of the old grudge he bears womankind, to celebrate the feminine in a pastoral hymn to Mother Earth and Father Sky, balancing *Ad Patrem* by *Ad Matrem*.

What poetry does not persuade us to accept, theology cannot coerce us to believe. The poetic effect of Book VII's images may seem stronger than the instructions of the admonitory angel advising Adam in Book VIII 'with contracted brow' (560). Raphael's advice not to trust the beautiful external form of Eve as if it were Highest Wisdom contradicts the implied message of Book VII's lyricism celebrating the divine perfection of earth and all her children. Adam admits to Raphael his feeling that in company with Eve:

> All higher knowledge in her presence falls
> Degraded, wisdom in discourse with her
> Loses discountenanced, and like folly shows...
>   (VIII. 551–3)

Raphael, apparently oppressed by worry based on experience of seeing his brother-angels 'fall/Degraded', and loaded with God's message, has to reply with a harangue distinguishing 'love' from 'passion', warning about the dire consequences of uxoriousness, and emphasising Adam's higher status than Eve on the scale of measurable value. Adam replies in terms of the proven identity of Eve with himself as 'both one soul', and in a wonderfully humorous moment turns back the archangel's probings upon himself: 'Love not the heavenly spirits, and how their love/Express they...?' (615–16). Adam seems to imply, very delicately, that perhaps Raphael does not know what he is talking about, because he has never experienced it. Raphael, of course, is undoubtedly theologically correct in issuing his warnings. But there is a secret sense—taught us by Book IV and the Orphic Book VII, and which we should never absolutely resign—in which it is right to say of Eve that 'All higher knowledge in her presence falls'. It is the intuitive or sexual *gnosis* which cannot be imparted by ratiocination, however, strenuous and earnest. But Adam cannot explain this to Raphael because it has its own silent language which does not translate into any other. As in the *Secret Discourse of Hermes to Tat*, an element of sublime humour enters with the teacher's inability to articulate what the uninitiated cannot in any case comprehend. Tat becomes incensed at the impotence of words to convey reality:

> *Tat.* Your words are riddles father; you do not speak to me as a father to his son—*Hermes.* This sort of thing cannot be taught, my son; but God, when he so wills, recalls it to our memory.—*Tat.* But what you say is impossible, father; it does violence to common sense...—*Hermes.* What can I say, my son? This thing cannot be taught...to such eyes as yours I am not now visible.—*Tat.* Father, you have driven me to raving madness...
>
> (*Hermetica*, p. 241)

And so it goes on, with the initiate expressing his suave relish for being in the know, and Tat in a state of escalating tantrum at his unreasonable exclusion from the divine secret. Finally, Tat goes silent. When he has finished being silent, he is declared to be reborn:

> I see myself to be the All. I am in heaven and earth, in water and in air; I am in beasts and plants; I am a babe in the womb, and one that is not yet conceived, and one that has been born.
>
> (*Hermetica*, p. 247)

He soon bursts forth into a hymn of praise. In *Paradise Lost*, of course, it is Raphael who plays Hermes' role ('Like Maia's son he stood,/And shook his plumes' [V. 285–6]) and Adam the disciple's. Nevertheless, hierarchy in the cosmos of Milton's poem is fluid rather than military: higher and lower may communicate as near-equals (that is the point of Raphael's sharing of Adam's meal), and the lower may have something special and unique in his experience to confer upon the higher.

Adam knows something Raphael does not at first admit to knowing. He tries to tell it in the approximate vocabulary: 'All higher knowledge in her presence falls'. Then he tries to hint, through invoking shared experience: 'Love not the heavenly spirits...?' In fact, Raphael understands the allusion: 'Total they mix' (627). This 'mixing' is the experience of the All, the Hermetic flow of imagination into all being. It constitutes the *gnosis* compared to which discourse of wisdom does stale to become an occupation for Bedlam. (The extreme of this experience is found in the deadly ratiocinations pursued by the fallen angels in hell, who 'reasoned high/Of providence...' [II. 558-9] in coils of endless argument, full of hard words. It implies our mutual separation.) In Paradise, Adam says and Milton demonstrates, knowledge is *eros*, the immediate and total mixing of knower and known, 'discountenancing' other kinds of knowledge which stop at the surfaces, or faces, of things. It is as if behind the doctrinally committed, punitive God who curses and expels Adam and Eve, there existed within the poem a God who is made in a revolutionary humanist image, coloured by Gnosticism and Hermeticism, who need never be lost to mankind. We recognise what Adam is trying to tell Raphael because *eros* survives the Fall, to be enjoyed and, perhaps, outside Eden's habitual joy, to be more fully appreciated, as a form of knowledge in its pristine condition, formulated at the end of the poem as 'A paradise within thee, happier far' (XII. 587). The Fall of Adam is apprehended by us as genuinely tragic and heroic because he falls for such good reason—Eve:

> How can I live without thee, how forgo
> Thy sweet converse and love so dearly joined,
> To live again in these wild woods forlorn?
> Should God create another Eve, and I
> Another rib afford, yet love of thee
> Would never from my heart; no no, I feel
> The link of nature draw me: flesh of flesh,
> Bone of my bone thou art, and from thy state
> Mine never shall be parted, bliss or woe.
>   (IX. 908-16)

Few can in their hearts believe that this grief-stricken reduction to his basic loyalty can or should be called 'false chivalry', 'corrupt patriotism'.[56] In a valid sense Eve is a real source of knowledge to Adam, in the 'highest' sense of all; she is himself, and in refusing to accept separation from what has been 'so dearly joined' he asserts his loyalty to his earliest emotional commitment, fulfilling his human nature by breaking out of Eden 'with kindly rupture', linked indissolubly with the feminine which was originally drawn from him, and is him: 'flesh of flesh,/Bone of my bone'.

CERES AND PROSERPINA

Such an implied heresy as I have outlined above is flamboyantly at odds with Milton's professed aim to justify the patriarchal God whose theology is laid out in Book III of *Paradise Lost*, with its respect for contract-law and the hierarchy of obedience. It flies in the face of *De Doctrina Christiana*. It contradicts Milton's own best and frequently expressed anti-female principles. St Augustine had remarked that woman was a bag of excrement; St Bernard of Clairvaux called his own sister a whore and a heap of dung.[57] With such illustrious patristic points of view behind him as authorities and guides, Milton might well have indulged his own legitimated spleen as a major constituent of *Paradise Lost*'s Christian ideology. It would then have stood as a far more retributive and punitive poem than it actually is. When we consider the venomous libels which the Christian and Pauline tradition permits its sons to utter against woman, and Milton's known tendency to exercise this right without restraint, both in day-to-day life and in his prose and some of his poetry, it is in the highest sense mysterious, that some more powerful compulsion drove the poet of *Paradise Lost* to honour the 'link of nature' that is man's life-line to the feminine. It is not so much a judicious mitigation, or inhibition of a misogynistic bias (for the 'feminine' parts of the epic do not feel at all inhibited) as an allowing of intense emotional affinity to pour across the entire cosmos of the poem. *Paradise Lost* reads as a unified whole. It does not seem to be experienced as a fratricidal struggle of incompatible points of view but rather as a passionate reconciliation of apparent contraries, an embodiment of the Renaissance *concordia discors* or *coincidentia oppositorum*.

I shall suggest in the final image contemplated here that allusion to the mythic structures which played such a powerful role in Shakespearean tragi-comedy and Spenserian feminine epic helped to mediate between Christian doctrine and other inspirations (both human and Hermetic) in shaping the redemptive structure of *Paradise Lost*. The forgiving spirit of the poem draws a ·poignant beauty from the assimilation of the story of Ceres and Proserpina to *both male and female* figures. The blame is in great measure drawn off the scapegoat shoulders of 'our general mother' to the Hades-figure of Satan through allusion to the generation of evil as a form of rape: the crime against the feminine. The Ceres/Proserpina story as a myth of restorative balance between upper, middle and chthonic powers contributes to the *felix culpa* theme: adjustment and the working out of justice are made emotionally tenable. The barriers between the various figures in the Christian story are broken down by allusion to a number of different figures in the Eleusinian story, reinforcing one of Milton's favourite theological positions: the closeness of God to man (and here, woman) in the figure of Christ the Mediator.[58] In this revolutionary interpretation of Scripture, not only class-barriers but also gender-barriers are questioned. Eve is alluded to both as a Ceres-figure and a Proserpina-figure, which no doubt we might have expected. But Christ is also presented through an unmistakable allusion as a Ceres-figure, seeking the lost soul of his mortal kin; and, by extension, as a Proserpina-figure, venturing into the grave itself on her behalf. Certainly, Milton's high-thinking Puritan rectitude continues in *Paradise Lost* as elsewhere, to cast doubt on the ethical and spiritual value of his classicism, which is habitually either denied ('*Not* that fair field of Enna', 'Thus they relate/*Erring*'), belittled or cast in the equivalent of parentheses; but the fluent classicism of *Paradise Lost*, and especially the Eleusinian component, carries with it a tenderness that centres it in our attention as a crucial body of imagery without which the poem's meanings cannot be fully glimpsed. The deepest effect of the Eleusinian references in *Paradise Lost* is its fostering of the reconciliation between the theological and the human and personal.

Satan's contribution to this structure is to act out the murderous role of Pluto/Dis, King of Hades, towards Eve as flower-maiden. The more this role is emphasised, the greater is our sense of his victim's guileless vulnerability. Satan begins to move upwards towards Eve in the middle of Book II, and from the first his journey is imaged in terms suggestive of sexual exploration through 'that abortive gulf' of the Abyss (441). The figure of Sin at the mouth of hell, forcibly entered by Death 'in embraces horrible and foul/Ingendering' (793–4), is an icon of violent sexual horror. Much of a reader's sense of the unfolding horror of the Fall of man is generated by this closing of distance between Satan and the unknowing Eve. It begins in his surging, scrambling climb up through Chaos in Book II, 'the womb of nature and perhaps her grave' (911), the word 'womb' being reiterated throughout the Book in association with confusion, noise and death. So far, Satan is at a great distance from humanity; yet in some real way he is already well advanced on his rape. Tiny in the immense perspective of the cosmos, he is potent as a sperm in its marathon up the black infinity of the birth canal. Milton is already forcing our minds to contemplate connections between Satan and generation, a 'ruinous' sexuality which cannot tell 'womb' from 'grave' since both are identically featureless and meaningless. Such a germ of infection is mathematically almost non-existent in the great perspective at the end of Book II. We cannot measure it when we are called to see the first impression of our world:

> This pendant world, in bigness as a star
> Of smallest magnitude close by the moon.
> (II. 1052–3)

Yet the contamination Satan bears seems all the more threatening when we see our own world so small, hanging from heaven by its slender golden chain. In spying Eve's home out, Satan imaginatively enters it. We share his vision, and though he is hardly a dot or fleck on that universal horizon, his subjectivity is as wide as the universe itself. The world has already gone in to him through the eye and become part of his predatory consciousness. In the closing moments of innocence, in Book IX, when Satan's marathon is so complete as to have brought him within yards of Eve's naked person and personality, the shock of possessive nearness is hardly more sinister. Through his voyeuristic eyesight, Satan eats the universe into his consciousness, and is himself spied on by the poet. The converse of this stealthy process of Satan's 'greedy eyes' eating up what they see and converting it into his own substance is Eve's experience of eating the fruit through which she is entered by the outsider's vision, raped away in her own person to an underworld knowledge. Milton is able to balance his account of this act in her favour by assimilating it to the Proserpina story, in which the puzzled maiden has very little choice:

> And as Demeter still held her dear child in her arms,
> her mind suspected trickery, and in awful fear she withdrew
> from fondling her and forthwith asked her a question:
> 'Child, when you were below, did you perchance partake
> of food?...'
> ....
>   'Aidoneus slyly placed
> in my hands a pomegranate seed, sweet as honey to eat.
> Against my will and by force he made me taste of it...'
>   (*Homeric Hymn to Demeter*, 390–4, 411–13)

Milton's Eve has to take a heavier, harder share of responsibility, for she is not the helpless child whose role Persephone plays, but a stronger, nearly fledged Christian soul who can bear responsibility. Nevertheless, the Proserpina allusion is useful to Milton in enabling him to unload some of the liberally dealt-out blame with which Christianity likes to honour Eve.

Indeed, through emphasis on the rape of innocence by knowledge, *Paradise Lost* manages to involve us all in collective responsibility, since poetry itself is a mode of knowing. At the moment of reading, since we enter Eden in such bad company, we convert the vision into the substance of our jaded fallen selves. As Satan brings his sensuality towards the Garden, he also smells what he sees. As Death snuffs up the scent of carnage on earth in Book X, slavering to 'lick up the draff and filth' (630), Satan's approach to Eve releases, so Satan receives in Book IV 'gentle gales' of 'native perfumes', 'balmy spoils' (156, 158, 159). The entry into Eden presents itself as a hideous travesty of the *Song of Solomon*, with Satan mocking the role of the yearned-for lover:

Awake, O north wind; and come, thou south; blow upon my
garden, that the spices thereof may flow out. Let my beloved come
into his garden, and eat his pleasant fruits.

(Song of Solomon, 4:16)

The *hortus conclusus* unconsciously draws its destroyer to enter
it, as if its delicious scents were the sighed-out imperatives of the
feminine voice in the Song's male-female dialogue. But the great
Old Testament love-poem emphatically speaks of the cultural
need and personal desire to protect the feminine from rough,
premature entry (8:8–9): the lyric voice appeals to the whole
tribe and family in ensuring her safety, whilst simultaneously
recognising that her beauty just by virtue of being itself is
exposed and vulnerable. Milton makes us feel a comparable
sense of collective family allegiance to the person of Eve, so
deeply identified with her closed garden-world. But because we
too have been betrayed into gaining entrance along with Satan,
we are called upon to protect the image of Eve against ourselves,
vaulting the wall of Eden in emulation of Satan's ludicrous high-
jump ('Due entrance he disdained' [180]), and unwillingly
implicated in the fanged animality with which he prepares to
shed blood ('As when a prowling wolf' [183]). We have to rely
upon the protection of the narrative voice, whose powerful
rectitude maintains a distance between Satan's perception and
our own, in order to guard against the blood-instinct evoked by
beauty in fallen creatures. The narrative voice withholds Eve
from scrutiny till the last possible moment, hiding her in the
penultimate seconds within veils-behind-veils of classical
similtudes:

> universal Pan
> Knit with the Graces and the Hours in dance
> Led on the eternal spring. Not that fair field
> Of Enna, where Proserpine gathering flowers
> Her self a fairer flower by gloomy Dis
> Was gathered, which cost Ceres all that pain
> To seek her through the world; nor that sweet grove
> Of Daphne by Orontes, and the inspired
> Castalian spring, might with this Paradise
> Of Eden strive...

(IV. 266–75)

Still we have not seen her. She remains enclosed within the future of the poem, an unseen mystery upon which we, and Satan, have not yet had a chance to feast our eyes. Satan's eyes have minutely catalogued Eden's streams, caves, flowers, trees—the Paradise that will later be called 'Her nursery' (VIII. 46)—but so far the poem has sealed her away in its own *hortus conclusus*. The sudden outburst of energy animating the complex epic simile, whose classicism veils the literal surface of the visible in Eden, suggests an access of mystery as proximity to Eve is at last attained. The graceful Botticellian tapestry of pastoral emblems, each glowing with meaning (Pan, Graces, Hours), suggests the Platonistic *trinitas conversoria sive ad supera reductoria*,[59] the last veil before the Truth herself is seen. But the pictures within the epic simile, evoking threatening stories concerning rape and tragic loss with only partial healing (Proserpine, Daphne) obliquely signal that the mystery is about to be broken. Eve's appearance is in fact preluded by a form of pastoral elegy, a trail of flowers such as in *The Winter's Tale* Perdita invoked from Proserpina:

> O Proserpina,
> For the flowers now that, frighted, thou let'st fall. . .
> (*The Winter's Tale*, IV. iv. 116–17)

naming the golden daffodils and primroses that illumine the earth on the far edge of winter (see pp. 158–9 above, and Cymoent, pp. 64–5 above). Eve is not precisely and directly Proserpina, of course, and Eden is explicitly '*Not* that fair field/Of Enna' (my italics). But the mere allusion to Proserpina's story calls up in a reader's mind a host of possible parallels, together with a perspective and attitude in terms of which the possible composite, Proserpina-Eve, may be judged. This mood is one of tenderness and regret, for neither in Ovid nor in any other source are we required to cast blame upon the Maiden for being raped. Whenever his poem connects Eve with the classical flower-maidens, then, the effect of the contact is to restrain the poet's tendency to cast blame. As flowers 'are gathered' without consent, so the 'fairest unsupported flower' (IX. 432) is 'deflowered' (IX. 901) without yielding a full consent.

The Proserpina story, like the Flora myth to which it

connects, offers images of healing and fruitfulness which Milton could assimilate to Eve's identity: *Chloris eram quae Flora vocor*. Sadness rather than shame, together with the promise of reparation, therefore characterises Milton's adaptation, so that pastoral elegiac tone and structure can guarantee the power of consolation and compensation for Eve's 'hapless' experiences. In *Lycidas* the dead boy is 'the hapless youth' (164); in *Paradise Lost* the narrator's tempered judgment of the heroine is no more incriminating than this: 'much deceived, much failing, hapless Eve' (IX. 404), the blame of the central 'failure' being surrounded by gestures away from this victim towards the rapist-figure of Satan/Dis, his potentially ennobling desire for Eve's physical beauty turned in the cauldron of frustration to molten rancour: 'the hot hell that always in him burns' (IX. 467). The epic simile in Book IV ('Not that fair field/Of Enna...') looks forward into the whole unfolding future of the poem, colouring our responses and shaping our expectations. Most crucially of all, the image of Eve as a Proserpina-figure is carefully and beautifully balanced by the poet's provision of a redemptive Ceres-figure, who undergoes 'all that pain/To seek her through the world'. The application of this image is complex, radical and far-reaching. It applies within the poem not only to Christ's atoning search through the means of the Easter of his Grace (III. 228) but also to God the Father's judgment on the errant world. God the Father partially blights the Paradise which he, like Ceres the grain-goddess, sustains; God the Son undergoes 'all that pain' to heal this blight. Christ most obviously takes on the attributes of the feminine. Milton recreates the male Trinity with a mysterious mother-component. This beautiful transformation is echoed in the application not only of the Proserpina component but also the Ceres-component of the myth to Eve. Motherless, she combines within herself the whole mother-and-maiden archetype, with unique fidelity to the myth's original meanings. For Eve is, of course, not *virgo intacta* like Proserpina; she is 'our general mother' like Ceres. Chaste as Proserpina, and as guileless, she loses her home; chastened by grief, loneliness and humiliation in Book X, she parallels Christ's offer to undergo 'all that pain' on man's behalf, with her own offer to atone for Adam. She speaks with Christ's voice, he speaks with hers.

The word 'grace' is recurrently associated with both figures, though in Eve's case it goes camouflaged as 'sweet attractive grace' (IV. 298), 'graceful innocence' (IX, 459), and does not declare itself as a precious individual version of Divine Grace, until the story calls for an act of redemption. The structure according to which human atonement can answer divine atonement takes the form of a glorious, subtle chiasmus, a cross figured from the third Book to the third from final Book:

> Behold me then, me for him, life for life
> I offer, on me let thine anger fall...
>
>   (III. 236–7)

> all
> The sentence from thy head removed may light
> On me, sole cause to thee of all this woe,
> Me me only just object of his ire.
>
>   (X. 933–6)

The first voice is Christ's to his Author, God; the second Eve's to her author, Adam. But it is the same language, a voice quiet with the sacred therapy that alone remedies the disjunction of the magical unity celebrated in Books IV and VII, in the 'Blest pair' sharing one another's sleeping life of divine *gnosis*, of Creation reflecting the Creator in its unflawed mirror. This voice of remedy has as the basis of its syntax the power to speak in the passive mood, or as the object of one's own sentence: 'me for him', 'On me.../Me me only'. Eve's use of this divine language is less composed, more forceful and passionate, involving both pity and contrition. Like Bunyan in his *Grace Abounding to the Chief of Sinners*, Eve speaks as a Puritan whose contrition is born from heart-shaking desolation. Light breaks on her while she is still in the shadow of death. The stressed 'all', the three stressed 'me's' communicate an utterly human version of the redemptive eloquence. Her words are distinguished by intuitive paradox. When she asks for the sentence to 'light' on her, the heavy penalty declares itself in weightless terms. From her darkness her words cast 'light'. Adam testifies rather eloquently to her status as the first reborn Puritan in *Paradise Lost* by at once rushing in to sabotage her speech in a hectic and ludicrous manner. Though Milton's narrative voice glosses his response as involving 'peaceful words', it sounds like a vicious rebuke:

> Unwary, and too desirous, as before
> So now of what thou knowest not, who desir'st
> The punishment all on thyself; alas,
> Bear thine own first, ill able to sustain
> His full wrath whose thou feel'st as yet least part,
> And my displeasure bear'st so ill...
>
> (X. 947–52)

Conceivably this could be heard as the voice of 'reason', though its grudging tone, unpleasant imperative, and the coiled up vindictiveness of the sting-in-the-tail ('And my displeasure') imply a very sour manner. Certainly it could not be heard as the voice of Grace. 'Bear thine own first' hurls Eve back into isolation. His evil-speaking 'Ill...ill' is based on a reading of the letter not the spirit of her language. Adam interprets a language overflowing from a full heart in communion of love intent upon breaking down 'the middle wall of partition', as language relating to behavioural probabilities judged by the law of precedent. He follows this up with a threat to race Eve to the mercy-seat if such a policy were likely to yield results—and, given his larger bulk and louder voice, he would inevitably win such a race—and 'expose' himself for both. Self-righteous and suspicious, Adam has still not found the lyric tone of Eden. The narrative voice endorses Adam's stance as very proper in the circumstances (Milton's tension between misogyny and feminine idealism is never more obvious), but Eve's speeches, which he could well have excised or distorted in perceiving the way they must govern a reader's sympathies, testify to his desire to redeem and sustain the original divine music in her speech. When, at the close of Book X, Adam's words become more mellow and pleasing, they do so because they approach the gracious tone of Eve's. He resolves that they should fall prostrate, ask forgiveness, 'with tears/Watering the ground' (X. 1089–90), demonstrating 'Sorrow unfeigned, and humiliation meek' (1092, 1104). Eve had fallen at Adam's feet, her hair flowing forwards 'with tears that ceased not flowing' (910), an embodied emblem of humility and a sign of Grace, necessary to

teach the haughty, kingly Adam a posture that always seems
foreign to his nature.

This close kinship between Christ's and Eve's voices is
essential to our recognition of the implications of the
Ceres/Proserpina image, which mediates between the two
figures. Eve and Christ can be imagined as acting out the roles of
both mythic counterparts. Eve will be Proserpina deflowered in
Book IX, Proserpina retrieved in Book X, pregnant with the
future. Christ will be Proserpina yielded down to Hades in his
foreseen bargain with God and Death:

> Father, thy word is past, man shall find grace;
> And shall Grace not find means, that finds her way,
> The speediest of thy winged messengers,
> To visit all thy creatures...
> ....
> Though now to Death I yield, and am his due
> All of me that can die, yet that debt paid,
> Thou wilt not leave me in the loathesome grave,
> His prey...
>
> (III. 227–30, 245–8)

The Divine Grace is most frequently rendered in iconography
by a feminine personification (see Ch. 3, 56n.). Spenser's
Charissa, Giles Fletcher's Mercie, Shakespeare's Hermione,
follow in this tradition. Suggested in Milton's Christ is a loving
universal motherhood which searches for God's children. Death
here is personified (like 'gloomy Dis') and Christ voluntarily
'yields' to 'him', *yielding* being deeply associated with Eve
throughout the poem (e.g. IV 309–10, 489). A 'yielding' nature
is seen throughout as a characteristic of the feminine, leaving her
open to guileful but also fruitful metamorphosis, as trees or
grain may be said to 'yield' seasonally. Christ yields himself
voluntarily to become prey; as 'Grace' he raises man. The
suffocating pain of the path he chooses is insisted upon, as Eve's
extreme pain is elaborated throughout the poem; in Book X the
paths meet in redemption.

In Claudian's *De Raptu Proserpinae*, perhaps the most
movingly dramatic of all classical accounts of the Ceres story,
this pain of Ceres is unforgettably demonstrated. Milton's

allusion to the rape which 'cost Ceres all that pain/To seek her through the world' explicitly directs us to the myth's literary tradition, assuming we are familiar with the famous accounts so as to recognise the depth of the pain involved. Milton is very close here to Claudian's *'quantasque oras/sollicito genetrix erraverit anxia cursu'* (I. xxxiii. 28–9). And like Claudian's, Milton's is a story of mental and spiritual ripening, leading to a growth of illumination in the goddess's mind, a new covenant between the underworld and the gods, which will have direct and propitious effect on mankind. The old aeon wanes; the new begins. Jupiter is at first construed as malignant in his sacrifice of Proserpina: 'The Father hath conspired against thee and betrayed thee to the realms of silence' (II. xxxv. 236). But the purpose of Jupiter is to quicken the underworld with love (I. xxxiii. 214ff.), and with the rape of Proserpina from an Enna described with such gorgeous lyricism that we understand what Milton intends by calling Eden yet more beautiful, the underworld is miraculously transformed. Acheron, its pitch-black river, flows with mother's milk (351). No children die on earth. The Father reveals to us that Proserpina's loss was essential so that humanity can move beyond the primitive stage to maturer civilisation. Ceres sees only her own aching loss, and criticises the cruelty of divine law, as a symptom of her bereavement: 'I saw the bryony pale/The roses fade, the lilies wither' (III. xxxvi. 240–1). The pastoral loss resembles the withering of the pastoral crown from Adam's hand when he sees Eve returning deflowered. Claudian's Ceres begins to recognise her own responsibility for leaving Proserpina exposed, and begins to accept her condition.

Milton's assimilation of the figures of Christ and Eve to the terms of this myth provides a similarly clarifying and reconciling focus. But just as importantly, it makes it possible for us to read *Paradise Lost* as a great fertility myth itself, in which the vegetation stories are a genuine and important component of the whole meaning. Fertility in the soul, or the poet's creating mind, are images of God's Creation; so is the womb of Eve. But in a real way the simple facts of the Garden of Eden—its plants, herbs, trees—are the lyrical and pastoral subject-matter of the poem, celebrated for their beauty and for our affinity and rooted attachment to them as the home and habitat of the species. You would think from some dry accounts that the poem is simply a blank verse rendering of theological arguments,[60] the Garden reducible to a plantation of allegorisations from Basil or Gregory or Augustine. But through Eve's recurrent characterisation as a nature-goddess, the mind's eye collects onto itself the intense greenness of the poem. As a garden-poem it is a 'green thought in a green shade'.[61] Eve links us to this rooted world of growing things where Adam does not. The Garden is full of her children, in that her attendance to its growth is felt as personal, reflective. When in Book VIII Adam invites Raphael to discourse to him on astronomy, Eve removes herself, to go:

> forth among her fruits and flowers,
> To visit how they prospered, bud and bloom,
> Her nursery; they at her coming sprung
> And touched by her fair tendance gladlier grew.
> Yet went she not, as not with such discourse
> Delighted, or not capable her ear
> Of what was high...
>
> (VIII. 44–50)

The latter proviso is, of course, crucial. She too is interested in, and capable of understanding, cosmology, but she would rather hear it intermingled with kisses and caresses than in the form of an abstract lecture. Milton is generally felt to have created a problem here, which he has trouble in solving satisfactorily.[62] For if Eve chooses to avoid the lecture, she is preferring the lower to the higher, and showing a flawed nature. Some of Milton's phrasing is undeniably unfortunate here, insinuating a coy leer in 'from his lip/Not words alone pleased her' (56–7). It is often felt that fussing among the plants is a fairly mindless choice of occupation, considering the tremendous intellectual powers the poet hastily ascribes to her. There are, of course, strategic narrative reasons why Eve has to be absent from the story in Book VIII (so that Raphael has a chance to warn Adam against overvaluing her). But the passage may be read in another way. Milton speaks of Eve's 'goddess-like demeanour' as she departs 'as queen' surrounded by 'graces' (59, 60, 61). This emphasis is generally interpreted as an allusion to Eve as a Venus figure (Fowler, 45n–63n), with justice. However, if we look back to the first allusion to the Graces in relation to a goddess-figure and to Eve, they are found prefiguring not Venus but the Ceres-Proserpina story (see p. 235 above). The erotic image retreats into the mother-image, caring for the growing world of vegetation which is her responsibility, 'her fruits and flowers'. Through dignifying the material world into a magically godlike quality, not antagonistic to spirit but a denser variant of it, Milton makes it possible for us to see that the tendance of 'fruits and flowers...bud and bloom' may express a variant form of wisdom and virtue. Raphael himself had communicated that truth through the image of a plant's organic continuity: 'So from the root/Springs lighter the green stalk...' (V. 479–80). The root is flesh, the stalk intermediate, the flower the spirit. All respire together, need and refresh one another: all is one.

Eve as Flora, Pomona or Ceres brings us into the deep growing centre of Eden, where the green of our life-cycle is rooted down and we feel the sap flow from origin to consummation. The Garden animatedly springs up towards her as she bends her power to it. Her likeness to Pomona is close and touching:

> Shee past not for the woodes
> Nor rivers, but the villages and boughes that bare both buddes
> And plentuous frute. In sted of dart a shredding hooke shee bare,
> With which the overlusty boughes shee eft away did pare
> That spreaded out too farre, and eft did make therwith a rift
> To greffe another imp uppon the stocke within the clift.
> And lest her trees should die through drought, with water of the springs
> She moysteth of theyr sucking roots the little crumpled strings.
>
> (*Ovid's Metamorphoses*, XIV. 713–20)[63]

Dedicated to her garden, Pomona is a fugitive, shy figure. Vertumnus woos her with the story of a girl turned to stone by her stony-hearted frigidity. After the tale, the apple-queen voluntarily yields to Vertumnus: the cycle of the orchard-world from apple blossom to harvest, and on to the bare boughs of winter, is thus initiated. Thus Milton's image of Pomona leads our minds out of the simplicity and retreat of Eden, with its fastidiously guarded safety, to the rich fruitfulness of a more mature (and inevitably fallen) culture. Milton's allusions to

Ceres run parallel, leading us to think of the initiation of the
cycle from dark ploughed fields, through to the grain-yield—the
one a green, the other a golden story. Eve's bower as more
fruitful than 'Pomona's arbour' (V. 378) or more beautiful than
'that fair field of Enna' may, as severe persons have insisted,
expose the dangerous fallibility of 'our general mother'. But the
poetic associations far more richly bless Eve with holding the
lyrical secret of a maturing good. She makes the Fall less
blighted, dramatising the maternal nature of God as 'our
nourisher' (V. 398) whose biblical source is God as nursing-
mother (Isaiah 49:15; Numbers 11:12–13), and which the
Church Fathers like Augustine and Clement elaborate as 'milk
flowing from the Father'.[64] In the great colour-scheme of
Paradise Lost, Milton continuously relates the figure of Eve to
this green light of the vegetational world glowing annually
through the surface of the planet. The dire warning of recurrent
winter is offset by the promise of the repeated miracle of 'the
earth's green cape' (VIII. 631), embodied in Eve as Pomona,
Flora and Ceres. The lesson which Michael must teach Adam in
the last two Books, of Temperance and punishment, is itself
tempered by the angel's affirmation that we are still to consider
ourselves at home on the autumnal earth:

> So mayst thou live, till like ripe fruit thou drop
> Into thy mother's lap, or be with ease
> Gathered, not harshly plucked, for death mature...
>   (XI. 535–7)

After the Fall, the seasons have been let loose on man, the planet
pushed out of true, the animals unleashed from their mutual
peace into predatoriness. But Michael can still affirm a 'natural'
world that man can willingly accept and which accepts him in a
mother-son relationship. It is only after his fall into isolation
that Adam receives the assurance of a 'mother's lap'. Adam in
old age will become the child he never was and return to a home
he never knew. Motherhood and all its consolation lies outside
Eden. Words like 'ripe' and 'mature' belong with it, together
with a gentleness which it might well seem to Adam worth the
struggle of falling to gain. The lines I have quoted show delicate
allusion to Pomona (the 'gathering' of ripe fruit in an orchard)

and to Proserpina ('harshly plucked'). As Proserpina in Book IV
'Was gathered' costing Ceres 'all that pain', so Adam will
'be.../Gathered' into the absorbing gentleness of a feminine
source, evoking the andogynous melting of genders which
Milton has centred on the Ceres story by making Adam's path
touch that of Proserpina very faintly, only to branch away ('*not*
harshly plucked'). The emphasis, like that of *King Lear* where
'Ripeness is all' (V. ii. 11), is on the possibility of maturing so as
to be ready for death, when this can be viewed as a timely re-
entry into the circulating life of the mother-planet. As in
Spenser's Garden of Adonis, at the very centre of the cycle of
fertility and decay is felt a process which is not wasteful or
threatening to individuality, but a resting-place for the self
within Time itself. Comfort is taken in the idea of return, which
for Milton is bound up with the mother-principle. Even in the
plainsong of the austere *Paradise Regained*, we can see it
operating in the relation between Christ the Son and Mary the
Mother. In the disciples' lament, 'our joy is turned' is translated
into the certainty 'Soon we shall see our hope, our joy, return'
(II. 37, 57); the final line of the poem completes the circle, where
Christ 'Home to his mother's house private returned' (IV. 639).
In *Paradise Lost* the promise is necessarily more oblique, yet it is
perhaps all the more distinctly felt through the complex of
allusive paradox which intensifies all the poem's meanings, until
bitter loss and new growth seem hardly distinguishable.
Eve turns from Adam:

> Thus saying, from her husband's hand her hand
> Soft she withdrew, and like a wood-nymph light
> Oread or dryad, or of Delia's train,
> Betook her to the groves, but Delia's self
> In gait surpassed and goddess-like deport,
> Though not as she with bow and quiver armed,
> But with such gardening tools as art yet rude,
> Guiltless of fire had formed, or angels brought.
> To Pales, or Pomona thus adorned,
> Likeliest she seemed, Pomona when she fled
> Vertumnus, or to Ceres in her prime,
> Yet virgin of Proserpina from Jove.
>
> (IX. 385–96)

As Eve mediates between Paradise and the outside world, the veil of classicism is again brought down around her, casting the green forms of the many-natured fertility goddess around her departure. Implicitly, she is a Venus-figure, but explicitly Venus' natural opposite and counterpart, Diana. As 'Delia', Diana is remembered from her divine birth on Delos, the elder of her twin, the sun-god Apollo, a classical type for Christ. As a Diana-figure, Eve is significantly not the *Diana Armata* of warrior-convention. Yet there is a powerful sense of the 'terrible Artemis' associated with her purity. Satan, like Actaeon intruding upon holy secrets, is struck 'with rapine sweet' (461) into a state of unwilled goodness at the sight. Our awareness of how purposefully Milton has avoided the martial 'armed Diana' emblem is reinforced when we are touchingly shown that instead of carrying Diana's aggressive tools of her trade, Eve has in her hand only primitive garden tools, 'art yet rude/Guiltless of fire'. yet the suggestion is heavy that this unpromethean satisfaction with childish technology invites and legitimates the natural desire for an art which is more than 'rude'. Claudian's Jupiter in *De Raptu Proserpinae* had spared Proserpina as a necessary sacrifice in order that mankind could progress to a new state of culture, based on seasonal sowing and reaping of seed-corn. Prometheus (translating 'forethought') is man's friend in providing the fire of artistry. Milton's provider of this new world of expanding knowledge is imagined as a girl in a natural scene, with the purity of Diana but the earnest sweetness of Ovid's Pomona: 'In sted of dart a shredding hooke shee bare' (see p. 243 above). And in the final triple image of Pales, Pomona and the composite Ceres/Proserpina, Milton elaborates this movement from a childhood to an adult civilisation. As Diana, goddess of the secluded and wildly virgin forest-world, Eve declares her affinity with Eden, the closed world of eternal childhood and spring. But as goddess of pastures (Pales), apple harvest (Pomona), corn (Ceres), her association is with the adult world of time, change, seasonal cycles. Our gaze is directed to the world outside Eden, the grazed meadows, orchards and wheat-fields of civilisation. The mother-and-maiden archetype (Ceres 'yet virgin of Proserpina') begins to enact the great round of loss and redemption, pointing to a rich pastoral world outside Eden, whose goodness is rooted in the Fall itself, and filled with

'The smell of grain, or tedded grass, or kine,/Or dairy' (IX. 450-1), a world liberated into culture.

Notes

1. INTRODUCTION

1. The references for the three quotations are as follows: Edmund Spenser, *The Faerie Queene*, III. xii. 46a; William Shakespeare, *Cymbeline*, V. v; John Milton, *Paradise Lost*, IV. 487-8.
2. Lisa Jardine, *Still Harping on Daughters. Women and Drama in the Age of Shakespeare* (Sussex and New Jersey, 1983), pp. 51-62, argues trenchantly for the patriarchy's limiting of female culture; but I think her claim is excessive.
3. *Ibid.*, pp.49-50.
4. *See* Don Cameron Allen, *Mysteriously Meant. The Rediscovery of Pagan Symbolism and Allegorical Interpretation in the Renaissance* (Baltimore and London, 1970), pp.23-24; Frances A. Yates, *Giordano Bruno and the Hermetic Tradition* (London, 1964), p.78.
5. *See* Yates, *Ibid.*, pp.62-80; D.P. Walker, *Spiritual and Demonic Magic from Ficino to Campanella* (Notre Dame and London, 1975 edn.) pp. 16-22; Wayne Shumaker, *The Occult Sciences in the Renaissance* (Berkeley, Los Angeles and London, 1972), p.203.
6. *See* J.L.E. Dreyer, *A History of Astronomy from Thales to Kepler* (London, 1953), pp.408-9, for notation of Kepler's planetary music.
7. Aristotle, *Metaphysics*, XII. ix, tr. Hugh Tredennick (Cambridge and London, 1927), Vol. II.
8. Patricia Vicari, 'The Triumph of Art, the Triumph of Death', in John Warden, *Orpheus. The Metamorphoses of a Myth* (Toronto, 1982), p.207.
9. Proclus, *The Elements of Theology*, tr. E.R. Dodds (Oxford, 1963), pp.63-5, expounds 'the whole in the part'; D.P. Walker, *The Ancient Theology. Studies in Christian Platonism from the Fifteenth to the Eighteenth Century* (London, 1972), pp.35-6.
10. *The Orphic Hymns*, tr. and ed. A.N. Athanassakis (Missoula, Montana, 1977), No. 6. *See* the account in W.Wili's 'The Orphic Mysteries and the Greek Spirit', in *The Mysteries. Papers from the Eranos Yearbooks*, ed. Joseph Campbell (New York, 1955), p.71, on the Orphic bisexual Creator.
11. *The Orphic Hymns*, 10:18-19.
12. Juliet Dusinberre, *Shakespeare and the Nature of Women* (London and Basingstoke, 1975), p.232; Jardine, *Still Harping on Daughters, passim*.

248

13. St. Augustine, *City of God, Against the Pagans*, II. iv, tr. G.E. McCracken (London and Cambridge, Mass., 1916), p.154.

14. G.B. Pico della Mirandola, *Oration: On the Dignity of Man*, tr. S. Davies and D. Brooks-Davies, in Stevie Davies, *Renaissance Views of Man* (Manchester, 1978), p.72.

15. *Areopagitica*, in *Complete Prose Works of John Milton*, gen. ed. Don M. Wolfe (New Haven and London, 1953–83), Vol. II, p.549.

16. *The Letters of Marsilio Ficino*, tr. Language Department of School of Economic Science, London (London, 1978), Vol. II, p.10.

17. *See* Jean Seznec *The Survival of the Pagan Gods, The Mythological Tradition and its Place in Renaissance Humanism and Art*, tr. B.F. Sessions (New York, 1953), pp.184–5.

18. Paracelsus, *Selected Writings*, ed. Jolande Jacobi, tr. N. Guterman (New York, 1951), p.100.

19. *See* Ian Maclean, *The Renaissance Notion of Woman* (Cambridge, 1980), p.12.

20. *Ibid.*, p.25.

21. *Ibid.*, p.24.

22. Quoted in Seznec, *The Survival of the Pagan Gods*, p.99.

23. Vincenzo Cartari, *Le Imagini de i dei de gli Antichi*, in *The Renaissance and the Gods*, ed. Stephen Orgel (New York and London, 1976), pp.110 and 116–17.

24. Edgar Wind, *Pagan Mysteries in the Renaissance* (London, 1958), pp.111–41; *see* Fig. 53 for Marco Zoppo's *Venus armata*. *See* Douglas Brooks-Davies, *Spenser's 'Faerie Queene'. A Critical Commentary on Books I and II* (Manchester, 1977), pp.64–5, 130–1, on Una and Belphoebe as *Venus virgo*.

25. Cesare Ripa, *Iconologia*, ed. E. Mandowsky (Hildesheim and New York, 1970), pp.336–7, 468.

26. *See* Wind, *Pagan Mysteries*, pp.100–10, and M.L. D'Ancona, *Botticelli's Primavera. A Botanical Interpretation Including Astrology, Alchemy and the Medici* (Fiorenze, 1983), pp.15–17, on the 'reading' of this picture, right to left.

27. D'Ancona, *Botticelli's Primavera*, pp.71–99.

28. Ovid, *Fasti*, V. 193–214, tr. J.G. Frazer (London and Cambridge, Mass., 1951).

29. *See* Barbara Gallati, 'An Alchemical Interpretation of the Marriage between Mercury and Venus', in D'Ancona, *Botticelli's Primavera*, pp.118–21.

30. *See* F.C. Blessington, *'Paradise Lost' and the Classical Epic* (Boston, London and Henley), pp.51–62, on the elevation of a female 'beloved companion' figure to heroic status.

31. *See* Charles Seltmann, *The Twelve Olympians and their Guests* (London, 1956), pp.102–7, on Ares/Mars.

32. *See* Francis A. Yates, *A Study of 'Love's Labour's Lost'* (Cambridge, 1936).

33. For this concept *see*, for example, J.E. Hankins, *Source and Meaning in Spenser's Allegory. A Study of 'The Faerie Queene'* (Oxford, 1971),

pp.22, 55, 187.

34. Pausanias, *Description of Greece*, tr. W.H.S. Jones (London and New York, 1918), Vol. 1, I. xxxviii. 7.

35. Francesco Petrarch, *On his own ignorance and that of many other people*, in *The Renaissance Philosophy of Man*, ed. E. Cassirer *et al.* (Chicago, Ill., 1948), pp.78-9.

36. *De legibus*, II. xiv. 36, in *De re publica; de legibus*, tr. C.W. Keyes (London, 1949).

37. Quoted in Carl Kerenyi, *Eleusis. Archetypal Image of Mother and Daughter*, tr. R. Manheim (New York, 1967), p.14.

38. *Hymn to Persephone, The Orphic Hymns*, No. 10.

39. *Hymn to Eleusinian Demeter, The Orphic Hymns*, lines 1-3, 12.

40. *See* Kerenyi, *Eleusis*, pp.10-12.

41. See W.F. Otto, 'The meaning of the Eleusinian Mysteries', in *The Mysteries*, ed. Campbell, Vol. 2, p. 16.

42. Claudian, *De Raptu Proserpinae*, in *Claudian*, tr. Maurice Platnauer (Cambridge, Mass., and London, 1922), Vol. 2, II. 221-2.

43. *The Third Part of the Countesse of Pembrokes Yvychurch*, in *The Renaissance and the Gods*, Vol. 13, p.26.

44. *Ibid.*, p.27.

45. *The Fountain of Ancient Fiction*, in *The Renaissance and the Gods*, Vol.13, Hiii.

46. Apuleius, *The Golden Asse*, tr. William Adlington, intro. Thomas Secombe (London, 1913).

47. *See* Plutarch, *De Iside and Osiride*, ed. J. Gwyn Griffiths (Wales, 1970).

48. *Ibid.*, p.51.

49. *See* R.M. Warnicke, *Women of the English Renaissance and Reformation* (Westport and London, 1983), pp.16-30.

50. *See* Jardine, *Still Harping on Daughters*, pp.37-67, for a statement of the most jaundiced possible case.

51. *The Correspondence of Sir Thomas More*, ed. E.F. Rogers (Princeton, 1947), p.122.

52. *See*, for some of these individuals, Pearl Hogrefe, *Women of Action in Tudor England* (Ames, Iowa, 1977).

53. *See* Ian Maclean, *Woman Triumphant. Feminism in French Literature 1610-1652* (Oxford, 1977), pp.1-27, for an able discussion of this discrepancy.

54. Henricus Cornelius Agrippa, *De nobilitate et praecellentia foeminei sexus...declamatio* (Antwerp, 1529).

55. *See* Dora and Erwin Panofsky, *Pandora's Box. The Changing Aspects of a Mythical Symbol* (New York, 1956), pp. 9-10, 68-78, for the two Pandoras.

56. For a sample of James' views, *see* his *Daemonologie* (Edinburgh, 1597).

57. Cyril Tourneur, *The Revenger's Tragedy*, III. v. 77, in *Three Jacobean Tragedies*, ed. Gamini Salgado (Harmondsworth, 1965).

58. *See* Francis A. Yates, *Shakespeare's Last Plays. A New Approach* (London, 1975), for this cult.

59. *See* Marina Warner, *Alone Of All Her Sex. The Myth and the Cult of the*

Virgin Mary (London, 1978).

60.   *See* E.C. Wilson, *England's Eliza* (Cambridge, Mass. 1939), *passim*; Francis A. Yates, *Astraea. The Imperial Theme in the Sixteenth Century* (London and Boston, 1975).

61.   Quoted by Wilson, *England's Eliza*, pp. 220–1.

62.   John Lyly, *Endimion*, III. iv. 169, in *The Complete Works of John Lyly*, Vol. III, ed. R. Warwick Bond (Oxford, 1973).

63.   *The Poems of Sir Walter Raleigh*, ed. A.M.C. Latham (London, 1951).

64.   *See* Douglas Brooks-Davies' analysis of Queen Anne's impersonation of Elizabeth under the motto *semper eadem*, in *The Mercurian Monarch. Magical Politics from Spenser to Pope* (Manchester, 1983), pp. 185–200.

65   Reproduced in Germaine Greer, *The Obstacle Race. The Fortunes of Women Painters and their Work* (London, 1979), p. 190.

66.   In Michael Drayton, *Works*, ed. J. William Hebel (Oxford, 1931), Vol. I.

67   *See* J.E. Neale, *Queen Elizabeth. A Biography* (London, 1957), p. 248.

68   *The Public Speaking of Queen Elizabeth*, ed. G.P. Rice (New York, 1951), p. 96.

69   For the theory of the king's 'body politic' and 'body natural', *see* E.H. Kantorowicz, *the King's Two Bodies. A Study in Medieval Political Theology* (Princeton,NJ, 1957).

70   *See* Aristotle, *Politics*, 1252B, 1259B; Cicero, *De re publica*, I.61.64, for the classical foundation of the *pater patriae* formulation.

71   ʼG.B. Gelli, *Circe* (1549), tr. H. Layng (London, 1745).

72   Thomas Middleton, *Women Beware Women*, ed. J.R. Mulryne (London, 1975), I. ii. 168–70.

73   *Doomes-Day, or, The Great Day of the Lords Judgment*, in *The Poetical Works of Sir William Alexander* (Manchester, 1926), Vol. 2, I. 64, p. 24.

74   Milton's own coinage: in *A Second Defence of the English People*, *CPW*, IV. i. p. 628.

2. SPENSER

1.   On *The Faerie Queene* as dream, *see* Graham Hough, *A Preface to 'The Faerie Queene'* (London, 1962).

2.   Quoted in A. Bartlett Giametti, *Play of Double Senses. Spenser's 'Faerie Queene'* (Englewood Cliffs, NJ, 1975), p. 16, though questioned by him. My biographical account generally follows Giametti.

3.   *See* Alastair Fowler, *Spenser and the Numbers of Time* (London, 1964), for example, pp. 142–4. In 'Emanations of Glory: Neoplatonic Order in Spenser's *Faerie Queene*', in *A Theatre for Spenserians*, ed. Judith M. Kennedy and James A Reither (Manchester, 1973), pp. 53–82, Fowler concentrates on the triad of Graces, not noting their extension into four.

4.   Fowler, *Spenser and the Numbers of Time*, p. 137.

5.   William Lilly, *Morals*, tr. Holland (1603), p. 767. *See also*: Plato, *Timaeus*, 31B–32C; S.K. Heninger Jr., *Touches of Sweet Harmony*.

Pythagorean Cosmology and Renaissance Poetics San Marino, California, 1974), pp. 146–200.

6. Sir Philip Sidney, *An Apology for Poetry*, ed. Geoffrey Shepherd (London, 1965), pp. 100–1.

7. *See*, for example, Humphrey Tonkin, *Spenser's Courteous Pastoral. Book Six of The 'Faerie Queene'* (Oxford, 1972), p. 8.

8. *Ovid's Metamorphoses. The Arthur Golding Translation (1567)*, ed. J.F. Nims (New York, 1965), III, 370ff.

9. *See* pp. 213 below for interpretation of the sleep of Adam and Eve as gnostic trance.

10. This discovery is recorded in A. Kent Hieatt's *Short Time's Endless Monument. The Symbolism of the Numbers in Edmund Spenser's 'Epithalamion'* (Washington, New York and London, 1960).

11. For the lineage of Hermaphroditus, see Abraham Fraunce, *The Countesse of Pembrokes Ivychurch*, 48a–49a, in *The Renaissance and the Gods*, Vol. 13, ed. Stephen Orgel (New York and London, 1976).

12. For significance of the hermaphrodite, *see* Macrobius, *Saturnalia*, III. viii, 1–3; Plato, *Symposium*, 181C; Cartari, *Imagini*, pp. 401–3; James Nohrnberg, *The Analogy* of *'The Faerie Queene'* (Princeton, New Jersey, 1976), pp. 601–5; C.S. Lewis, *Spenser's Images of Life*, ed. Alastair Fowler (Cambridge, 1967), pp. 15–16; Angus Fletcher, *The Prophetic Moment. An Essay on Spenser* (Chicago and London, 1971), p. 199. *See also* Marie Delcourt, *Hermaphrodite. Myths and Rites of the Bisexual Figure in Antiquity* (London, 1961).

13. *See* Lewis, *Spenser's Images of Life*, pp. 42–4, 58–60.

14. Nicholas Cusanus, *The Cloud of Unknowing*, ed. James Walsh (London, 1981), for example, pp. 251–2.

15. *See*, for this motif, Carol Schreier Rupprecht, *The Martial Maid. Androgyny in Epic from Virgil to the Poets of the Italian Renaissance* (Yale Ph.D. dissertation, 1977); A. Bartlett Giametti, 'Spenser: From Magic to Miracle', in *Four Essays on Romance*, ed. Herschel Baker (Cambridge, 1971), p. 17; and Giametti, *Play of Double Senses*, p. 102.

16. *See* Frances A. Yates, *Giordano Bruno and the Hermetic Tradition*, p. 62.

17. Giordano Bruno, *The Expulsion of the Triumphant Beast* (1484), tr. A.D. Imerti (New Brunswick, 1964), p. 236.

18. Yates, *Giordano Bruno and the Hermetic Tradition*, pp. 288–9.

19. For full, condensed treatment of this theme, *see* Robin Headlam Wells, *Spenser's 'Faerie Queene' and the Cult of Elizabeth* (London, Totowa, NJ, 1983), especially pp. 14–21; 74–90.

20. *See* P.J. Alpers, *the Poetry of 'The Faerie Queene'* (Princeton, NJ, 1967), p. 373, on Book III's dissolution of the difference between pastoral and heroic.

21. *See* Maureen Quilligan, *Milton's Spenser. The Politics of Reading* (Ithaca and London, 1983), pp. 185–199, on the gender of the reader of Book III.

22. Quoted from *The Manner of the Coronation of King Charles the First of England*, ed. Christopher Wordsworth, Henry Bradshaw Soc., 2 (1892),

p. 43. *See* Douglas Brooks-Davies, *The Mercurian Monarch*, pp. 34–7, for fuller treatment of this passage.

23. Noted by Virginia Ramey Mollenkott in *The Divine Feminine. The Biblical Imagery of God as Female* (Crossroad, NY, 1983), p. 36.

24. On Britomart as embodied *concordia discors*, see Kathleen Williams, *Spenser's 'Faerie Queene'. The World of Glass* (London, 1966), pp. 86–96.

25. By Maurice Evans, in *Spenser's Anatomy of Heroism. A Commentary on 'The Faerie Queene'* (Cambridge, 1970), p. 153.

26. *See* Natalis Comes, *Mythologiae* (Venice, 1567), 'De Adoni', pp. 161–2; 'De Baccho', pp. 145a–56a.

27. *See* Marcel Detienne, *The Gardens of Adonis. Spices in Greek Mythology* (Sussex, 1977), pp. 52–3.

28. *Ibid.*, p. 55.

29. Fraunce, *Yvychurch*, p. M2.

30. *Ibid*, p. M3.

31. Ad de Vries, *Dictionary of Symbols and Imagery* (Amsterdam and London, 1974), see under *dolphin*.

32. And see p. 241 below.

33. *See* Carl Kerenyi, *Asklepios. Archetypal Image of the Physician's Existence*, tr. Ralph Manheim (New York, 1959).

34. Leonard Barkan, *Nature's Work of Art. The Human Body as Image of the World* (New Haven and London, 1975), p. 23.

35. On Florimell as a Psyche figure, *see* A.C. Hamilton's 'Spenser's Treatment of Myth', in *Critical Essays on Spenser from ELH* (Baltimore and London, 1970), p. 91.

36. *See* Janet Spens, *Spenser's 'Faerie Queene'. An Interpretation* (New York, 1934), p. 84, on the nature of Florimell.

37. S.K. Heninger, *A Handbook of Renaissance Meteorology with Particular Reference to Elizabethan and Jacobean Literature* (Durham, NC, 1960), p. 89.

38. Marsilio Ficino, *Five Questions Concerning Mind*, in *The Renaissance Philosophy of Man*, ed. E Cassirer *et al*, p. 209.

39. *Hermetica*, ed. and tr. Walter Scott (Oxford, 1924), Vol I, Libellus VII. 2a. p. 173.

40. Ficino, *Commentary on Plato's 'Symposium'*, tr. S.R. Jayne (Missouri, 1944), p. 159.

41. *See* Thomas P. Roche's beautiful treatment of this theme in *The Kindly Flame. A Study of the Third and Fourth Books of Spenser's 'Faerie Queene'* (Princeton, NJ, 1964), pp. 159–62, 193.

42. I must thank my friend Andrew Howdle for first drawing this iconography to my attention.

43. For the nature of Diana, *see* Comes, *Mythologiae*, pp. 82–5.

44. The tradition of the two Helens stems from Stesichorus' palinode. *See* Nohrnberg, *The Analogy of 'The Faerie Queene'*, pp. 114–19, 572–4, 604, 630.

45. For yellow as a Venerean colour, *see* Douglas Brooks and Alastair Fowler, 'The Meaning of Chaucer's *Knight's Tale*', *Medium Aevum*,

Vol. XXXIX (1970), No. 2, p. 143.

46. Kathleen Williams' phrase in ' "Eterne in Mutabilitie": The Unified World of *The Faerie Queene*', in *That Soveraine Light. Essays in Honour of Edmund Spenser*, ed. W.R. Mueller and Don Cameron Allen (New York, 1952), p. 45.

47. Robert L. Reid, 'Man, Woman, Child or Servant: Family Hierarchy as a Figure of Tripartite Psychology in *The Faerie Queene*', in *Studies in Philology*, 78 (1981), pp. 370–90.

48. While later critical patriarchs have peremptorily discounted such a suggestion, the great Anglican C.S. Lewis could contemplate its possibility with serenity (*Spenser's Images of Life*, p. 59).

49. Frances A. Yates, *The Art of Memory* (London, 1966), offers the definitive account of the Renaissance theory of memory.

50. C.S. Lewis' account in *The Allegory of Love. A Study in Medieval Tradition* (New York, 1958 edn.), pp. 297–360, remains unsurpassed.

51. Roche, *The Kindly Flame*, p. 78.

52. *See* D.P. Walker, *Spiritual and Demonic Magic from Ficino to Campanella*, pp. 12–44.

53. *See* Clifford Davidson, 'The Idol of Isis Church', *Studies in Philology*, 66 (1969), pp. 70–86; René Graziani, 'Elizabeth at Isis Church', *Publications of the Modern Language Association (of America)*, 79 (1964), pp. 376–89.

3. SHAKESPEARE

1. My biographical statements are based on S. Schoenbaum's *William Shakespeare. A Documentary Life* (Oxford, 1975).

2. Murray M. Schwarz, 'Shakespeare through Contemporary Psycho-analysis', in *Representing Shakespeare. New Psychoanalytic Essays*, ed. Murray M. Schwartz and Coppelia Kahn (Baltimore and London, 1980), p. 28.

3. Richard P. Wheeler, ' "Since First We Were Dissevered": Trust and Autonomy', *Representing Shakespeare*, p. 164.

4. *See* Stevie Davies, *Images of Kingship in 'Paradise Lost'. Milton's Politics and Christian Liberty* (Missouri, 1983), pp. 164–70, for a summary of sources.

5. *See* Charles Nicholl's perceptive account of the father-daughter relationship in alchemical terms, in *The Chemical Theatre* (London, Boston and Henley, 1980), pp. 201–18.

6. *See* Imerti's Introduction to Bruno's *Expulsion of the Triumphant Beast*, pp. 24–46, for helpful material on Sophia's role as Earthly Wisdom.

7. On the dream-dimension of the Last Plays, *see* Derek Traversi, *Shakespeare. The Last Phase* (London, 1954), p. 18.

8. Giambattista Guarini, *Il compendio della poesia tragicomica*, tr. EM Waith, *Pattern of Tragicomedy in Beaumont and Fletcher* (New Haven, 1952), p. 48.

9. Joan Hartwig, *Shakespeare's Tragicomic Vision* (Baton Rouge, 1972), p. 31.

10. *See* Carol Gesner, *Shakespeare and Greek Romance. A Study of Origins* (Lexington, 1970), pp. 56–61, 153.

11. *See* C.L. Barber, 'The Family in Shakespeare's Development: Tragedy and Sacredness', in *Representing Shakespeare. New Psychoanalytic Essays*, ed. Murray M. Schwartz and Coppelia Kahn (Baltimore and London, 1980), p. 194.

12. Michael Drayton, *Poly-Olbion*, Song XIII, 19–24, in *Works*, ed. J. William Hebel, Vol. IV.

13. Coppelia Kahn, *Man's Estate. Masculine Identity in Shakespeare* (Berkeley,, LA, and London, 1981), *passim*.

14. For full treatment of this theme, *see* C.L. Barber, *Shakespeare's Festive Comedy. A Study of Dramatic Form and its Relation to Social Custom* (Princeton, New Jersey, 1959).

15. For mercury as feminine, *see* C.G. Jung, *Alchemical Studies*, tr. R.F.C. Hull (New York, 1970), p. 321; (having attributes of Venus), p. 226n.

16. Giordano Bruno, *The Heroic Frenzies*, tr. Paul Eugene Memmo, Jr. (Columbia thesis, 1959), p. 229.

17. Richard P. Wheeler, *Shakespeare's Development and the Problem Comedies. Turn and Counter-Turn* (Berkeley, Calif., and London, 1981), pp. 83, 175.

18. For this theme, *see* Marjorie B. Garber, *Dream in Shakespeare. From Metaphor to Metamorphosis* (New Haven and London, 1974), pp. 142ff.

19. *See* Wheeler, *Shakespeare's Development and the Problem Comedies*, pp. 81–6, for a feeling treatment of this theme; also Coppelia Kahn, 'The Providential Tempest and the Shakespearean Family', in *Representing Shakespeare* and in her *Man's Estate*, pp. 151ff.

20. Francesco Colonna, *Hypnerotomachia. The Strife of Love in a Dream* (1592), tr. R.D., ed. Lucy Gent (Delmar, NY, 1973), p. 62.

21. *See* Peter G. Phialas, *Shakespeare's Romantic Comedies. The Development of their Form and Meaning* (Chapel Hill, 1966), p. 111, for the derivation of the name Titania from Ovid's Diana in *Met.*, III. 173..

22. As the founding father of Athens, we would expect Theseus to be idealised: Phialas accepts such a view (*Shakespeare's Romantic Comedies*, p. 123), and Ruth Nevo wittily excuses Theseus' endorsement of paternal tyranny in *Comic Transformations in Shakespeare* (London and New York, 1980), pp. 96–7. I do not think Shakespeare venerates the status quo thus in Theseus.

23. *See* Ruth Nevo on 'Titania's wrong-headed "incorporation" of the Indian boy' (*Comic Transformations*, p. 105). Even Barber seems to assume the rightful nature of the bargain in *Shakespeare's Festive Comedy*, p. 193. *See* Dusinberre, *Shakespeare and the Nature of Women*, pp. 259–60.

24. For Shakespeare's use of the Psyche story, *see* Alex Aronson, *Psyche and Symbol in Shakespeare* (Bloomington and London, 1972), p. 139.

25. *See* C.G. Jung, *Psychology of the Unconscious* (London, 1922), pp. 135, 146–7, 149.

26. Howard B. White, *Copp'd Hills Towards Heaven. Shakespeare and the Classical Polity* (The Hague, 1970), p. 98. This account does not

perceive the Eleusinian basis of the famine in Tharsus (p. 101), misreads Ephesus as a Pauline miracle (p. 107), and wishes to see the magus Cerimon as a 'Baconian scientist' (p. 106).

27. Pliny, *Natural History*, ix. 2.
28. In *The Poems and Letters of Andrew Marvell*, ed. H.M. Margoliouth, Vol. I (Oxford, 1971).
29. Although, on the role of memory, *see* Douglas L. Peterson, *Time, Tide and Tempest. A Study of Shakespeare's Romances* (San Marino, California, 1973), pp. 214–49.
30. *See* Carl Kerenyi, *Eleusis*; R. Gordon Wasson *et al.*, *The Road to Eleusis. Unveiling the Secret of the Mysteries* (New York and London, 1978), for fullest reconstruction of details.
31. Howard White, *Copp'd Hills Towards Heaven*, pp. 53–4.
32. *See* Richard Cody's beautiful and learned *The Landscape of the Mind. Pastoralism and Platonic Theory in Tasso's 'Aminta' and Shakespeare's Early Comedies* (Oxford, 1969), p. 132.
33. Rosalie Colie, *Shakespeare's Living Art* (Princeton, NJ, 1974), pp. 268ff.
34. *See* Cody, *The Landscape of the Mind*, p. 34.
35. Ficino, *Opera*, i.p. 528 (*De Vita*); ii, p. 1374 (*In Phaedrum*).
36. *See* Wind, *Pagan Mysteries in the Renaissance*, p. 41.
37. *See* Kahn, *Man's Estate*, pp. 1–10, 153, 216, on the female and nurture.
38. *See Countesse of Pembrokes Yvychurch* (III), p. 26a.
39. Campanella, Poetica, in *Tutti le Opere*, ed. Luigi Firpo (Italy, 1954), p.1005. For magic music through which man can link up with the spheres, *see* Ficino, *De vita coelitus comparandi* on music as air/spirit picking up the *spiritus mundi*; Pietro Pomponazzi, *De incantationibus*; Fabrio Paolini, *Hebdomades*. For fuller treatment, *see* D.P. Walker, *Spiritual and Demonic Magic*, *passim*.
40. *See* Dorothy Koenigsberger, *Renaissance Man and Creative Thinking. A History of Concepts of Harmony, 1400–1700* (Sussex, 1979), pp.173–207.
41. Quoted in Nicholl, *The Chemical Theatre*, p.197.
42. *Ovid's Metamorphoses. The Arthur Golding Translation* (1567), ed. J.F. Nims (New York, 1975).
43. Hesychius, *Hesychii Alexandrini Lexicon*, rev. J. Alberti and M. Schmidt (Jena, 1858), Vol. I, p.193.
44. Plato, Letter 7, 334, in *Phaedrus and Letters VII and VIII*, tr. W. Hamilton (Harmondsworth, 1973).
45. Colin Still in *Shakespeare's Mystery Play. A Study of 'The Tempest'* (London, 1921) and *The Timeless Theme. A Critical Theory Formulated and Applied* (London, 1936) identified, I think erroneously, *The Tempest* as the Eleusinian play. Still's method, producing a 'final solution' of the allegorical levels of *The Tempest* in terms of Lesser and Greater Mysteries (*Shakespeare's Mystery Play*, p.14) is fanciful, appealing anachronistically to Warburton as an authority, and to 'natural symbolism' (p.86ff.), the Eleusinian structure as innate. He plays little attention to the feminine foundation of the myth.

46. *See* Kahn, *Man's Estate*, p.216.

47. E.g., R.G. Hunter in *Shakespeare and the Comedy of Forgiveness* (New York and London, 1965), p.198.

48. *See* Tom Driver, *The Sense of History in Greek and Shakespearean Drama* (New York, 1960), pp.168ff., for useful material on relation between Shakespearean tragi-comedy and Greek drama, especially Euripides.

49. On connection between Bacchus and Proserpina, *see* Comes, *Mythologiae*, pp.150, 155a; on sacrifice associated with Bacchus, p.151a; on Athenian Dionysian processions, p.153.

50. *See* Robert Graves, *Greek Myths* (Harmondsworth, 1960 edn.), Vol I, 'Dionysius' nature and deeds', pp.103–111.

51. A.P. Riemer, *Antic Fables. Patterns of Evasion in Shakespeare's Comedies* (Manchester, 1980), p.151.

52. *Ibid.*, p.158.

53. For the role of Hecate in the mother-maiden triad, *see* Nor Hall, *The Moon and the Virgin. Reflections on the Archetypal Feminine* (London, 1980), pp.189–215.

54. *See* n. 45 above.

55. *See* Charles Seltmann, *Riot in Ephesus. Writings on the Heritage of Grace* (London, 1958).

56. For the overwhelmingly feminine iconography of Grace, see Cesare Ripa, *Iconologia*, p.195; Rosemund Tuve, *Allegorical Imagery. Some Mediaeval Books and their Posterity* (Princeton, 1966), pp.153–154, 206–209.

57. Coppelia Kahn's analysis of this aspect of *Macbeth* is persuasive (*Man's Estate*), pp.151–4.

58. Julian the Apostate, *Hymn to the Mother of the Gods, The Works of the Emperor Julian*, 483–4, tr. W.C. Wright (London and Cambridge, 1954); Frances Yates in *Astraea. The Imperial Theme in the Sixteenth Century* (London, 1975), comments on the Ceres component of the Astraea motif, through the ear of corn in Astraea's hand (*virgo spicifera*), pp.30–2, 59, 77–8.

59. *See* Wasson, *The Road to Eleusis*, p.103.

60. In *The Theban Plays*, tr. E.F. Watling (Harmondsworth, 1947).

4. MILTON

1. John Phillips, *The Life of Mr. John Milton*, in *The Early Lives of Milton*, ed. Helen Darbishire (London, 1932), p.33.

2. Edward Phillips, *The Life of Mr. John Milton* (1694) in *Early Lives*, p.77.

3. *Ibid.*, p.78.

4. *See* A.N. Wilson, *The Life of John Milton* (Oxford, 1983), pp.218–19.

5. John Aubrey, *Minutes of the Life of Mr John Milton, Early Lives*, p.6.

6. *See* Milton's comments on *Hercules Furens* as Seneca's mouthpiece in *Defence of the English People* (*CPW*, IV. i. p.446): 'it is the custom of

poets to place their own opinions in the mouths of their great characters'.

7. William B. Hunter, Jr., *Milton's 'Comus'. Family Piece* (Troy, NY,1983), pp.12–15.

8. For Milton's grudging respect for Hobbes, *see* Aubrey, *Minutes*, in *Early Lives*, p.7. On his Christian militancy, see Arthur E. Barker, *Milton and the Puritan Dilemma* (Toronto, 1942) and Christopher Hill, *Milton and the English Revolution* (London, 1977).

9. Alfred 'turn'd the old laws into english...I would he liv'd now to rid us of this norman gibbrish', *Commonplace Book* (*CPW*, I, p.424). *See* my *Images of Kingship in 'Paradise Lost'*, pp.39ff.

10. *See* D.P. Hall, *The Antinomian Controversy, 1636–38. A Documentary History* (New York, 1957), p.179; Keith Thomas, *Religion and the Decline of Magic* (London, 1971); Lawrence Stone, *The Family, Sex, and Marriage in England, 1550–1800* (New York, 1970); Roberta Hamilton, *The Liberation of Women. A Study of Patriarchy and Capitalism*; Maureen Quilligan, *Milton's Spenser*, pp.222–31.

11. See *Reason of Church Government* (1642), *CPW*, Vol. I, pp.807–8.

12. A point of view stated with admirable succinctness in *Eikonoklastes* (1649) where he says of Charles I's letters that 'to sumn up all, they shewed him govern'd by a Woman' (*CPW*, III, p.538). On Puritan attitudes to Henrietta Maria, *see* Christopher Hill, *The Century of Revolution, 1603–1714* (London, 1969), pp. 67–72.

13. On the Muse as Son, *see* William B. Hunter, Jr., 'Milton's Muse', in *Bright Essence* (Salt Lake City, 1973); and *see* Merritt Y. Hughes, 'Milton and the Symbol of Light', *Studies in English Literature*, IV (1964), pp.1–33.

14. *See* Rosemond Tuve, *Images and Themes in Five Poems by Milton* (Cambridge, Mass., 1967) for a still unparalleled treatment of nature in *Lycidas*.

15. Carl Kerenyi, *Dionysos*, p.133.

16. Euripides', *The Bacchae* presents the fatal absence of discrimination on the part of the Dionysian cult between human and animal sacrifice (1751–67) in *The Bakkhai*, tr. Robert Bagg (Amherst, 1978).

17. *See* Jane Ellen Harrison, *Prolegomena to the Study of Greek Religion* (1903) (New York, 1955), p.459, for the meaning of the quiet of Orpheus.

18. For Milton's Platonism, *see* Irene Samuel's classic study, *Plato and Milton* (Ithaca, New York and London, 1947).

19. *Conclusiones*, No. 6, interpreted by Wind in *Pagan Mysteries*, p. 56.

20. Wind, *Pagan Mysteries*, p.61.

21. *Ibid.*, p.40.

22. *See* Fowler, *Paradise Lost*, I. 17–22n in *The Poems of John Milton* (Oxford, 1968), ed. John Carey and Alastair Fowler. Fowler also perceives the 'deliberate allusion to the Hermetic doctrine that God is both masculine and feminine', citing Cusanus.

23. For Ficino, 'Mind' 'remains light in its brightest form, without

motion, but engraved with all the principles of everything' (*Commentary on Plato's 'Symposium', Renaissance Views of Man*, p.49).

24. *See* Proclus, *Elements of Theology*, Proposition 67, tr. and ed. E.R. Dodds (Oxford, 1963), for 'the whole in the part'.

25. The most inspiring critical work on this topic is Michael Lieb's *The Dialectics of Creation. Patterns of Birth and Regeneration in 'Paradise Lost'* (Massachussetts, 1970). *See also* John Shawcross, 'The Metaphor of Inspiration in *Paradise Lost*', in *The Upright Heart and Pure. Essays Commemorating the Tercentenary of the Publication of 'Paradise Lost'*, ed. A.P. Fiore (Pittsburgh, 1967), for the sexual overtones of inspiration.

26. Hermetic influence on Milton is suspected by Christopher Hill in *Milton and the English Revolution*, pp.5–6, 37, 110, 324, 400. It is derived from Fludd by Frances Yates in *The Occult Philosophy in the Elizabethan Age* (London, Boston and Henley, 1979), pp.177–81.

27. Pico, *Oration*, in *Renaissance Views of Man*, p.67 (based largely on the Hermetic *Asclepius*).

28. *See* n.13 above.

29. Plato, *Republic*, 395D, in the edition by G.M.A. Grube (London and Sydney, 1981 reprint): 'imitations...become part of one's nature and settle into habits of gesture, voice and thought.' Grube's commentary on the Platonic notion that what we 'impersonate' in poetry we also become, is invaluable (pp.63ff. and 72ff.)

30. *See* C.G. Jung, *Four Archetypes*, tr. R.F.C. Hull (London, 1972), pp.15–44.

31. The idea of the female's womb as 'man's world' is a constant feature of alchemy, e.g., Paracelsus, 100.

32. Comparable with the 'frozen loins' noted by Christopher Ricks in *Milton's Grand Style* (Oxford, 1963), p.51.

33. Cornelius Agrippa, *Philosophy of Natural Magic. Three Books of Occult Philosophy or Magic*, ed. W.F. Whitehead (New York, 1971), p.128.

34. Compare *Paradise Lost*, III. 583–6 with Ralph Cudworth's sunny God 'kindling, cheering, quickening, warming, enlivening hearts' in *A Sermon of 1647* in *The Cambridge Platonists*, ed. C.A. Patrides (London, 1969), p.105.

35. Pseudo-Dionysius (Dionysius the Areopagite), *The Mystical Theology and The Celestial Hierarchies*, editor unnamed (Godalming, 1965).

36. *See* for this tradition, Nicholas Cusanus, *De Docta Ignorantia*, in *Unity and Reform. Selected Writings of Nicholas de Cusa*, ed. J.P. Dolan (Chicago, Ill., 1962), p.68; Frances Yates' brilliant exposition of the Dionysian *vita negativa* in *Giordano Bruno and the Hermetic Tradition*, pp.117–29.

37. *Images of Kingship in 'Paradise Lost'*, pp.195–7.

38. *See* J.M. Evans, *Milton and the Genesis Tradition* (Oxford, 1968), especially pp.70–7.

39. Giordano Bruno, *The Heroic Frenzies*, tr. Paul Eugene Memmo, Jr.

(Columbia PhD), p.312; and *see* J.C. Nelson *Renaissance Theory of Love. The Context of Giordano Bruno's 'Eroici Furori'* (New York, 1958), pp.163-233.

40.   *Paradise Lost*, V. 404-505; Bruno, *Concerning the Cause Principle and One* in *The Infinite in Giordano Bruno*, tr. Sidney Greenberg (New York, 1950), p.286; and *see* A.M. Paterson, *The Infinite Worlds of Giordano Bruno* (Springfield, Ill., 1970), p.45.

41.   Though it is also appreciated by other readers as the essence of desirable femininity, for example, John Peter, *A Critique of 'Paradise Lost'* (Archon, 1970), p.95.

42.   *Pimander*, 21-30, *Hermetica*, pp.127-31; and Yates, *Giordano Bruno and the Hermetic Tradition*, p.240.

43.   For the emblem of 'Vanity', *see* I.J. Halkett, *Milton and the Idea of Matrimony* (New York and London, 1970), pp.106, 107; M. Nicolson, *John Milton. A Reader's Guide to his Poetry* (New York, 1963), p.242.

44.   In *Renaissance Views of Man*, p.50.

45.   For fuller treatment, *see* my 'The Quest for the One: Eve and Narcissus in *Paradise Lost*', *Studies in Mystical Literature*, Vol.3, No.I (January, 1983), pp.1-17. *See also*: Louise Vinge, *The Narcissus Theme in Western European Literature up to the Early Nineteenth Century*, tr. R. Dewsnap (Lund, 1967) pp.123-7; Patricia A. Parker, *Inescapable Romance. Studies in the Poetics of a Mode* (Princeton, NJ, and Guildford, 1979), pp.114-23, for Eve's choice as 'the Augustinian evening of angelic choice'.

46.   Bruno, *The Heroic Frenzies*, Part I, Dialogue 4.

47.   Hill, *Milton and the English Revolution*, pp.75-6, 324-33.

48.   *See* William B. Hunter, Jr., 'Eve's Demonic Dream', *A Journal of English Literary History*, Vol. xiii (1946), pp. 255-265, for the tradition of dream and devil lore.

49.   Gafurius, *Practica Musica*, considered in Wind, *Pagan Mysteries*, pp.112-13.

50.   John Phillips, *The Life of Mr. John Milton*, in *Early Lives*, p.33.

51.   Bruno, *The Expulsion of the Triumphant Beast*, p.236.

52.   *Ibid.*, pp.235-8. These passages present Bruno's classic statement that '*natura est deus in rebus*', in which the Divinity is spoken of as 'she' (p.238) and to be found 'in all things, one fecund Nature, preserving mother of the universe'.

53.   A gendered equivalent of Bruno's Sophia's teaching that 'the beginning, the middle, and the end, the birth, the growth, and the perfection of all that we see, come from contraries, through contraries, into contraries, to contraries' (*The Expulsion of the Triumphant Beast*, pp.90-1).

54.   S.K. de Rola, *The Secret Art of Alchemy* (London, 1973), see Plates.

55.   Hermes Trismegistus, *Emerald Table*, Ibid., p.17; and *Ars chemica*, 'Tractatus aureus Hermetis' in C.G. Jung, *Alchemical Studies*, tr. R.F.C. Hull (New York and London, 1970), pp.147-8.

56.   *See* Douglas Bush's edition of *Paradise Lost*, 908-10n.

57.   For Augustine's attitude to sex as essentially sinful even within

marriage, see *City of God*, Book XIV, Chs. 16–28; for St Bernard's misogyny, *see* M. Payen, *Discussion*, in *Cahiers de civilisation medieval* 20 (1977), p.128 (Bernard on 'le sac d'ordures').

58. *See De Doctrina Christiana, CPW*, VI, Book I, Ch. 5.
59. *See* Wind, *Pagan Mysteries*, p.106.
60. I tactfully refrain from naming names.
61. On this theme, *see* Kathleen M. Swaim, 'Flower, Fruit, and Seed: A Reading of *Paradise Lost*', *Milton Studies*, Vol. V, pp.155–76.
62. John Peter, *A Critique of 'Paradise Lost'*, pp.102–3.
63. *Ovid's Metamorphoses. The Arthur Golding Translation* (1567), ed. J.F. Nims (New York, 1975).
64. *See* Virginia Mollenkott, *The Divine Feminine*, pp.20–25.

Select Bibliography

Allen, Don Cameron, *Mysteriously Meant. The Rediscovery of Pagan Symbolism and Allegorical Interpretation in the Renaissance*, Baltimore and London, 1970

Apuleius. *The Golden Asse* (1566), tr. William Adlington, intro. Thomas Secombe, London, 1913

Bruno, Giordano. *The Heroic Frenzies*, tr. and intro. Paul Eugene Memmo, Jr., Columbia, 1959

—— *The Expulsion of the Triumphant Beast* (1584), tr. A.D. Imerti. New Brunswick, 1964

Campbell, Joseph (ed.), *The Mysteries. Papers from the Eranos Yearbooks*, tr. Ralph Manheim, 2 vols., New York, 1955

Cartari, Vincenzo, *Le Imagini de i Dei gli Antichi*, in *The Renaissance and the Gods*, ed. Stephen Orgel, New York and London, 1976

Claudian, *Works (De Raptu Proserpinae)*, tr. Maurice Platnauer, 2 vols., London and New York, 1922

Cody, Richard, *The Landscape of the Mind. Pastoralism and Platonic Theory in Tasso's 'Aminta' and Shakespeare's Early Comedies*, Oxford, 1969

Comes, Natalis, *Mythologies*, Venice, 1567, in *The Renaissance and the Gods*, ed. Stephen Orgel, New York and London, 1976

Cusanus, Nicholas, *Unity and Reform. Selected Writings of Nicholas de Cusa*, ed. John Patrick Dolan, Chicago, Ill., and Crawfordsville, Ind., 1962

Darbishire, Helen (ed.), *The Early Lives of Milton*, London, 1932

Davies, Stevie, *Renaissance Views of Man*, Manchester, 1978

—— *Images of Kingship in 'Paradise Lost'. Milton's Politics and Christian Liberty*, Missouri, 1983

Delcourt, Marie, *Hermaphrodite. Myths and Rites of the Bisexual Figure in Classical Antiquity*, London, 1961

Drayton, Michael, *Works*, ed. J. William Hebel, Oxford, 1931

Dusinberre, Juliet, *Shakespeare and the Nature of Women*, London and Basingstoke, 1975

Elizabeth I (Queen of England), *The Public Speaking of Queen Elizabeth*, ed. G.P. Rice, New York, 1951

Euripides, *The Bakkhai*, tr. Robert Bagg, Amherst, 1978

Ficino, Marsilio, *Opera Omnia*, 2 vols, Monumenta Politica et Philosophica Rariora, Series I, Turin, 1962

Fowler, Alastair, *Spenser and the Numbers of Time*, London, 1964

Gelli, Giovanni Battista, *Circe*, tr. H. Layng, London, 1744

Hall, D.D., *The Antinomian Controversy, 1636–38. A Documentary History*, Middleton, Conn., 1968

Hall, Nor, *The Moon and the Virgin. Reflections on the Archetypal Feminine*, London, 1980

Heninger, S.K., Jr., *Touches of Sweet Harmony. Pythagorean Cosmology and Renaissance Poetics*, San Marino, Calif., 1974

Hermes (Trismegistus), *Hermetica*, ed. Walter Scott, Oxford, 1924

Hesiod, *Theogony*, tr. and ed. Dorothea Wender, Harmondsworth, 1973

Hesychius, *Hesychii Alexandrini Lexicon*, Rev. J. Alberti and M. Schmidt, 2 vols, Jena, 1858, 1861

Hill, Christopher, *Milton and the English Revolution*, London, 1977

Homer (attrib.), *The Homeric Hymns*, tr. Apostolos N. Athanassakis, Baltimore and London, 1976

James I (King of England), *Daemonologie*, Edinburgh, 1597

Jardine, Lisa, *Still Harping on Daughters. Women and Drama in the Age of Shakespeare*, Sussex and New Jersey, 1983

Jung, Carl Gustav, *Alchemical Studies*, New York and London, 1970

Kahn, Coppélia, *Man's Estate. Masculine Identity in Shakespeare*, Berkeley, Calif., and London, 1981

Kerenyi, Carl, *Asklepios. Archetypal Image of the Physician's Existence*, tr. Ralph Manheim, New York, 1959

—— *Dionysos. Archetypal Image of Indestructible Life*, tr. Ralph Manheim, London, 1976

—— *Eleusis. Archetypal Image of Mother and Daughter*, tr. Ralph Manheim, New York, 1967

Lewis, C.S., *Spenser's Images of Life*, ed. Alastair Fowler, Cambridge, 1967

Lieb, Michael, *The Dialectics of Creation. Patterns of Birth and Regeneration in 'Paradise Lost'*, Cambridge, Mass., 1970

Linche, Richard, *The Fountain of Ancient Fiction*, in *The Renaissance and the Gods*, ed. Stephen Orgel, Vol. XIII, New York and London, 1976

Maclean, Ian, *The Renaissance Notion of Woman. A Study in the Fortunes of Scholasticism and Medical Science in European Intellectual Life*, Cambridge...Sydney, 1980

—— *Woman Triumphant. Feminism in French Literature, 1610–1652*. Oxford, 1977

Mollenkott, Virginia Ramey, *The Divine Feminine. The Biblical*

Imagery of God as Female, New York, 1983

Nelson, John Charles, *Renaissance Theory of Love. The Context of Giordano Bruno's 'Eroici Furori'*, New York, 1958

Nohrnberg, J.C., *The Analogy of 'The Faerie Queene'*, Princeton, NJ, 1976

Orpheus (attrib.), *The Orphic Hymns*, tr. and ed. A.N. Athanassakis, Missoula, Mont., 1977

Ovid. *Ovid's Metamorphoses. The Arthur Golding Translation* (1567), ed. J.F. Nims, New York, 1965

Panowsky, Dora and Erwin, *Pandora's Box. The Changing Aspects of a Mythical Symbol*, New York, 1956

Paracelsus, *Selected Writings*, ed. Jolande Jacobi, tr. Norbert Guterman, New York, 1951

Patrides, C.A., *The Cambridge Platonists*, London, 1969

Pausanias, *Description of Greece*, tr. W.H.S. Jones, 6 vols., London and New York, 1918

Petrarch, Francesco, *On his own ignorance and that of many other people*. Tr. H Nachod in *The Renaissance Philosophy of Man*, ed. E. Cassirer *et al.*, Chicago, Ill., 1948

Plato. *Phaedrus and Letters VII and VIII*, tr. W. Hamilton, Harmondsworth, 1973

—— *Republic*, tr. G.M.A. Grube, London and Sydney, 1981

—— *Symposium* tr. W. Hamilton, Harmondsworth, 1951

Plutarch, *De Iside et Osiride*, ed. J. Gwyn Griffiths, Wales, 1970

Pseudo-Dionysius (Dionysius the Areopagite), *The Mystical Theology and the Celestial Hierarchies*, editor unnamed (Godalming, 1965).

Riemer, A.P., *Antic Fables. Patterns of Evasion in Shakespeare's Comedies*, Manchester, 1980

Ripa, Cesare, *Iconologia*, intro. Erna Mandowsky, Hildesheim and New York, 1970

Samuel, Irene, *Milton's Platonism*, Ithaca, NY, and London, 1947

Schoenbaum, S., *William Shakespeare. A Documentary Life*, Oxford, 1975

Seltman, Charles, *Riot in Ephesus. Writings on the Heritage of Greece*, London, 1958

Seznec, Jean, *The Survival of the Pagan Gods. The Mythological Tradition and its Place in Renaissance Humanism and Art*, tr. B.F. Sessions, New York, 1953

Shumaker, Wayne, *The Occult Sciences in the Renaissance*, Berkeley, Calif., 1972

Sophocles, *The Theban Plays*, tr. E.F. Watling, Harmondsworth, 1947

Stone, Lawrence, *The Family, Sex, and Marriage in England, 1500–1800*, New York, 1977

Tuve, Rosemund, *Allegorical Imagery. Some Mediaeval Books and their Posterity*, Princeton, NJ, 1966

Walker, D.P., *The Ancient Theology. Studies in Christian Platonism from the Fifteenth to the Eighteenth Century*, London, 1972

—— *Spiritual and Demonic Magic. From Ficino to Campanella*, Notre Dame and London, 1975

Wasson, R. Gordon *et al.*, *The Road to Eleusis. Unveiling the Secret of the Mysteries*, New York and London, 1978

Wells, Robin Headlam, *Spenser's 'Faerie Queene' and the Cult of Elizabeth*, London and Canberra, 1983

Wind, Edgar, *Pagan Mysteries in the Renaissance*, London, 1958

Yates, Francis A., *Giordano Bruno and the Hermetic Tradition*, London, 1964

—— *The Occult Philosophy in the Elizabethan Age*, London, Boston and Henley, 1979

Index

Acidalius, Valens, 10
Adam, 26, 74
Adonis, 55–6, 63–4, 74, 99
    Garden of, 5, 55, 69ff, 72, 81–2,
    86ff, 210, 226
    and Marinell, 65ff, 70, 84, 99
Aesculapius, *See* Eleusinian
    Mysteries
Agrippa, Cornelius, 25–6, 204
Alcestis, 156, 163
alchemy, 2, 5–6, 9–10, 52, 69, 86,
    102, 114, 197, 203, 205–6, 211,
    226–7
Alexander, Sir William, 35
Alfred (King), 258n
Allen, D.C., 248n
Alpers, P.J., 252n
Amazons, 32–3, 121, 220
androgyne. *See* hermaphrodite
Apollo, 10, 76, 105, 161, 163, 216,
    246
Apuleius, 22–4, 41, 53, 68, 82,
    91–3, 120, 124, 129
Arden, Mary, 110
Arethusa, 21
Ariosto, Ludovico, 49–50
Aristophanes, 18
Aristotle, 4, 24, 39, 55, 106, 194,
    197, 225, 251n
Aronson, A., 255n
Arthurian Revival, 28
Ascham, Roger, 25
Aubrey, John, 176, 185
Augustine, St., of Hippo, 7, 231,
    242

Bacchus/Dionysos, 163–5
    and Maenads, 180, 189ff, 204,
    220, 258n
Barber, C.L., 255n
Barkan, L., 253n
Barker, A.E., 258n
Basil, St., 242
Berecynthia, 7
Bernard, St., of Clairvaux, 231
Bible, 201, 216
    Gen., 10, 58, 86, 89, 145, 193–4,
    220; Acts, 167–8; Eph., 7;
    Isa., 31, 244; Jonah, 139;
    Judges, 186; Luke, 152;
    Matt., 108; Num., 244; Song
    of Songs, 234–5
Blessington, F.C., 249n
Boadicea (Queen), 179–80
Boiardo, Matteomaria, 49–50
Botticelli, Sandro, 44
    Birth of Venus, 14; *Mars and
    Venus* 14–5; *primavera*, 11ff.,
    13–14; Venus Urania in, 13;
    See coincidentia oppositorum
Boyle, Elizabeth, 37, 41–2, 44, 82
Britomartis, 34
Brooks-Davies, D., 249n, 251n,
    253n
Bruno, Giordano, 3, 7, 10, 52, 53,
    75–6, 78, 107, 115–16, 143, 210,
    215, 223, 260n
Bunyan, John, 238
Bush, D., 260n

cabbala, 2, 4, 207

266

Calliope., *See* Milton

Campanella, Tommaso, 150

Cartari, Vincenzo, 11, 21, 24, 120, 252n

Cartimandua (Queen), 179

Ceres/Demeter, 10, 17ff, 49, 61, 65, 67, 91, 121, 127–8, 142, 144–5, 152–74, 245f
  as corn-goddess, 20, 136; as Demeter Hermione, 153–5; as Demeter Law-Giver, 153f, 154f, 171; *See* Eleusis, Eleusinian Mysteries, Proserpina

Christ, 10–11, 187
  as Apollo, 246; as Ceres, 237, 240–1; maiden-Christ, 149; as Proserpina, 237

Claudian, 18, 20, 67, 142, 241, 246

Cicero, Marcus Tullius, 18, 19, 21, 120, 149, 251n

Circe, 17, 32, 190

Cody, R., 256n

Colie, R., 138, 256n

Colonna, Francesco, 120–1

Comes, Natalis, 11, 123, 253n, 257n

coincidentia oppositorum, 5, 64, 231
  Belphoebe and Amoret as, 81; Britomart as, 6, 58; Cupid and Psyche as, 185; hermaphroditic Venus as, 46ff; Mars and Venus as, 14; Mercury and Venus as, 14; Proserpina-Ceres-Hecate as, 12; twins as, 105; Venus and Diana as, 12, 79ff, 136; Viola as, 114; Zephyrus and Chloris as, 14

concordia discors, 58, 139, 151, 231

Cudworth, Ralph, 259n

Cupid (Amor), 14, 80, 96, 97, 122

and Psyche, 22, 39, 41, 87, 91–3, 129, 185

Cusa, Nicholas de, 48, 207

Cybele, 45, 61

Daedalus, 46, 103–4

D'Ancona, M.L., 13, 249n

Dante Alighieri, 40, 160

Davidson, C., 254n

Davies, Sir John, 28

Davies, S., 208, 249n, 259n, 260n

Dekker, Thomas, 28, 29

Delcourt, M., 252n

Detienne, M., 253n

Diana/Artemis, 11, 12–13, 21, 23, 34, 79ff, 105, 115, 121, 123, 125–8, 132, 140, 151, 219, 245–6
  as *Venus virgo*, 12; *See coincidentia oppositorum*, moon, sea

Dionysius II (Tryant of Sicily), 154

Donne, John, 6, 163

Drayton, Michael, 30, 110

Dreyer, J.L.E., 248n

Driver, T., 257n

Drummond of Hawthornden, William, 38

Dusinberre, J., 248n

Echo, *See* Narcissus

Eleusinian Mysteries, 17–21
  Aesculapius and, 69; Arethusa in, 20–1; Christian antagonism to, 19; Christian synthesis of, 17; in Cicero, 18–19; in Claudian, 18, 20; in *Homeric Hymns*, 18–19; as mother-and-daughter religion, 19–20, 109, 162–3, 192; in *Orphic Hymns*, 18–19; in Pausanias, 18; in Shakespeare, 21, 129–74; in

Sophocles, 18–19; secrecy of, 17, 18–19

Eleusis, 11, 104, 193
in Milton, 19, 21; in Shakespeare, 19, 21, 119, 128ff, 150, 156, 161; in Spenser, 19; vision at, 18–19, 150–1

Elizabeth I (Queen), 10, 16, 24–7, 37ff, 77, 82, 103–4, 122–3, 178, 180, 185;
as Amphitrite, 53; as Astraea, 24, 28; as Belphoebe, 24; as Britomart, 33–4, 52–3, 56ff; as Cynthia, 24, 29; as *dea abscondita*, 29–30; as Deborah, 28; as Diana, 28, 29; as Gloriana, 28f, 54, 82, 121; as Isis, 28, 102–3; as Judith, 28, 30–1; as *mater patriae*, 31, 32, 61, 103; motto of, 28; as pelican/Christ, 32; as Phoebe, 24; as Sacred Virgin, 28, 61, 121; as *Venus virgo*, 82; as warrior, 30–1, 34, 33–4, 53; white rod of, 58

Elizabeth Stuart (Princess of England), 28

Euridice. *See* Orpheus

Euripides, 18, 162–3, 189–90

Erasmus, Desiderius, 25

Evans, J.M., 259n

Evans, M., 253n

Eve, *passim*
as Diana, 246; as Garden, 210, 242; as Pomona, 243–6; as Venus, 242, 246; *See* Flora, Milton

Fell, Margaret, 183

Ficino, Marsilio, 3, 7, 9, 44, 51, 73, 99, 139, 143, 214, 258–259n

Venus Urania in, 13

Fletcher, A., 252n

Flora/Chloris, 13–15, 157, 236–7
as fertility goddess, 21, 84; Milton's Eve as, 236–7, 244–5; the two Floras, 27; *See* Botticelli, *coincidentia oppositorum*

Fowler, A., 40, 251n, 253n–254n, 258n

Fraunce, Abraham, 20–1, 64, 153, 253n, 256n

Garber, M., 255n

Gelli, G.B., 32–3, 34

Gentileschi, Artemisia, 30

Gesner, C., 255n

Giametti, A., Bartlett, 251n, 252n

Giraldi, L.G., 11

Gloriana, *See* Elizabeth I, Spenser

gnosis, 24, 44, 69, 101, 108, 147, 199, 210, 213–14, 219, 224, 229, 238
See Hermetica

Graces, 11, 12–14, 38ff, 235–6, 242
in Ficino, 51; the four Graces, 37–54

Graves, R., 257n

Graziani, R., 254n

Greene, Robert, 28

Greer, G., 251n

Gregory, St., 242

Guarini, G.B., 109

Halkett, I.J., 260n

Hall, D.P., 258n

Hall, N., 257n

Hamilton, A.C., 253n

Hankins, J.E., 249n

Harrison, J.E., 258n

Hartwig, J., 254n

Hecate, 12, 21, 28, 121, 125, 128, 166–71, 190

See Ceres, *coincidentia oppositorum,* Proserpina,moon

Helen of Troy, 80 (the twoHelens), 153

Heninger, S.K., 71, 251n, 253n

Henrietta Maria (Queen), 185,258n

Henry Stuart (Prince of Wales),28

hermaphrodite, 1–2, 5–6, 14, 34,41, 44–52, 70–1, 100–2, 105,108, 195–6
in alchemy, 5–6, 114, 152, 226; Amoret and Scudamore as,39, 100–2; angels as, 6, 196; the artist as, 111, 195ff; Britomart as, 39, 50ff, 58ff,95, 147; God as, 5, 195ff, 198–9; Muse as, 193–9, 207; Nature as, 38–49, 71, 89, 148;in Orphism, 5; Pericles, as, 147–8; Psyche and Cupid as, 39; Venus as, 45–9, 95; *See* Milton, Spenser

Hermaphroditus, 44

Hermes/Mercury, 13, 111–14, 124,127
Autolycus as, 157; as bisexual figure, 14; as combined with Athena, 14; as combined with Venus, 14, 102; Raphael as, 229; Viola as, 111–17

Hermes Trismegistus, 3, 47, 72, 114, 165, 199, 260n

Hermetica, 2, 41, 72–3, 89, 113, 141, 147, 214, 229
Asclepius, 51, 101, 116, 141, 165, 211; *Pimander,* 4, 5, 47, 116, 198, 213, 260n

Hermeticism, 2–4, 100ff, 108, 141, 163, 202, 211–4, 229
mors osculi in, 4, 101; *See* magus

Hermione, 152–5, 160, 165–6

See Ceres

Hesiod, 186

Hesychius, 153

Hieatt, A. Kent, 252n

Hill, C., 215, 258n, 259n

Hobbes, Thomas, 258n

Hogrefe, P., 250n

Homer, 187, 192, 202

Homeric Hymns, 18, 111–12, 128, 136, 146, 161, 234

Hough, G., 251n

Howdle, A., 253n

Hughes, M.Y., 258n

humanist, woman as, 24–6

Hunter, R.G., 257n

Hunter, W.B., 178, 258n, 260n

Hutchinson, Anne, 183

Hyacinthus, 76, 88

Isis, 7–9, 22–4, 61, 82, 102–3, 109, 120–9, 145
in Apuleius, 21–4; as female law, 43, 102–3; Hermia and, 124–5; as humanist quest for truth, 8–9; in mythographers, 22; as white magician, 28; as wisdom (Minerva), 24

Isocrates, 18

James I and VI (King), 28, 250n
and witchcraft, 27–8

Jardine, L., 6, 248n, 250n

Jonson, Ben, 38

Julian the Apostate, 171

Julius II (Pope), 17

Jung, C.G., 255n, 259n, 260n

Jupiter/Zeus, 5, 10, 76, 83, 92, 96, 98, 186, 241, 246

Kahn, C., 110, 255n, 256n, 257n

Kantorowicz, E.H., 251n

Kepler, Johann, 4

Kerenyi, K., 189, 250n, 253n,256n, 258n
king, as *pater patriae*, 31, 106
Koenigsberger, D., 256n
Krinagoras, 18

Leda, 76, 96–7
Lewis, C.S., 40, 252n, 254n
Lieb, M., 259n
Lilly, William, 251n
Linche, Richard, 21, 24
Lyly, John, 28, 29

Maclean, I., 249n, 250n
Macrobius, 120
Maenads. *See* Bacchus
magus,
    as black magician, 95–6, 98,
        216; poet as magus, 4–5,
        95–104, 139–40;
        Shakespeare's Paulina as,
        165–174; *See* Isis
Marlowe, Christopher, 16, 17, 96
Mars Ares, 14–15, 16, 17, 34
    See coincidentia oppositorum
Martia (Queen), 180–1
Marvell, Andrew, 130, 139, 256n
Mary Stuart (Queen of Scots), 53
Mary (Virgin) 1, 4, 10–11, 20,
    79,83
    as Second Eve, 57; *See*
        Elizabeth I
matriarchy, 24, 32, 58, 179–80
Medici, Catherine de, 10, 30
Michelangelo Buonarroti, 17
Middleton, Thomas, 33
Milton, Anne (daughter of the
    poet), 176
Milton, Deborah (daughter of the
    poet), 175, 176, 185–6
Milton, John,
    Ad patrem, 185, 222, 228;
        Arcades, 178; *Areopagitica*,

8–9; *Christian Doctrine*, 186,
    231, 261n; *Colasterion*, 181;
    Commonplace Book, 180,
    258n; *Comus*, 178, 185,
    190–1; *Defence of the English
    People*, 186, 257n; *Doctrine
    and Discipline of Divorce*,
    181, 182–3, 195; *Of
    Education*, 178–9;
    Eikonoklastes, 178, 258n;
    History of Britain, 179–81;
    Lycidas, 21, 69, 138, 180, 186,
    187–90, 194; *Paradise Lost*, 1,
    7, 13, 15, 36, 48, 67, 87, 101,
    107, 108, 177, 180, 182–3,
    184–5, 186–262; *Paradise
    Regained* 221, 245; *Reason of
    Church Government* 258n;
    Samson Agonistes, 177,
    199–200; *Second Defence*, 35,
    180, 186, 251n;
    Tetrachordon, 181–4, 196,
    212; Calliope in Milton, 21,
    138, 187ff; Dalila in, 176, 177,
    200; Eve in, 15, 26, 35, 182–3,
    184–5, 192, 201, 204, 208–62;
    Furies in, 188; Garden of
    Venus in, 15, 209ff;
    hermaphrodite/androgyne
    in, 35–6, 195ff; Hermeticism
    in, 198–200, 209–17, 229; Isis
    in, 8–9; Orpheus in, 138, 163,
    188–92, 195, 207–8, 222ff;
    Urania in, 187, 219–21; *See*
    Christ, Eleusis
Milton, John (son of the poet),175
Milton, Mary (daughter of the
    poet), 175
Minerva/Athena, 9, 20, 24, 45, 46,
    111, 205
Mnemosyne, 89, 186
Mollenkott, V.R., 253n, 261n
moon, 121ff, 197

as goddess Luna, 10–11, 67; as feminine principle, 21ff, 120ff; as Lucina, 67, 127; waning as Hecate, 21, 127, 204; *See* sea

Moses, 2, 10–11, 192

Mother (Great), 7, 53, 202
as mother earth and mother nature, 45–7, 64, 83, 94, 148, 197, 221–31, 227–8, 244–5

Muses, 89, 186ff, 192, 207
See Milton

Narcissus, 44, 88, 190, 214–15

Neale, J.E., 251n

Nelson, J.C., 260n

Nevo, R., 255n

Newton, Sir Isaac, 197

Nicholl, C., 254n, 256n

Nicolson, M., 260n

Nohrnberg, J., 252n, 253n

Odysseus, 17, 32, 34

Orpheus, 3, 43–4, 163–4
as founder of mystery religions, 4; as lover of Euridice, 17, 43–4, 156; as magus-poet, 4–5, 43, 138–9, 191; and Proserpina, 141–2; synthesised with Christ, 17, 189; *See* Euridice, Milton

Orphic Hymns, 2, 4, 5, 18–19, 46, 65, 134, 139, 148, 170, 195

Osiris, 8–9, 23–4, 102–3, 109, 124
as patriarchal law, 43; *See* Isis

Otto, W.F., 250n

Ovid, 14, 18, 44, 144, 152–3, 156, 158, 243

Pales, 21, 245–6

Pandora (the two Pandoras), 27

Panowsky, D. and E., 250n

Paolini, 3

Paracelsus, 10, 114, 226, 259n

Parker, P.A., 260n

pastoral (as feminine), 13, 21, 223,246

Paterson, A.M., 260n

patriarchy, 180

Paul, St., 7, 167–8, 183

Pausanias, 18, 153

Peele, George, 28

Peter, J., 260n, 261n

Petrarch, Francesco, 18

Phanes, 5

Phialas, P.G., 255n

Phillips, Edward, 175, 257n

Phillips, John, 175, 257n., 260n

Philomela, 141–2, 208

Pico (G. Pico della Mirandola), 3, 8–9, 11, 42, 141, 163, 191

Pindar, 18

Plato, 3, 162
Letters, 154; *Meno*, 130; *Phaedrus*, 4, 66; *Republic*, 27, 52, 111, 172, 259n; *Symposium*, 4, 90, 105, 252n

Platonism, *passim*

Pliny, 129

Plutarch, 22, 24

polytheism, 11ff

Pomona, 21, 243–6

Powell, Mary, 175, 176

Praxiteles, 103–4

Proclus, 248n., 259n

Prometheus, 27, 246

Proserpina, 11, 18–23, 64, 65, 99, 119, 125, 141–52, 158–9, 231–46
and Adonis, 64–70; daffodil emblem of, 21, 64–5, 76, 96–7; underworld, 21, 121–2, 127; as waning moon (queen of underworld) 21, 121–2, 127; *See* Christ, *coincidentia oppositorum*, Hecate, moon, Orpheus

Protestantism (and woman), 24, 28, 183
Pseudo-Dionysius (Dionysius the Areopagite), 207
Psyche, 22, 68, 93, 129
  See Cupid
Puritanism, 10, 220, 224, 232, 238
Pythagoras, 4

queen, as *mater patriae*, 31-2
  as nursing mother, 32; as warrior woman, 30ff
Quilligan, M., 252n

Raleigh, Sir Walter, 29, 38, 54
Reid, R.L., 85
Rice, G.P., 251n
Ricks, C., 259n
Riemer, A.P., 166, 167, 257n
Ripa, Cesare, 12, 249n, 257n
Ripley, George, 152
Roche, T.P., 97, 253n, 254n
Rola, S.K. de, 260n
Roper, Margaret, 25
Rupprecht, C.S., 252n
Rufus, Mutianus, 10-11, 28

Sadler, Hamnet and Judith, 105
Samuel, I., 258n
Schoenbaum, S., 254n
Schwartz, M.M., 254n
sea (as female archetype). 67-9, 79, 118-19, 129ff
  Diana and, 79; Venus and, 79-80
Seltmann, C., 249n., 257n
Semiramis, 32-3
Seznec, J., 249n
Shakespeare, Hamnet, 105
Shakespeare, Judith, 105
Shakespeare, Susannah, 105
Shakespeare, William, *As You Like It*, 6, 110, 117

Comedy of Errors, 109, 168;
  Cymbeline, 1-2, 6, 140, 170;
  Henry IV, Part I, 15; *Henry V*, 15-16; *King Lear*, 16, 35, 93, 106-7, 133-4, 144, 147;
  Love's Labour's Lost, 16, 123;
  Macbeth, 169-70; *Merchant of Venice*, 6, 117; *Midsummer Night's Dream*, 22, 24, 106, 109, 120-9, 136, 143, 155;
  Much Ado, 26; *Othello*, 35, 126; *Pericles*, 4, 69, 107, 118, 129-52, 168, 202; *Sonnets*, 90, 106; *Tempest*, 5, 118, 119, 130, 140, 156, 167, 170;
  Twelfth Night, 6, 59, 109, 110, 111-19, 127; *Venus and Adonis*, 80, 226; *Winter's Tale*, 13, 19, 21, 35, 49, 103, 106, 108, 118, 126, 128, 132, 140, 141, 152-74, 189
Shawcross, J., 259n
Shrewsbury, Elizabeth Countess of, 77-8
Shumaker, W., 248n
Sicily, 20-1, 152-4
Sidney, Sir Philip, 42, 88, 172
Sophocles, 18, 19, 133, 149, 172
Spens, J., 253n
Spenser, Edmund, *Amoretti*, 37, 41-2, 43, 67, 82, 146
  Epithalamion, 37, 41, 43-4;
  Faerie Queene, 1, 2, 5, 12, 15, 33-5, 37-104, 163, 210, 219, 232; *Fowre Hymnes*, 43, 160;
  Letter to Raleigh, 7, 68;
  Prothalamion, 37, 38;
  Shepheardes Calendar, 13, 29, 39-40, 65, 138; amoret in *FQ*, 39, 47, 81, 82, 91, 93-102; Belphoebe in, 26, 69, 81ff; Britomart in, Ch. 2, *passim*; Cymoent in, 21, 64ff,

97, 119; Florimell in, 15, 27, 50, 70ff, 96, 97, 99; Gloriana in, *passim*; hermaphrodite in, 38–54; Una in, 17, 27; *See* Adonis, *coincidentia oppositorum*, Eleusis, Graces

Spenser, Elizabeth (mother of the poet), 37

Spenser, Elizabeth (sister of the poet), 37

Spenser, Peregrine (son of the poet), 37

Stesichorus, 253n

Still, C., 256n, 167

Swaim, K.M., 261n

Tamburlaine, *See* Marlowe

Tasso, Torquato, 49, 50

Tellus, 10–11

Theocritus, 21, 153

Thomas, K., 258n

Tiresias, 187

Tomyris, 32–3

Tonkin, H., 252n

Tourneur, Cyril, 28

Traversi, D., 254n

Tuve, R., 257n., 258n

Urania. *See* Milton

Venus/Aphrodite, 11, 13–15, 16–17, Ch. 2 *passim*, 114, 186, 246
  as fourth Grace, 37–41; garden of, 13–15, 66ff., 86–93; as hermaphrodite, 38–51; as mother, 45, 47, 88ff; *Venus*

Urania, 13, 27; *Venus barbata*, 45; *Venus genetrix*, 46, 189; *Venus Pandemos*, 27; *Venus virgo*, 58, 82; *See coincidentia oppositorum*, Botticelli, Hermes, Elizabeth I, Spenser

Vicari, P., 248n

Vinge, L., 260n

Virgil, 49, 51

Vries, A. de, 253n

Walker, D.P., 248n, 254n

Warner, M., 250n

Warnicke, R.M., 250n

warrior-woman, 49–50
  in Boiardo, 49–50; Britomart as, 16, 33ff, 50–3, 58ff, 97; in Tasso, 49–50: in Virgil, 49–50; *See* Elizabeth I

Wasson, R.G., 256n, 257n

Webster, John, 28

Wells, R.H., 252n

Wheeler, R.P., 254n, 117

White, H., 129, 136

Wili, W., 248n

Williams, K., 253n, 254n

Wilson, A.N., 257n

Wilson, E.C., 251n

Wind, E., 249n, 256n, 258n, 261n

Wordsworth, C., 252n

Yates, F., 249n, 251n, 252n, 259n, 260n

Zephyrus, *See* Flora

Zeuxis, 103–4